D1484370

SACRED SPACE
for the Missional Church

SACRED SPACE
for the Missional Church

Engaging Culture through

the Built Environment

William R. McAlpine

WIPF & STOCK · Eugene, Oregon

SACRED SPACE FOR THE MISSIONAL CHURCH
Engaging Culture through the Built Environment

Wipf & Stock
An Imprint of Wipf and Stock Publishers
199 W. 8th Ave., Suite 3
Eugene, OR 97401

www.wipfandstock.com

ISBN 13: 978-1-60899-468-7

Manufactured in the U.S.A.

Contents

List of Illustrations | vi

Foreword by John Swintonn | vii

Preface | ix

Acknowledgments | xv

Chapter 1 Is There a Place for a Place Called Church? | 1

Chapter 2 The Church, the Gospel, and Culture: Defining Mission | 9

Chapter 3 A Historical Framework for Sacred Space | 33

Chapter 4 A Theological Framework for Sacred Space | 72

Chapter 5 The Significance of Place in Fulfilling of the Mission of the Church | 105

Chapter 6 Missional Challenges and Opportunities in the Twenty-first Century | 133

Chapter 7 Where We Need to Be | 164

APPENDIX A—*Sacred Space Walk: A Guideline for Personal Reflection* | 179

Bibliography | 181

Subject and Author Index | 199

Illustrations

Figures

1.1 Transformative Reflection Model | 5

3.1 The Central Door on the Western Façade, St.-Denis | 47

3.2 Exterior of Central United Church | 62

3.3 Interior of Central United Church | 63

5.1 The Experience of Place | 128

7.1 Community Building Space, First Alliance Church | 170

7.2 Spaces That Invite Unhurried Reflection, First Alliance Church | 171

7.3 View of the Seating Arrangements in First Alliance Church | 174

7.4. Transformative Reflection Model Revisited | 176

Tables

3.1 Dominant Church Structures | 34

3.2 Historical Feature, Influence, and Strategy | 69–70

Foreword

THIS IS AN IMPORTANT book. Carefully and thoughtfully Bill McAlpine brings to our consciousness something that is obvious yet crucial: space matters. Space is foundational for God's creative purposes. Without space: that emptiness that provides room for God's creative power, nothing could come into existence. Most theologies focus on that which inhabits space, but actually space in and of itself, is equally as important. The space we inhabit is created space; meaningful space. That created space is where the Spirit hovers; it is a sacred space.

Space not only provides the context for creaturely life, it also forms the boundaries between us. Without space healthy relationships are not possible. It is as we meet in the space between us, as Martin Buber put it, that we come to know who we are and what it means to love and be loved. In the same way, the church needs space in order that it can relate to the world. Without it the church will lose its identity and collapse into the world. It is the space between church and world that reveals the identity of both. The space between the church and the world is, at least in potential, a sacred point of meeting; a place where we learn to recognise Jesus: a space for mission. The difference between church and world is not the moral virtue of one or the lack of such in the other. Rather it is the simple fact that the church has noticed who Jesus is and the world has yet to do so. The church provides the sacred space, or perhaps better, sacred spaces, where the love of God can be revealed and the meaningfulness of creaturely existence can be revealed to those who have not yet noticed Jesus. It is the fundamental task of the church to seek to draw the world's attention to the sacredness of the spaces within and between them and to create relational and physical space that reveals the love of God in ways that will draw people into relationship with God. Is that not the essence of mission?

I think, at least in part, that this is the fundamental missiological dynamic that Bill McAlpine's reflections on the nature of such sacred space captures. With great care, he draws our attention to the fact that the spaces that we minister within are consecrated: declared holy and devoted to the God who comes to us in Christ. Such space has both shape and meaning and the two are deeply intertwined. It *really* matters what we do with our worship space. It *really* matters how and why we design our churches in the ways that we do. It *really* matters what kind of space we choose to bring people into. Why? Because the sacred spaces that the church creates, within and between, are powerful reminders of the fact that we live in a different time from the rest of the world. Within the business-oriented mindset of Western societies, time is conceived as always coming towards us and disappearing behind us. Time marches on. We may catch a glimpse of it as we look back and we may plan for it as we look forward, but rarely do we take the time to stop and recognise the significance of the present moment. The sacred spaces of the church are places where we are called to remember that we live in eschatological time and to recognise that time matters. Space is the container for the revelation of such eschatological timefullness. The ways in which we create our architectural space impact upon the ways in which we create our relational space, and our relational space is the place where people begin to meet Jesus. It's strange how little theological attention has been given to the sacredness of space. I am grateful to Bill McAlpine for helping redress this shortfall. I hope and I pray that this book initiates a long and fruitful conversation that will help all of us to live lovingly in the sacred spaces that have been given to us.

JOHN SWINTON
University of Aberdeen
20/12/2010

Preface

THERE IS AN AUTOBIOGRAPHICAL dimension influencing the pages that follow in terms of both motivation and methodology. I entered the pastoral ministry with the Christian and Missionary Alliance in Oshawa, Ontario, Canada in April 1975. I had little knowledge and virtually no interest in the relation between sacred places and the mission of the church. After more than fifteen years of pastoral experience, which included involvement in two major building projects at two different churches, I had given little thought to the subject.

In the late autumn of 1999, a veil began to lift from my thinking. My wife and I, along with a teaching colleague of mine, were asked to serve on the building committee that would lead our church into an ambitious, multi-million dollar relocation and building program. My wife and I accepted; my colleague had to decline. But in his refusal he admonished the leadership to ensure that the committee included a theologian. The suggestion prompted mild bewilderment and the simple question, "Why?" Such a response is reflective of many pastors and lay leaders within my own tradition, including myself, up to that point.

This suggestion of including an intentional, theological dimension to a "brick and mortar" project was instrumental in launching me on a reflective journey. Over the next several years, this journey blossomed into the most challenging and extensive academic investigation of my life to that point and, subsequently, a radical realignment of some of my own plausibility structures.[1] The concept of theological intentionality in

---

1. "Plausibility structures" is a term that features prominently in some of the writings of Lesslie Newbigin and Peter Berger, both of whom have influenced my thinking over the years.

the architecture of church buildings finds a wider acceptance in many traditions outside my own heritage within evangelical Protestantism. Yet I am aware of a longing, which appears to be surfacing among evangelicals,[2] for qualities in our built sacred places that respond to more than pragmatic, utilitarian criteria. I now find myself comfortable talking in epistemological and ontological terms with respect to the built environment and in particular, the sacred places we call churches.

The following investigation of the relation between sacred space and the mission of the church explores the issue through the lens of historical and theological frameworks. It also pursues a dialectic path with representatives from religious studies and the social sciences. Many evangelicals have evidenced an alarming degree of ambivalence with respect to sacred places[3] while others refused to even consider the built environment as anything beyond a receptacle in which church life occurs.

Much of the research informing the following pages has spanned textual resources across a spectrum of eras and traditions, but a substantial portion of the work behind the book was qualitative case study research involving two churches representing two disparate traditions within Christianity: a Roman Catholic church and a congregation within the Christian and Missionary Alliance in Canada. The two congregations were chosen on the basis of their well-articulated mission statements and their involvement in major relocation and building projects, providing excellent contexts to examine how their missions were embodied in and informed the design of their new physical facilities. A description and analysis of that research material is presently being worked into a five-year longitudinal study due to be completed within the next year and, therefore, is not included in this volume.

The reflective transformative methodology[4] that I use has been born out of reflectively engaging the critical correlational approach to practical theology developed by two key scholars, David Tracy and Don S. Browning. My Protestant heritage and tradition has dialogued with the Roman Catholic tradition. The intent was to better understand my own tradition, to develop a deeper appreciation for Roman Catholic faith and praxis, and to discover principles to assist the Christian church

---

2. I am thinking particularly of the Canadian context of my own experience.

3. This has included questioning whether there really is or should be such a thing as "sacred space."

4. This is described in detail in the first chapter.

in moving toward the authentic and effective embodiment of her mission in her sacred places, unhindered by traditional barriers.

If this whole endeavor had utilized a unilateral methodology, I am convinced the outcome would have varied significantly. Restricting research to theological or biblical sources to the exclusion of other disciplines would have fostered shallower, myopic results. Limiting the qualitative dimension to one tradition would have compromised the potential richness and wisdom gained. The dialogical engagement of a variety of sources and traditions provided the fertile ground for the informed reflection necessary for transformation to effectively take place.

The link between mission and sacred place can facilitate either one-way or two-way movement. The dictum that form follows function is a one-way street demanding challenge. A synergistic dynamic needs to exist between mission and sacred places. Unless this is intentionally attended to, the dynamic can easily devolve into an adversarial, counterproductive reality. Sacred places should be considered an enabling aspect of the church's mission rather than merely the context in which it is acted out.

Given the disconcerting increase in the numbers of people departing from institutional religion and local churches in particular and opting instead for personal, individual spirituality, some might question the necessity of a book like this. Such an investigation might be ill-timed if not anachronistic altogether. The reality is there are numerous examples within the universal church that are defying the current, well-documented migration away from institutional religion. As a result, church buildings continue to be constructed, underscoring the need for transformative reflection on the role of sacred places in the fulfilment of the church's mission.

Our approach, then, will be as follows: chapter 1, "A Place for a Place Called Church," lays out one of the foundational elements of the book by arguing that despite the reality that the church, in essence, is people, built environments dedicated to the mission of the church can legitimately be called *church*.

The second chapter, entitled "Church, the Gospel, and Culture: Defining Mission," will explore our present situation as the church in the Global North by unpacking the terms "church" and "mission" in particular and considering the significant relationships between church, gospel, and culture. By so doing, we will address the issue of the church's foundational and essential mission.

In chapter 3, "A Historical Framework for Sacred Space," we will take a glance backward in history and explore five salient structures or architectural expressions that have evolved as the church has grown through the centuries to our present day. Rather than simply attempting to underscore what was done well or poorly, the purpose of this historical survey is to gain an understanding of and appreciation for the various factors that contributed to various expressions and influenced the shifts from one architectural paradigm to another.

Chapter 4, "A Theological Framework for Sacred Places," explores the concept of sacrality, specifically how it relates to the particularity of place or space through the lens of theological reflection. Voices from outside the theological disciplines, including the works of Rudolph Otto, Emile Durhkeim, and Mircea Eliade, are brought into the conversation with biblical scholars and theologians in an effort to understand the meaning, function, and impact of the sacred. The majority of the chapter, however, is dedicated to a consideration of sacred space in the Old and New Testaments.

The fifth chapter, "The Significance of Place in Fulfilling the Mission of the Church," explores numerous ways in which place impacts the human experience by reflecting theologically on the contributions of social scientists. Consideration is given to the fact that beyond pragmatic or functional dimensions, place also can have meaning; it can foster healing impact and can influence desired actions. These insights are then brought to bear on the mission of the church and underscore why the missional church can only ignore the significance of sacred space at major cost.

In chapter 6, "Challenges and Opportunities in the Twenty-first Century," we explore an array of significant realities that could serve either to hinder or augment an effective integration of a theology of sacred space and the mission of the church. Phenomena as varied as the house church movement, the internet and cyberspace, ecumenical dialogue, and the design of shopping malls are all brought into the discussion.

The final chapter, "Where We Need to Be," draws some conclusions from the historical-theological reflection engaged throughout the book and addresses the "So what?" question in terms of implications for the missional church in the twenty-first century. In this chapter, we also tackle the thorny issue of cost and the legitimacy of multi-million dollar edifices in a world of profound need.

It is my sincere hope that readers find this book helpful and that as they engage with its content, whether in agreement or not, they will be challenged to consider seriously the organic link between the church's mission and the sacred spaces where the church gathers, from which we fulfill our God-given mandate.

Acknowledgments

ALTHOUGH WRITING A BOOK is essentially a solo mission involving protracted periods of solitary work on the part of the author, it is highly unlikely that such a project would ever see completion in the absence of the contributions and support of so many other people, more than can be adequately acknowledged here. I am deeply grateful to Rev. Dr. John Drane and Prof. Rev. John Swinton, who supervised and encouraged me through the whole dissertation process at the University of Aberdeen in Aberdeen, Scotland. Their subsequent confidence that this project could prove beneficial on a broader scale both in the academy and beyond has provided incentive in ways they could not imagine. Numerous friends and colleagues who serve in many capacities literally around the world have been outstanding conversation partners, and not always from the position of agreement. To them I extend profound thanks. But the ones who have been my greatest fans while at the same time paying the highest price throughout this entire journey are my dear wife Heather and our four grown children, Todd, Tamara, Tim, and Taylor. Their willingness ten years ago to have their lives rearranged in order to release me to embark on this adventure, and their subsequent tolerant endurance of my occasional passionate tirade on the theology of sacred space, leaves me humbled and truly without the means to adequately say thanks. They have helped me to discover the sacred places that are the most precious to me.

Chapter 1

Is There a Place for
a Place Called Church?

I N MANY WAYS, A book like this would have
been easier to write two to three decades ago
when the connection between theology and the built environment was
a basic assumption in Roman Catholic thinking and virtually a non-
issue in much of Protestant thinking. I am convinced, however, a book
of this nature has never been more important than our present day for
the simple reason that churches continue to erect buildings but unfortunately with little or no theological reflection informing the process. The
purpose of this book is to encourage continued reflection and discussion on issues relating to theology and the built environment among
students and professors in a number of academic disciplines. In addition it is intended to provide some practical suggestions and guidance
for pastoral and lay leaders of churches considering building new or
renovating existing facilities by considering the vital link between the
church's mission and the built environment in which the church functions, that is, sacred space.

The immediate purpose here is twofold: first, the provision of a
clear working definition of the term "missional church" as it will be
used throughout the following pages, and secondly, the establishment
of the fact that sacred space does exist and furthermore is vital to the

fulfillment of the mission of the church. I am well aware that the need for buildings dedicated to the gathering of Christians is being called into question more and more, and, to some degree, understandably so. Inherited architectural paradigms, like some inherited theological paradigms, carry far less currency than in previous generations. For example, the framework that insisted on a large space dedicated to a couple of liturgical events per week has been revisited and found wanting in more and more denominations. Few if any would argue the point that fundamentally the church is not a building; it is people. However, to conclude from that statement that there is therefore no need for buildings dedicated to the ministry and mission of the church is, in my mind, to relinquish sound reasoning.

MISSIONAL CHURCH: POINT OF DEPARTURE

Like several other terms that have made appearances recently such as "postmodern" or "seeker-sensitive" or "emergent," the expression "missional church" has gained increased popularity in a number of disciplines over the past few years. But when the title of any book includes the phrase "missional church," one cannot assume that all readers will understand or appreciate how or why an author intends to use it. Even a cursory survey of the impressive number of works dedicated to the missional church that have been published recently would leave one with an interesting array of nuances and interpretations. Therefore, the starting point will be to clarify what is meant by the term "missional church" for our purposes here.

In recent times this term has been used generally to describe or designate the functions of the church that are outwardly oriented as opposed to activities and ministries that are more internally focused, such as teaching and preaching, the sacraments, and fellowship among the saints. Although related, the terms "missional" and "missions" have been kept distinct in a way that would see missionary activity as it has been historically and typically understood, that is, falling under the broader rubric of *mission*. In other words, the term "missions" is but one expression of mission. The concept of a missional church is often set in opposition to the attractional paradigm or seeker-sensitive approach in which the unchurched are invited to attend a corporate gathering designed with them in mind. The missional approach is informed by a desire to minimize the church's "home-field advantage" by engaging in mission outside the confines of a church building or campus, in places where the unchurched person is more likely to feel less threatened (such as private homes, pubs, or restaurants).

Because one finds similar missional strategies offered in the writings of advocates of the Emergent church there may be a tendency to consider the two equivalents. Although the Emergent phenomenon (or "conversation," as some call it) embraces a missional motivation, and therefore merits serious consideration, it lies outside the parameters and purposes of this book.[1]

Much of the rhetoric that places the church building primarily within the realm of the pragmatic belies an understanding of mission that is activity oriented. If, in our thinking, mission has to do with what we are called to *do* in this world, then it is logical and understandable to perceive the buildings we use as inert containers designed to assist us do what we are called to do. However, foundational to a proper understanding of the role of the built environment for the missional church is a proper grasp of what mission is. For that reason we need to carefully consider the essence and nature of the mission of the church, to which more detailed attention will be given in chapter 2.

At times the concept of a missional church has been considered to be one of several models or paradigms included among others already mentioned, such as the seeker-sensitive church or the Emergent church (and also the liturgical church). I would argue that this kind of categorization represents an imposed, artificial human construct that has the potential to foster a truncated concept of the church. Any church that is not missional is not a church in the biblical sense. The very essence of the church demands mission. Therefore, mission is not solely or primarily what we *do* as the church; it is what we *are*. The church *is* mission. Therefore, operating from a missional stance may impact programming, but it is not contingent upon or limited to effective programs. Likewise, missional thinking and convictions may give birth to strategies and influence structures, but, again, there is no such thing as a strategic or structural template that is unequivocally missional. Having said that, it

---

1. I would strongly encourage those interested in understanding the essence and significance of the Emergent Church to consult primary sources, that is, read the works of Emergent leaders themselves, such as Doug Pagitt, Tony Jones, Brian McLaren, and Dan Kimball, for instance, and not rely solely on second-hand assessments.

is important that we guard against an either-or approach that elevates doing or being over the other. Mission is both.

In summary, then, the missional church operates on the wavelength of God's overarching redemptive purposes in the world for the glory and honor of his name. It is not solely concerned with activity, that is, what we do; it is concerned with being, that is, who and what we are. Let me put it this way: the missional quality of the church reflects both our identity (who we are) and our purpose (what we are called to do). We cannot separate identity from purpose. One does not trump the other, since being the missional church will irresistibly manifest itself in doing, and that doing will be carried out in the particularity of identifiable contexts.

I am writing from the conviction that there is still a place for such structures that may legitimately be called churches, at least within the context of the West, or what John Drane has referred to as the "Global North."[2] Since one of the goals here is to address the existence of sacred space and deal with the appropriateness of designating a building with the label "church," we need address the fundamental issue of function. If, as I am contending, there is a place for church buildings, what function (or functions) do they serve?

THE FUNCTION OF A BUILDING CALLED "CHURCH"

According to Peter Hammond, the function of the church building is not to convert a visitor into a worshiper. It is not to become a place that provokes admiration or provides a worship experience for its visitors. In Hammond's mind, such things are secondary and derivative in terms of the nature of church buildings. "The first purpose of building a church is a purely practical one; to provide a shelter for the liturgical assembly of a particular Christian community."[3]

Perspectives such as these are sustainable only if one considers a church building primarily, if not exclusively, as the *domus ecclesiae*, that is, the house where the church meets and nothing else. However, if one also considers the church building as *domus Dei*, a place where God dwells,[4]

2. Drane, *After McDonalization*, 3.

3. Hammond, *Liturgy*, 29.

4. On the issue of dwelling see Gorringe, *Built Environment*, 26–49 and 79–113, and Harries, *Ethical Function*, 152–66.

then there is room to consider it as the concrete representation of the beliefs of those who gather in it. In other words, the church building can be considered a symbol of the mystical body of Christ. Hammond believes, however, that this will only be possible if and when church structures reflect a "genuine understanding of the nature of the Christian community and its liturgy."[5] He believes, furthermore, that it is highly inappropriate to concern ourselves with the finer points of Christian symbolism in the absence of buildings that *work* for corporate worship.[6]

The manner in which the following arguments are going to unfold is as follows: rather than looking imaginatively from our present realities into the future, we are going to cast a thoughtful glance backward first, then revisit our present situation, and finally, in the light of what we have discovered or rehearsed, offer suggestions for the future.

Taking a historical glance over our shoulder is not likely to answer all our questions. In fact, if it works well, it may raise more important questions than when we started. But it is often questions that have not been considered previously that open up new understandings and appreciation for present situations that, in turn, facilitate an informed approach to future possibilities.

With this in mind, the methodology offered in this book and the way we are going to address the significance of sacred space to the missional church can be presented as follows:

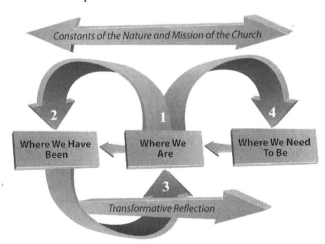

FIGURE 1.1. *Transformative Reflection Model (graphics by George Toth).*

5. Hammond, *Liturgy*, 30.
6. Ibid., 30.

1. Where we are currently: present ecclesial praxis[7]

2. Where we have been: Scripture and tradition, and past ecclesial praxis

3. Where we are—revisited: ecclesial praxis and present situation with opportunities and challenges; incorporating dialogue from theological and biblical studies with that from relevant disciplines outside the field of practical theology

4. Where we need to be: on the basis of reflective assessment, risking change for twenty-first-century ecclesial praxis by developing and adopting philosophical and concrete approaches consistent with and embodying revealed Scriptural truth

Implicit in this diagram are the following assumptions: previously, where we have been (#2) was where we need to be (#4), which became where we are (#1) before becoming where we have been (#2). Similarly, where we need to be (#4) will subsequently become where we are (#1) then, ultimately where we've been (#2). Thus, the directional arrows point from the right to left.

Throughout the entire process of transformative reflection, two procedural aspects influence the rhythm and the outcome. First, transformative reflection encapsulates the prime objective of practical theology, which is change or transformation, brought about in part through the self-evaluative process of reflection. Second, the anticipation, formulation, and implementation of change should not imply the eradication of all that has formed and embodied where we are or where we have been.

Regardless of where we are, in the process there are constants with respect to the nature and mission of the church which must essentially remain integral and connected throughout time. Van Reken posits the preaching of the Word, the sacraments, and church discipline as the three nonnegotiable elements without which the church cannot be the church.[8] I concur with Van Reken's convictions on the Word and the sacraments, but I do not think that church discipline is on the same, nonnegotiable level.

---

7. My use of the term "praxis" here, as opposed to *practice*, has been informed by Swinton and Mowat's work *Practical Theology and Qualitative Research* and Browning's *Fundamental Practical Theology*.

8. Van Reken, "Mission," 2.

If a transformative reflective[9] approach is consistently and properly engaged, there will indeed be times when where we are (#1) and where we need to be (#4) are virtually identical. Minimizing the inconsistency or disparity between where we are and where we need to be is one of the critical functions of practical theology and must be viewed as a perpetual process. Equilibrium must harmonize the where we are–where we've been connection and the where we are–where we need to be connection. Our present situation (where we are) is always informed and shaped by our history (hindsight), but the connection between these two must not be permitted to exercise a hegemonic influence that minimizes or jeopardizes vision for the future, foresight, or reflection on where we need to be.

Similarly, foresight or a visionary commitment to where we need to be must not render wise historical praxis (hindsight gained from where we have been) redundant, unproductive, or necessarily obsolete. Although the transformation that may arise between where we have been and where we need to be may be so significant or extensive that familial resemblance is virtually negligible, the organic connection between the two cannot be denied or eradicated.

It should also be underscored that all three locations, if you will— that is, where we have been, where we are, and where we need to be— always possess an element that is contextually specific. Appropriate criteria for determining where we need to be will vary from place to place, even within relatively close geographic proximity. Thus, at this point the dialogue of disciplines outside the field of practical theology is particularly pertinent to include within the process of transformative reflection.

This model is not only conducive to doing practical theology on an academic level, however. I suggest it can be applied by virtually any local church that finds itself in the planning process of renovating current facilities or adding new ones. More on this is found in the final chapter.

As stated earlier and as has often been said, the church is not a building; it is people. In essence I would agree. But I would also argue that nothing of that essence is violated when referring to a building that is dedicated to liturgical and missional purposes as a church. A parallel example is found in the word "home." In one sense the word refers to a

---

9. I use the term "transformative reflection" to designate a form of reflection that induces action, resulting in transformation.

place of permanent residence, or a place where one is at ease or flour-ishes. In another sense, it refers to the relationships and dynamics in that occur in that place. When one speaks of a "broken home," the reference is not to a building that needs repair. It refers to the distressed relation-ships, the social unit that occupies that place. What would a student be referring to when she says she is looking forward to going home for the summer? Is it the physical structure also referred to a "house," or her family? In all likelihood, it is both.

One of my Greek professors used to remind us regularly that us-age always trumps etymology. It is dangerous to attempt to establish the meaning of a word and its subsequent significance and application solely on the basis of etymology, that is, the history of a word's discernable ini-tial use and how that usage has changed. Having said that, in the case of the word "church," it is helpful to be mindful that like the German word *Kirche* and the Scottish expression *kirk*, the word does find its heritage in the Greek word *kuriakos* and its cognates, which mean "of or belong-ing to the master or lord." We find that word used only twice in the New Testament: once in 1 Corinthians 11:20, where it describes the Lord's Supper, and once in Revelation 1:10, where it is used in reference to the Lord's Day. In neither instance is the word used in reference to the church as is the word *ecclesia*. It is not entirely unreasonable, then, to refer to a built environment dedicated to God's mission in the world, or sacred space, as a church, a space belonging to the Lord.

By incorporating the phrase "missional church" in the title of this book, I realize that I join the ranks of several before me who have written on the subject and on whose shoulders I need to stand in delineating my own perspectives. All of us who have the passion and time to write about the missional church bring something unique to the discussion table that is born out of our own experience, spiritual giftedness, theology, and personalities. What I have found absent from the vast majority of excellent works on the topic, and which I am convinced is germane to and deserves to be included in the conversation, is the built environment, particularly sacred space. The importance of the built environment to the missional church is what I hope to unpack in the chapters that fol-low. I also hope to demonstrate how the two are organically linked and, therefore, mutually affective.

Chapter 2

The Church, the Gospel, and Culture: Defining Mission

OUR PRESENT SITUATION:
WHERE WE ARE, REALLY

ALTHOUGH THERE IS SOME compelling evidence to suggest that the apparent decline of the Western church is but a harbinger of its ultimate demise, not all social scientists, theologians, and church leaders would agree. Following more than thirty years of research in the Canadian context, Canadian sociologist Reginald Bibby has concluded that the church and religion is not on the decline but rather it has a major role to enact in what he calls "the emerging Canadian religious renaissance."[1] Much of the negative prognosis has been evoked by secularization theory, which enjoyed wide acceptance particularly during the 1950s and 1960s. The essence of secularization theory posits: "Modernization necessarily leads to the decline of religion, both in society and in the minds of individuals."[2]

Peter Berger does not deny that some secularizing effects have been fostered by modernization, but points out that counter-secularization movements have also arisen. Berger views the assumption that modernity inevitably leads to the decline of religion as a seriously flawed

1. Bibby, *Restless Churches.*
2. Berger, *Desecularization,* 2.

9

perspective. Berger proposes that two strategies of response to secularization are open to religious institutions: rejection or adaptation.[3] Based on Berger's research, religious institutions that have resisted adapting to the demands of a secular world are the ones that have survived.[4] He states it this way: "Experiments with secularized religion have generally failed; religious movements with beliefs and practices dripping with reactionary supernaturalism (the kind utterly beyond the pale at self-respecting faculty parties) have widely succeeded."[5]

It would be difficult to identify one single denomination or religious group that has not experienced some degree of numerical hemorrhaging, fostering subsequent generations of people that have come to be known as "the unchurched." Researcher George Barna, leading director of the Barna Research Group Limited, has defined the unchurched person as one who has "not attended a Christian church service at any time during the past six months, other than special events such as weddings and funerals."[6] There is very little evidence, however, to support the assumption that these people have little or no desire for spiritual experience or have somehow abandoned a faith they once possessed. In fact, quite the opposite seems to be the case.

Alan Jamieson's research among evangelical, Pentecostal, and other charismatic churches in New Zealand has demonstrated that only about 1 percent of people leaving the church have done so as a result of rejecting or abandoning their faith. Almost 50 percent of people leaving the institutional church eventually become what he terms "reflective exiles," a descriptor for those who have not left the church rashly or thoughtlessly but continue to walk a spiritual journey and continue to embrace their faith.[7] Barna's research in the American context echoes Jamieson's findings, suggesting that at least 20 percent of unchurched people would

---

3. Ibid., 3.

4. Ibid., 4.

5. Ibid.

6. Barna, *Grow Your Church*, 23.

7. Jamieson, *Churchless Faith*, 64–65. Jamieson bases his use of the term "exile" on the work of T. A. Veling, who suggests that although generally associated with an imposed or forced position, there is also a voluntary or optional genre of exile, when people chose escape.

call themselves "born again." According to Barna's calculations, that represents more than fifteen million Americans.[8]

What represents both a challenge to and an opportunity for the church today is the reality that many of the people who have left the church have not necessarily forsaken a belief in God, nor is it true that they no longer have a felt need or desire for an experiential spirituality. My concern here is to address a disconcerting gap in research efforts on the part of the Western church relative to the significance of sacred space for the fulfillment of the mission of the church in an age of apparent decline in the numbers of those who associate themselves with any local congregation. There is no shortage of research material addressing the question of why churches have failed to retain their members and attract new ones, nor is there a dearth of resources offering programs and theologies designed to stem the tide of declining growth and attendance.

A critical element I see missing in the research realm of practical theology, however, is a commitment to discover of the vital role fulfilled by the built environment in the accomplishment of the church's mission. People continue to choose church buildings as the venue of choice for significant events such as weddings and funerals. Does this not suggest that in the minds of many people, sacred space is still considered important, even if only occasionally?

Sacred place has been relegated primarily to the pragmatic realm within parts of the Western church, and evangelicalism in particular. It has apparently been deemed nonessential or at best of secondary importance. Without insisting that sacred place dominate this aspect of practical theology, I would argue the contrary position, demonstrating that the church cannot thrive, let alone fulfill its mission in the twenty-first century, without a comprehensive understanding of the praxis component inherent in the theology and hermeneutic of the built environment. In an effort to bring the connection between sacred space and the mission of the church into sharper focus, we will begin with a brief consideration of the threefold relationship between the culture, the gospel, and the church.

8. Barna, *Grow Your Church*, 26.

MISSION: THE CHURCH IN CONTEXT

It is difficult to seriously dispute the assertion that we are living in a post-Christian society.[9] The relationship between the church and this post-Christian society is a profound and serious issue demanding thoughtful consideration and robust dialogue within the church and beyond. Virtually since its inception, the church, either by choice or necessity, has grappled with the degree and manner in which it should engage the culture of its day. In considering this relationship between church and culture, it is essential to bear in mind what John Stott and Robert Coote state: "It is literally impossible to evangelise in a cultural vacuum. Nobody can reduce the biblical gospel to a few culture-free axioms which are universally intelligible."[10]

An Appreciation for Culture

Culture is a complex reality. The manner in which a person chooses to define it is obviously influenced by one's own experience and assumptions. An anthropologist approaches the study of culture with a different agenda and set of presuppositions than a behavioral scientist, a theologian, or missiologist, notwithstanding the common ground that exists between them all.[11] Personal prejudices affect our interpretation and experience not only of culture in general but also of the specific aspects within it, including the built environment.

Literature from various disciplines, including theology, anthropology, and missiology, is replete with a wide array of definitions. Clifford Geertz perceives culture as "a system of inherited conceptions expressed in symbolic forms by means of which human beings communicate, perpetuate, and develop their knowledge about, and their attitudes towards, life."[12] From his perspective, culture has a foundation that is profoundly conceptual; not excluding the behavioral aspects of culture, he explains how inherited concepts are expressed through a system of symbols, which form the more tangible aspects.

---

9. See Hunt, *Alternative Religions*, 7.

10. Stott and Coote, *Down to Earth*, xi.

11. Stanley Hauerwas concurs: "For example, it surely makes some difference that I write as a Christian schooled by the habits of American academe. What I say about the church as the body of Christ cannot help but be shaped by that context" (Hauerwas, *In Good Company*, 22).

12. Geertz, *Interpretation of Cultures*, 89.

Michael Gallagher suggests that culture is the dimension in which a child learns and develops and attains its potential.[13] He argues that the transmission of culture from one generation to the next involves more than the communication of concepts; since humans are symbol-using animals, "Symbols rather than concepts are the natural vehicles for mediating the meanings and values embodied in cultures."[14]

It is significant to note the semiotic thread present in these and many other descriptions of culture that could be given. To understand and appreciate any given culture, a person must discover and interpret the symbolic content of that culture. One of the essential means to gaining an understanding of the semiotics of a culture is through attention to the built environment, both religious and nonreligious. It would appear that the semiotic expression of culture is intimately intrinsic to our humanness. I would argue that the built environment, and in particular sacred spaces associated with and produced by a culture, provides one of the most significant windows into understanding that culture.

Do absolute or universal symbols exist, or do symbols change? According to Aylward Shorter, culture is embodied in and transmitted through a pattern of symbols, "a pattern *capable of development and change* and it belongs to the concept of humanness itself."[15] Yet despite the fluidity of culture, one can still tease out three main components: symbol, myth or narrative, and ritual.[16] "Symbols, with their variety of meanings, are born because they respond to the subjective needs of people and their experience of life."[17] Cultural symbols are not necessarily imposed on individual members of a culture but rather develop or evolve as the subjective needs of the people within it mutate.

It is within the concrete context of culture that the gospel is embodied. "It represents a way of life for a given time and place, replete with values, symbols, and meanings, reaching out with hopes and dreams, often struggling for a better world."[18] A vital element of culture is its significant social or relational component. According to H. Richard Niebuhr,

---

13. Gallagher, *Clashing Symbols*, 6.

14. Ibid., 15.

15. Shorter, *Theology of Inculturation*, 5 (italics added).

16. Arbuckle, *Refounding*, 38.

17. Arbuckle, *Earthing*, 15.

18. Schreiter, *Local Theologies*, 20.

anything that is purely private, neither contributing to nor benefiting from social life, is not a part of culture; "social life is always cultural."[19]

Some such as Lesslie Newbigin believe that the individualism so rampantly characteristic in Western culture represents the deepest source of the contemporary malaise presently plaguing today's society.[20] The apparent freedom offered by individualism is a denial of one God-given reality fundamental to our human nature, namely, that "we grow into true humanity only in relationships of faithfulness and responsibility toward one another."[21]

The variety of perspectives on culture presented here illustrates that attempts to offer a precise, universally accepted definition is onerously challenging. Exacerbating the challenge is the fact that culture changes, often at such a rate and magnitude that the ability to remain current eludes even the most skilled social scientists. The proliferation of subcultures within most societies only increases the enormity of the challenge in understanding culture and interpreting its impact.

A related issue that could be discussed at some length pertains to the question of whether culture is the product of human creativity and activity or vice versa. Michael Gallagher perceives humanity as both the subject (shaper) and the object (goal) of culture. "Christianity in particular has been a creator of culture because of the value it places on the transcendence of the human person."[22]

Unfortunately, one of the most serious wounds the church has historically suffered has been self-inflicted by her choice to neglect or minimize the significance of culture, ignoring the vital position it occupies in the fulfillment of her God-given mission. The lamentable result has been a tendency within the Western church to perceive the Euro-American expression as the most authentic one, the one that more accurately mirrors the Scriptures—fostering a mindset that cultures outside that context are incapable of offering added value to the dialogue or to any evangelistic endeavor.

Charles Kraft suggests that missionaries have not intentionally sought to be disloyal to biblical principles, nor were they knowingly disrespectful of the cultures to which they ministered. "They merely lacked

19. Niebuhr, *Christ and Culture*, 33.

20. Newbigin, *Gospel in a Pluralist Society*, 231.

21. Ibid.

22. Gallagher, *Clashing Symbols*, 50.

the ability to understand and appreciate the significance of cultural differences. They approached their task from a monocultural, ethnocentric point of view. They see their ways as superior and 'Christian.' Whether consciously or unconsciously, they regarded other cultures as inferior to their own home cultures."[23] Any suggestion of an unadulterated, pure gospel runs the risk of failing to recognize that there really is no such thing as a gospel that is not culturally informed.[24]

Such attitudes belie the failure of these well-intentioned pioneers to recognize that their own experience of the gospel message within the cultural forms in which they lived it out was vastly different from the culture of the original recipients of the gospel. As Kraft points out,[25] culture and cultural forms used to convey sacred truth in and of themselves are not sacred. Yet God continues to use an abundance of cultural forms to convey his changeless truth. Receiving cultures are primary stakeholders in the process of how the gospel should be conveyed in their context.

Professor Samuel Huntington of Harvard University believed that what he called the Velvet Curtain of culture has become a more influential dividing line than any Iron Curtain of ideology.[26] Perhaps the apparent demise of the church's contribution to a sense of meaningfulness in society today is due in part to the church's failure to recognize and come to grips with this truth.

How then does culture relate to the significance of sacred space? A culture cannot be understood or fully appreciated without consideration of the built environments within it. The reverse is also true; an appreciation of built environments cannot be acquired in the absence of an understanding of the culture in which they are situated. Establishing the vital role of sacred space in relation to the mission of the church can only be accomplished successfully as culture, and its potential to influence and be influenced, is incorporated into the facilitation of that mission. Culture should also be evaluated and addressed in the process of constructing built environments, which optimise the mission's fulfilment.

---

23. Kraft, "Church in Culture," 212.
24. See Newbigin, *Gospel in a Pluralist Society*, 142.
25. Kraft, "Church in Culture," 223.
26. Cited in Gallagher, *Clashing Symbols*, 3.

An Understanding of the Gospel

The mission of the church not only requires an appreciation for and understanding of culture. It must also be accompanied by a proper understanding of the gospel. In particular, two dimensions of the gospel need to be considered, both of which are related to and influenced by sacred space, namely, content and effect. Although the word "gospel" in essence connotes "good news," universal agreement among theologians and biblical scholars on what the good news is, both in terms of what the gospel means (content) and what it is intended to do (effect), is difficult to establish. Yet the gospel is or should be the very core or hub of everything the church is and does.

Jesus's whole ministry was gospel oriented. All three synoptic writers describe on numerous occasions Jesus's teaching ministry as a presentation of the good news, the gospel.[27] But in the writings of the apostle Paul we also see the gospel centering on Christ himself, evidenced in part by Paul's use of the expression "the gospel of Christ" (Rom. 15:19). The content of the gospel in Paul's mind is abundantly clear, particularly in portions such as his letter to the Galatians. The remedy for the alienation that exists between humanity and God is available solely through faith in the death and resurrection of Christ. The gospel, therefore, is based on the grace or unmerited favor of God through Jesus Christ. Those who embrace this gospel of grace become the possessors of hope (Col. 1:23) and peace (Eph. 6:15).

Paul's ministry was governed by a commitment to the gospel that had a marked sense of obligation. This is made clear in his statement, "Woe is me if I do not preach the gospel!" (1 Cor. 9:16). The health and longevity of churches established under Paul's missionary endeavors were contingent upon a commitment to this gospel, which was anchored on the birth, life, teachings, death, resurrection, and promised second coming of Jesus Christ.

The majority of people adhering to some form of the gospel would typically admit that change is an inherent and resulting aspect of the good news. If we believe that the gospel will bring about change, or conversion, how will the evidence of that change be perceived in an individual's life? Will it be swift and radical, or as Arbuckle suggests, "a life-long striving towards self-transcendence, in the midst of failures

---

27. See Matthew 9:35; Mark 1:14–15; and Luke 7:22 for examples.

and imperfections"?[28] A thoughtful study of conversions brought about by an encounter with the gospel would likely reveal that no single template of universal applicability exists, either for individuals or for various cultural contexts. Biblical and anecdotal resources provide evidence for significant diversity in the manner and in the rate at which change occurs. This may prove more problematic for the modern Western mind, which prefers predictability and logical sequence expounded in certain key principles or spiritual laws.

One must also discern the gospel's potential for both corporate and societal transformational influences. Is the expected cultural impact simply the sum total of all individual experiences? Missionaries occasionally have encountered less-than-enthusiastic responses from North American churches when they recount stories of entire villages responding to the gospel and converting to Christianity all at one time. The Western conversion paradigm perceives the individual as the focal point, insisting that certain responses must occur in the proper sequence: acknowledgement of sin, repentance, confession, regeneration, justification, sanctification, and so on. This persuasion arises with a bias toward or emphasis on individualism, characteristic of the Western mindset. Significantly, the mass conversions experienced in many third-world countries resonate more readily with biblical accounts (e.g., the "conversion" of Nineveh, recorded in the book of Jonah, and Pentecost, when some three thousand people responded to the apostle Peter's preaching, recorded in Acts 2) than it does with the Western understanding of conversion.

A historical tension between missiologists and anthropologists has often centered on the issue of what constitutes a legitimate encounter between the gospel and a culture. Anthropologists have resisted any introduction of the gospel or any ideology that would in any way impinge on, denigrate any aspect of, or demand change of any sort within the receiving culture. The insistence that change occur is perceived as arrogant and imperialistic. Therefore the introduction of the gospel into any culture is going to be viewed as intrusive to some degree.[29]

A major challenge faced by today's church is how to maintain the gospel and the receiving culture in a proper and symbiotic tension, that is, without being disloyal to the gospel as revealed in Scripture or paternalistic or demeaning in the approach to those cultures. Despite many

28. Arbuckle, *Earthing*, 190.
29. Kraft, "Church in Culture," 214.

significant benefits brought about by the introduction of Christianity to other cultures, some question whether the more negative dimensions of missionary expansion have not outweighed the benefits.[30]

The gospel's ability to influence change both individually and corporately does not imply that those conveying its message should ignore or seek to remove all vestiges of the culture to which they go. But we should also avoid the dangerous tendency to recognize only the good in that culture. Robert Schreiter refers to this as "cultural romanticism," a mindset that "assumes that there is no sin in the world, that people cannot be and are not often cruel to one another, and that culture contact/ change is always a bad thing."[31]

The gospel must advance both in terms of the sharing of its content and the actualizing of its desired effect. The mission of the church involves more than the mere conveyance or translation of propositional truth if it is to be loyal to Scripture and relevant to today's world. It must aim at introducing people to an experience of God, and into a community of godly persons resonating with who they are, without violating the manner in which God has revealed himself or his purpose and preferences for them. In order for these objectives to be achieved and to ensure that the theology is adequate to the local situation, it is imperative that "one must listen to the religious responses already present in the culture."[32] It is in these existing responses that we are likely to discover some profound indicators of the fact that God is already at work in that culture.

Besides the more positive dimensions such as the promise of peace of mind, healing, and relief from anxiety, there is another side to the gospel message. The cross of Christ, central to the Christian gospel—which speaks of God's mercy, love, and willingness to forgive—also speaks eloquently of God's judgment. As John C. Bennett asks, "Is it not the essence of the Christian gospel that healing and judgment belong together?"[33] One finds an unparalleled demonstration of this balance in the life and ministry of Jesus Christ.

The incarnation of Christ also provides insight into the effect of the gospel. The gospel message communicates God's intersection with

---

30. Drane, *Cultural Change*, 105.

31. Schreiter, *Local Theologies*, 29.

32. Ibid., 123.

33. Bennett "Prophetic Critic."

human history in the person of his son Jesus Christ and the work he accomplished while on earth. The incarnation provides the "how," the specific strategy to introducing the gospel into any context. I would agree with Stephen Bevans,[34] who suggests that the incarnational nature of Christianity necessitates the contextualization of theology. He states, "Incarnation is a process of becoming particular, and in and through the particular, the divinity could become visible and in some way (not fully, but in some way) become graspable and intelligible."[35]

A danger to be aware of and avoided in embracing an incarnational emphasis is the tendency to minimize or neglect the ascension as a pivotal aspect of Christ's incarnation. The aspect of divine immanence is clearly born out in the truth of Christ's incarnation, while the ascension makes it clear that divine transcendence is equally central to the gospel.

Michael Gallagher notes a similar distinction between older spiritualities, which he sees as "vertical roads of questing for God beyond this world," and newer ones that "stress a this-worldly fullness of life, as an experience of Christian faith."[36] It is possible that some newer spiritualities would readily embrace the incarnational dimension of the gospel, emphasizing immanence and present experience while marginalizing the transcendent. These two emphases are also readily discerned by comparing the architectural expressions of the twelfth century cathedral with any number of church buildings constructed or renovated during the past few decades. Through elements such as proportion and lighting, the cathedral affects an awareness of transcendence. In contrast, many churches being constructed in our day have been informed by the core value of community and intimacy, which is reflected in the use of softer colors and materials and seating arrangements that intentionally enhance awareness of and engagement with other worshipers.

Robert Schreiter conveys the relation between the incarnation and the gospel masterfully when he says,

> Gospel is always incarnate, incarnate in the reality of those who bring it to us, and incarnate in those who help us nurture the beginnings of faith. Church is a complex of those cultural patterns in which the gospel has taken on flesh, at once enmeshed in the local situation, extending through communities in our own time

34. Bevans, *Models of Contextual Theology*, 7.

35. Ibid., 8.

36. Gallagher, *Clashing Symbols*, 137.

and in the past, and reaching out to the eschatological realization of the fullness of God's reign . . . the gospel without church does not come to its full realization; the church without gospel is a dead letter. Without church there is no integral incarnation of the gospel.[37]

But it must be kept in mind that Christianity is not the gospel. As Lesslie Newbigin states, "Christianity is what generations of us have made of the gospel, and we know we have often made a mess of it."[38] The gospel is not limited to the vast array of experiences known to occur among people who have embraced it, important as the existential aspect is. Rather, the gospel is a declaration of the work of God in space-time, in human history, through the incarnation of Christ. The impact of this declaration on the design and use of sacred space within the mission of the church must not be minimized or rendered inconsequential.

An Acceptance of the Church

Schreiter's comment on the indispensable nature of the church in the incarnation of the Gospel prompts closer consideration of its nature as it relates to both the gospel and culture. Clarification of the term "the church" is critical, as many different images and connotations emerge in people's thinking. Many recall specific physical buildings, from chapels to cathedrals, in which significant rites of passage or regular rituals have occurred. For others, the term may connote an organizational or denominational entity, while for others it may refer to a specific group of people with whom they gather on a regular basis.

In terms of the church universal, one can legitimately think in terms of a transcultural entity, since it refers to the company of all believers from all time in all places. However, it is impossible to think this way when focusing on the local expression of the church. Every local church bears cultural birthmarks that are not only linguistic in nature but also liturgical, organizational, and often architectural. Rather than viewing these cultural dimensions as hindrances or moral deficiencies needing refurbishment or removal, they must be recognized as essential ingredients to an authentic expression of the church within the context and time of that given culture.

37. Schreiter, *Constructing Local Theologies*, 21.
38. Newbigin, *Signs Amid the Rubble*, 113.

I. Howard Marshall comments,

> Certainly, while it is sin-denying, Christianity is not world-deny-
> ing. The New Testament attitude to cultural values is a positive
> one. . . . Contrary to traditional evangelical eschatology, the God
> revealed by the New Testament writers surely has in mind the
> conservation and transformation of human culture and human
> society in the world to come.[39]

Because of this, it behooves the church to be cognizant of the media
of the cultures in which it is located. We need to identify the "modes and
the content of public communication and exchange of verbal and visual
ideas."[40] But it is also vital that we have a deep understanding of the
nature of the church and be able to answer the following important and
relevant question: How exactly is the church to be that kind of presence
in today's society?

A New Testament Church?

"New Testament church" is a term used widely in reference to the gathering and functioning of Christians as recorded in the book of Acts and
the Epistles. It becomes apparent even before the end of the book of
Acts, let alone after reading the various letters written by the apostles,
that within the first few decades of the church's existence, significant differences began to arise. Different churches struggled with a wide variety
of internal issues[41] as well as rather divergent external pressures.

Relatively little biblical text is dedicated to detailed descriptions of
or prescriptions for service formats, liturgies, or liturgical space, leaving
a significant amount of freedom for a variety of expressions at the local
church level. The term "New Testament church" is applicable only in a
broad and general sense. As Newbigin points out, one characteristic of all
churches referred to in the New Testament is that they were known in two
dimensions: their relation to God through Christ and their location.[42]

---

39. Marshall, "Culture and the New Testament," 31.

40. Miles, *Image as Insight*, 28.

41. The Corinthian Church confronted issues as unfortunate as incest (1 Cor. 5),
insensitive drunken behaviour at the Lord's table (1 Cor. 11) and a flawed understanding and exercise of spiritual gifts (1 Cor. 12–14), whereas the Galatian Churches dealt
with the insistence by some, on circumcision and other aspects of the Mosaic Law, as
an essential aspect of personal salvation.

42. Newbigin, *Gospel in a Pluralist Society*, 229.

A Dynamic Equivalent Church?

In the universal and essential sense, common traits mark the church regardless of location or culture. But to insist on transcultural uniformity in the manner in which the church expresses itself locally is to misunderstand the nature of the church and to misrepresent the manner in which Christ has chosen to establish it. At the local level, the church must not only be seen as accurately reflecting the essence of the gospel message; it must also do so in a manner that is easily understood and reflects the culture in which it is located. One of the most obvious vehicles through which people are often introduced to the church for the first time is the building where a local congregation gathers.

Rather than striving for a precise duplication of the first-century church, a more realistic endeavor in our present day would be to aim for what has been described as a "dynamic equivalent church." Kraft offers the following characteristics of what that would look like: "(1) conveys to its members truly Christian meanings; (2) responds to the felt needs of its society, producing within it an impact for Christ equivalent to that which the first century church produced in its society; and (3) appropriates cultural forms that are as nearly indigenous as possible."[43] This demands the development of expressions of the gospel that not only preserve the integrity of the biblical message and teaching but also bear the marks of cultural authenticity and relevance. As many churches have discovered, this is not always a simple challenge.

A Reciprocal Engagement

What, then, should the relation between culture, the gospel, and the church be like? Is the gospel transcultural and thus impervious to any possible influence by cultures? Is any change or impact resulting from an encounter between the gospel and culture unilateral? To some, the suggestion that the gospel could be susceptible to cultural influence may represent a violation of biblical legitimacy. However, many see the possibility and even the necessity of a symbiotic relationship between the gospel and culture. The position of Pope Paul II, for instance, was very clear: "The synthesis between culture and faith is not just a demand of culture, but also of faith. . . . A faith which does not become culture is a faith which has not been fully received, not thoroughly thought through, not

43. Kraft, "Church in Culture," 224.

fully lived out."[44] The gospel is never expressed into thin air, but always within a cultural context, thus cultures not only need to be evangelized but the gospel needs to be inculturated. Gallagher expands further: "To advocate that faith should become culture means simply that the gospel can and should permeate the ethos of a people, its essential attitudes, its institutions, and all its structures."[45]

In the World Council of Churches publication *Study Process on Gospel and Cultures, 1995*, we read, "The gospel transcends every culture, but is never accessible apart from its embodiment to specific cultures."[46] Such convictions are not the products of this past century alone. Michael Gallagher cites a famous seventeenth-century church document, which echoes the 1997 sentiments of I. Howard Marshall:

> Do not bring any pressure to bear on these people to change their manners, customs and practices, unless these are obviously contrary to religion and morality. There is nothing more absurd than to want to bring France to China—or to bring Spain or Italy or any part of Europe. Carry none of that but rather faith, which neither despises nor destroys the way of life and the customs of any people, when these are not evil things. On the contrary, faith desires that these traditions be conserved and protected.[47]

The above observations representing Roman Catholic, ecumenical, and evangelical perspectives underscore the need to discern carefully the alternative methods and techniques that are appropriately relevant to the plurality of cultures to which the gospel needs to be taken. The values, perspectives, people, and other relevant aspects of those cultures must be incorporated within efforts to discover and implement the strategies and tactics utilized to introduce the gospel in a manner which allows people to embrace it as their own rather than as an alien intrusion or transplant.

At some point, translation must take place, but it must go beyond a more obvious, superficial, linguistic level into the deeper intrinsic cultural aspects of function and meaning. In order to discover function and meaning, symbols and other cultural texts must be understood and intentionally incorporated into the translation process. Effective

44. Cited in Gallagher, *Clashing Symbols*, 53.

45. Gallagher, *Clashing Symbols*, 54.

46. Cited in ibid., 63.

47. Cited in ibid., 102.

translation is dependent not only on an accurate exegesis of the texts in which the gospel has been invested but also requires an exegesis of the culture to which it is being conveyed.

Robert T. Rush offers an interesting metaphor contrasting pre- and post-Vatican II missionary work.[48] Before Vatican II, the missionary could be likened to a pearl merchant who had a treasure (the gospel) to bring to a culture. Following the Council, the perspective on evangelization was altered, such that the missionary was like a treasure hunter who came to seek and discover the treasure God had already invested in that culture. This method was more characteristic of what Stephen Bevans refers to as an anthropological model of practical theology: "Culture shapes the way Christianity is articulated."[49]

This is not to imply that the conviction held by some, including J. I. Packer, that "the content of the gospel message must always control the method of its communication,"[50] is no longer relevant. Although Newbigin believes that it is incumbent upon the church to consider intently the needs and desires of people in an effort to understand their situation, he does warn,

> Neither these desires and needs, nor any analysis of the situation made on the basis of some principles drawn from other sources than Scripture, can be the starting point for mission. The starting point is God's revelation of himself as it is witnessed to us in Scripture.[51]

Packer's concern is that cultural sensitivity and a concern for relevance not dominate to the point of detracting from the essence and necessity of the gospel message. With that I concur. At the same time I agree with Michael Gallagher, who states, "Ideally the gospel transcends all cultural embodiments, but in reality a pure encounter with a culture-free gospel is impossible."[52] The outcome of any effort to introduce the gospel to a given culture must be a message that is marked by theological soundness within cultural authenticity. In order for that end to result, the church must not only be willing to speak and give something; it must incorporate within its means an earnest willingness to listen and receive something.

48. Rush, "Pearl Merchant," 6–10. Cited in Bevans, *Models*, 49.

49. Bevans, *Models*, 49.

50. Packer, "The Gospel," 97.

51. Newbigin, *Gospel in a Pluralist Society*, 153–54.

52. Gallagher, *Clashing Symbols*, 103.

The point being emphasized here is that no presentation of the gospel is ever culture free. From the beginning of the church's history, the gospel has always been embodied in a culture. "The idea that one can or could at any time separate out by some process of distillation a pure gospel unadulterated by any cultural accretions is an illusion."[53]

Failure to invest the effort necessary to understanding or appraising the world in which the church is located runs the risk of rendering the gospel incomprehensible. At the same time, a second potential response the church must avoid in its efforts to fulfill its mission is allowing culture or society to set the agenda and determine the issues. "The result then is that the world is not challenged at its depth but rather absorbs and domesticates the gospel and uses it to sacralize its own purposes."[54]

One must accept the fact that times and circumstances will arise when the church, out of loyalty to the gospel, will need to be a dissenting body, challenging societal mores and structures. There will also be times when the church needs to be a "church for the nation or the parish."[55] The challenge is to know which posture is appropriate and when, especially when we keep in mind that a gospel that is not a public gospel is no gospel at all.

The challenge that must be confronted honestly is expressed by Gallagher's question: "In what spirit should faith view a dominant culture that, either openly or more silently, denies many of the values that are at the core of the Christian vision?"[56] By its very nature, the gospel calls for demarcation between evil and good. A preoccupation with the more marketable, positive aspects of the gospel, therefore, has raised concern with some that the church seems to have neglected her role as prophetic critic. In a relativistic, pluralistic society, the lines between good and evil are not always easily drawn and will rarely find universal acceptance.

Robert Schreiter describes and addresses two potential responses to this issue.[57] One approach is *syncretism*, which "has to do with the mixing of elements of two religious systems to the point where at least one, if not both, of the systems lose their basic structure and identity."[58]

53. Newbigin, *Foolishness*, 4.

54. Newbigin, *Gospel in a Pluralist Society*, 152.

55. Ibid., 196.

56. Ibid., 112.

57. Schreiter, *Local Theologies*, 144–45.

58. Ibid., 144.

Appealing to many within a pluralistic context, this approach eventually crumbles when faced with a scenario involving opposing or colliding values. One must be aware that any attempt to be relevant may succumb to the pull of syncretism. On the other hand, an effort to avoid syncretism may degenerate into irrelevance.[59]

Thus, another approach taken is what is known as *dualism*.

> In dual systems a people follow the religious practices of two distinct systems. The two systems are kept discrete; they can operate side by side. . . . Conversion to Christianity has usually meant putting all other religious systems aside, but in these instances significant parts or even the entirety of a second system is maintained.[60]

A dualistic approach is far more likely to find acceptance within a postmodern world view in which apparently contradictory positions can be juxtaposed far more easily than in a modernistic framework.

In either of these approaches, we are brought back once again to the question of what conversion really is and what role the church should play within a given culture. Can a person be truly converted while continuing to engage in centuries-old cultural customs, which seem to run counter to scriptural teaching? It is essential to maintain a balance between the roles of the church as prophetic critic and as messenger of healing.

In all efforts to maintain this essential balance in the roles of the church, it is imperative that we remain sensitive to the receiving cultures. Cultural insensitivity runs the risk of allowing the church and its theology to become little more than a conduit of external domination. We come perilously close to assuming a docetic posture, acting as though our Lord never did become flesh.[61] Karl Rahner would add his strong sentiment, "Faith risks self-destruction if it fails to create the forms of faith demanded by a new culture."[62]

MISSION AND MISSIONS

This brief consideration of the significance of and interplay between culture, the gospel, and the church leads naturally into the foundational

59. Lesslie Newbigin, *Foolishness*, 7.

60. Schreiter, *Constructing Local Theologies*, 145.

61. See Ibid., 20.

62. Cited in Gallagher, *Clashing Symbols*, 109.

issue of the mission of the church. It will be on this understanding of the essentials of the church's mission that the following chapters will be based. The terms "mission" and "missions" are often used interchangeably, but doing so tends to limit their application and weakens the significance of both.

For the purpose of clarity, it is important that "the mission of the church" as it is used here be distinct and distinguished from the more narrowly focused term "missions." The reason for this is that there appears to be a subtle shift from the use of the word "missions" to "mission" in the thinking and conversations among missiologists and theologians. Although missionary activity[63] constitutes a significant aspect of the mission of the church, it does not represent the aggregate. There is good indication that a universal understanding and acceptance of what the missional nature of the church really means and entails remains elusive. For example, many still default to missionary activity as the sum total of what it means to be as a missional church. The mission of the church exceeds the realm of proclamation and includes an ontological dimension; the mission of the church determines not only what it does but also what it is in its essence.[64]

Mission, for some, continues to be identified with evangelistic endeavors. Rick Warren, popular author and founding pastor of Saddleback Community Church in Lake Forest, California, one of America's largest and best-known churches, summarizes Christ's purpose for his church with five key words:[65]

Magnify	We celebrate God's presence in worship.
Mission	We communicate God's Word through evangelism.
Membership	We incorporate God's family into our fellowship.
Maturity	We educate God's people through discipleship.
Ministry	We demonstrate God's love through service.

All of the above five dimensions are sufficiently generic to be applicable in virtually any church setting, but in the purpose statement of the Saddleback

---

63. I am referring to the proclamation activity of taking the gospel to those who are deemed in need of receiving it, under the rubric of "missions."

64. In a similar way, Stanley Hauerwas states, "The church does not *have* a social ethic, but rather *is* a social ethic" (Hauerwas, *In Good Company*, 22).

65. Warren, *The Purpose-Driven Church*, 107, italics added. Warren's penchant for alliteration is at times distractingly obvious throughout this book.

Community church, mission is intentionally connected with outreach or evangelism. As Craig Van Gelder points out, the flaw in this approach is its fixation on *activity*, on what the church does.[66] Furthermore, historically, and to some degree still today, people have thought of mission in terms of evangelistic activity that may be supported by the local church but is ultimately carried out by people beyond the boundaries of their homeland. As such, missionary activity is considered to be one of several responsibilities associated with the mandate of the church.

Identifying the "Essential" Mission of the Church

It could be argued that the church has historically approached its mission from an adversarial or a pathological posture. The adversarial position sees the world as the opponent to be overcome, while the pathological perspective sees the world as sick and in need of healing. Although both positions contain some truth and do reflect reality, both are incomplete. Both of these are born out of an interpretation of the apostolic nature of the church, enshrined in statements including the Nicene Creed.

The Apostolic Nature of the Church

Of the four qualifiers relative to the church contained in the Nicene Creed, "We believe in one holy catholic and apostolic church," the term "apostolic" is particularly germane to our purposes thus far. There are at least three ways in which the term can be interpreted. It can refer to the succession from the apostle Peter through the laying on of hands;[67] the foundation laid for the church through the teachings of the apostles of Jesus Christ;[68] or it can be based on an interpretation of the word *apostolos*, which emphasizes the aspect of being sent. What is noteworthy about the latter view is that the predominant context in which mission occurs is beyond the walls of the church.[69]

Because God is a sending God—God sent his own Son, his Son sent his apostles, and the Father and Son sent the Spirit—the whole concept of being sent must be woven into the very fabric of who we are as the missional church. This "sent-ness," if you will, is what fosters and

---

66. Van Gelder, *Ministry of the Missional Church*, 16–17.

67. This is the position commonly held by the Roman Catholic Church and by some within the Anglican Church.

68. Van Reken, "Mission of the Local Church," 348.

69. Yannoulatos, "Rediscovering Our Apostolic Identity," 12.

necessitates what Reggie McNeal calls our "thereness."[70] Rather than seeing ourselves primarily as a sending body, we must see ourselves as a body that is *sent*.

The Mission of God

Another approach to gaining an understanding and fuller appreciation of the church's mission is to reflect on God's prime concern for the world: *missio Dei*, or God's mission. According to one of the major contributors to this whole conversation, David Bosch, the concept of mission as the activity of God was first articulated by Karl Barth in a paper he presented at the 1932 Brandenburg Missionary Conference.[71] Mission should never be a reflection solely of human ingenuity or sincerity. Since then, others have rallied around the concept that mission is born in the heart of God.[72] We can be indicted all too often for operating from a deistic posture, acting as though God, having started the ball rolling, has subsequently retired to the bleachers and left us on our own with little or no direct involvement in our world and lives.

God's mission is larger than the church. Arguably the prime instrument for God's mission is the church, but it is not limited to the church. "The *missio Dei* is God's activity, which embraces both the church and the world, and in which the church may be privileged to participate."[73] God's mission is cast in eternity—from the foundations of the earth—and is cosmologically oriented, rather than exclusively anthropologically or ecclesiologically.

In light of the Christ event, *redemption* surfaces as *missio dei*. The alienation between humanity and God, resulting in the subsequent need for reconciliation, is a prominent theme featured in virtually every part of Scripture. The way this revelation informs or is reflected in the understanding of the mission of the church has been and continues to be a debated issue.

Van Reken, representing the Christian Reformed tradition, argues that although the mission of the local church should reflect God's overall mission in the world (redemption), there is still great latitude in terms

70. McNeal, *Missional Renaissance*, 25.

71. Bosch, *Transforming Mission*, 389.

72. See, for example, van Gelder, *Ministry of the Missional Church*, 85–88, and Drane, *After McDonaldization*, 59–92.

73. Bosch, *Transforming Mission*, 391.

of what that will actually look like at the local level.[74] Just as individuals are called to specific ministries based upon personal giftedness and calling, we need to consider and accept the possibility that individual denominations and/or local churches are likewise called to specifically emphasize certain aspects of mission unique to their particular context.

Although evangelism is not the sole purpose for the church's existence, it must remain central and influential to all it does. Manifesting a reflection of God's salvific, redemptive purposes exceeds the concern for the eternal welfare of individual souls.[75] Redemption is not limited to eschatological realities, but it must also address existing conditions and be marked by a need for justice, healing, and reconciliation. Nor is God's mission focused exclusively on humanity; all of creation is the beneficiary of God's redemptive work.[76]

An important missional question relates to how epitomizing evangelism as the pivotal function of the church would affect other dimensions, including the administration of the sacraments, worship, and even the preaching of the Word.[77] Van Reken argues that counter-productivity will inevitably be the result. The same principle may apply to the inordinate elevation of any number of other functions of the church, including preaching, worship arts, or the sacraments. Van Reken is convinced that although other organizations can and should be involved in evangelism, the preaching of the Word, the administration of the Lord's Supper, and the sacrament of baptism are to be conducted only within the context of the church.[78] Since God's grace is received through these functions, Van Reken concludes, "It would seem that the mission of the church is to be God's chosen (dare I say, *elect*?) agent for special grace."[79]

God's mission, then, is informed and characterized by grace, the extension of unmerited favor to the undeserving. If the mission of the church is to reflect the *missio Dei*, then the function of the church is to be the means through which God's special grace is dispensed.

---

74. Van Reken, "The Mission of the Local Church," 352.

75. I am using this term here in a way that reflects my own evangelical heritage, that is, in reference to the spiritual, invisible part of our humanness that outlives our earthly human bodies.

76. Romans 8:20–21

77. Van Reken, "Mission of the Local Church," 358–60.

78. Ibid., 361.

79. Ibid.

In light of these perspectives, the church could extend to include such things as fellowship, worship, pastoral counseling, healing, or even exercise classes and instruction in art or self-defense. Furthermore, the whole dimension of social action needs to be integrated intentionally and wisely into the mission of the church. Is it not completely reasonable to include any and all of these activities within the realm of the distribution of the special grace of God?

The church exists to reflect and continue the mission of God on earth, particularly as this was demonstrated through the incarnate life and ministry of Jesus. It must be devoted to addressing the reality of the alienation between God and humanity. The consequences of that alienation, such as injustice and brokenness, must be a concern to the church as well as eternal destinies.

Mission Statements: Localizing Mission

Relatively recently, attention has been given to the formulation of mission statements within local churches. Currently, mission statements are not exclusive to ecclesiastical bodies; many major corporations have well-thought-out and very clearly delineated mission statements. McDonald's fast food restaurants in the United Kingdom all operate under a mission statement that indicates its aim is to be the UK's best fast service restaurant experience. British Airways, in establishing its new corporate identity, has announced its new corporate mission to be the undisputed leader in world travel for the next millennium.

Inherent in both of these corporate statements is a commitment to affecting change in people's behavior. Mission statements represent an articulation of purpose, answering the questions "Why are we here?" and "What are we trying to accomplish?" McDonald's and British Airways both aim to have people willingly alter or arrange their plans in order to adopt the products and services they are offering. One of the hallmarks of contemporary literature on leadership is the call for vision casting, a pivotal leadership quality. This is the ability to articulate the organization's ultimate form, or the desired contextual expression of its *raison d'etre,* in a manner that infects its members with an enthusiasm and confidence that the vision can and should be accomplished.

Some within the church today discern a flaw in the concept of context-specific mission statements and suggest that it renders no church accountable.[80] This raises the question of whether there is a missional aspect that is transculturally and trans-temporally applicable. In other words, is there an aspect of mission without which a church cannot be a church? What I have attempted to establish in this chapter and will continue to develop in the following chapters is that mission addresses two issues of unequivocal importance: the first is a matter of *identity*, or who we are; the second one is the issue of *purpose*, or what we are here to do.

An understanding and appreciation of a church's mission is a prerequisite to determining a church's activities. The nature of the activities undertaken by the church will affect the types of built environments in which those activities are optimally accomplished. Foundational to both the mission and the activities of the church is a biblical ecclesiology. Built environments that hinder the accomplishment of a church's mission lack the integrity and the authenticity that are fundamental to sacred places. Sacred place is an essential consideration with respect to the church's mission in our world in the twenty-first century. To move this examination forward we will turn our focus backward in time and construct a historical framework for sacred places.

---

80. Van Reken, "Mission of the Local Church," 346.

Chapter 3

A Historical Framework for Sacred Space

REVISITING WHERE WE HAVE BEEN

IF THE CONCERN MOTIVATING any church body to renovate or build their ministry spaces is to enhance effectiveness in mission now and in the future, why invest the effort to gain an appreciation of historical developments from centuries past? The reason for such an investigation is not primarily to learn from our predecessors' mistakes and avoid their apparent blunders. Rather by considering some of the salient shifts and developments marking the design and construction of spaces used by the church from the New Testament era through the medieval period to the contemporary church buildings currently utilized, I also intend to distill benefits from what has been done well.

In this chapter we will consider five prominent types of structures that have been utilized by the church through the centuries, investigating first how each was influenced by the cultural realities of their respective time and secondly how they reflected the beliefs of the church and assisted in the fulfilment of her mission and the expression of her faith. This investigation is based on the premise that church buildings provide one of the most effective means of gaining insight into a church's belief system and mission. Jeanne Halgren Kilde says it well: "Indeed, church buildings are dynamic agents in the construction, development, and persistence of Christianity itself."[1]

I have elected to focus on five structural genres, which have emerged as prominent features or dominant centres of the church's activities, rather than investigating period styles of church architecture and adopting the nomenclature often associated with them.[2] The reason for this approach is that it is more conducive to an assessment of the relationship between the existing spiritual beliefs and the spatial expressions within church structures.

These dominant church structures can be described as follows:

TABLE 3.1. *Dominant Church Structures*

Time Frame	Dominant Structure[*]
First to fourth centuries	Private Home
Fourth to twelfth centuries	Basilica
Twelfth to sixteenth centuries	Cathedral
Sixteenth to twentieth centuries	Reformed Experiments
Twentieth century to present	Multi-purpose and the Megachurch

* There are residual traces of features associated with structures of a previous era(s); rather than clearly distinct characteristic shifts, the progression was analogous to the color scheme of a rainbow.

Although in some instances the transition from one era to the next occurred somewhat abruptly, other shifts have emerged over longer durations. Of particular interest to our purposes are the transitions in the role, structure, and design of Christian sacred places and the factors contributing to their development.

PRIVATE HOME

During the first three centuries, the essential role of the private dwelling in the establishment and early development of the church is not difficult to understand. Sharing meals together was a common activity when the

1. Kilde, *Sacred Power*, 3.

2. The terms referred to include Byzantine, Romanesque, Gothic, Renaissance, Reformation, and Baroque/Rococo.

church gathered together,[3] a practice based on the frequent mention of the early church doing so in the Book of Acts.[4] Fellowship around a meal that was accompanied by teaching and/or discussions was common within the early church as well as in the broader culture of the day. Obviously, the most conducive environment for fellowship and teaching of this nature was the private dwelling.

Many reasons are suggested for the private dwelling featuring prominently as the primary venue for early church gatherings. Harold Turner's summary[5] captures them effectively. First, the paucity and poverty of early believers rendered the construction of church buildings economically infeasible.[6] Second, the Christian church was born into a culture that was religiously pluralistic and frequently hostile,[7] rendering construction of dedicated liturgical environments unreasonable. This cultural reality dictated that Christians assume a more inconspicuous profile.[8] Finally,

3. Hurtado, *Origins of Christian Worship*, 41.

4. Refer to Acts 2:42, 46; 11:3; 20:7, 11; Galatians 2:11–12. In 1 Corinthians, Paul admonishes the Church against associating with those whose lifestyles contradict their profession of faith as believers, specifying that they are not even to eat a meal with such a person.

5. Turner, *Temple to Meeting House*, 158.

6. J. G. Davies attributes the absence of church buildings during the first three centuries to "paucity, poverty, and persecution" (Davies, *Secular Use*, 1–2). He argues that the absence of church buildings reflected a theological conviction of the early church that embraced the unity of the sacred and the profane. I do not find Davies's suggestion incontrovertible.

7. J. G. Davies also represents those believing that persecution under Roman authorities was not a significant factor. "The popular idea that during the first three centuries Christianity was under such continuous persecution that its adherents were driven to worship in secrecy in the catacombs and other hiding places does not conform with the facts . . . the persecutions which were carried out under imperial orders were not many, and in the aggregate occupied a very small part of the three centuries over which they extended" (Davies, *Origin and Development*, 12–13).

8. Although most gatherings took place in homes, at times the Church was forced underground. Underground mausoleums (catacombs) were established in various Roman Empire locations, allowing citizens to bury their dead, where Christians met unnoticed by authorities. A community believed to be from the second century was discovered in the catacombs of Naples in southern Italy. Rumours of cannibalism and child sacrifice circulated about early church practice because of the retreat to public burial sites. This venue significantly dictated the activities of the early church. Discoveries uncovered in some catacombs reveal certain forms that characterized later church architecture. A chapel found in the S. Sotere Cemetery consisted of three areas: nave, chancel, and apse. In the Capella Greca, a similar rectangular structure was found, with an apse at one end and paintings symbolizing scenes from John's Gospel (Stewart, *Simpson's History*, 2).

Turner suggests that the intimate context of the private dwelling was more reflective of the teaching of Jesus and the early understanding of the church as the new temple of God. He argues that this new self-awareness, fostered by the teaching of Jesus, "abrogated the Jerusalem temple and all such sacred places."[9] Although I cautiously concur with his first two suggestions, Turner's argument does not convince me that the emergence of the private home as the prime venue for the early church constitutes an intentional abandonment of or aversion to the temple.

Scholars are not in unanimous agreement on the specific spaces within private homes that proved the most conducive to the church's activities. Gregory Dix suggests that certain spaces within first-century homes, such as atriums and other adjacent or nearby areas, had already been used to honour pagan gods before the development of Christian congregations after Pentecost (Acts 2).[10] He proposes that these spaces were easily adapted to Christian worship, including baptism and the Eucharistic meal.[11] Louis Bouyer strongly disagrees, suggesting that the only location suitable for Christian worship within a private dwelling during Roman times was a lengthy, oblong room, which typically served as the dining area.[12] Archaeological evidence suggests that the average home commonly included a dining area inadequate to accommodate more than eight or nine people.[13] Although both Dix and Bouyer present interesting arguments in support of their particular views, neither are compelling enough to settle the issue, particularly when limited archaeological evidence exists to sustain either viewpoint.

A further reason for ambiguity is that our understanding of the liturgical spaces of the early church is limited. Scripture provides minimal informative detail regarding the design specifics of spaces used in early Christian worship. Apart from the description in Acts 20 of the

---

9. Turner, *Temple to Meeting House*, 158.

10. "Here ready at hand was the ideal setting for the Church's 'domestic' worship at the Eucharist. . . . The quaint old images of the household gods and their altar must go, of course, along with the sacred hearth and its undying fire. All else was exactly what was needed" (Dix, *Shape of the Liturgy*, 22–23).

11. Similarities between the Tabernacle and Temple of Ancient Israel and the worship centers of foreign nations of the same period suggest that the structure of ancient Israel's sacred places were not inherently unique to its spirituality.

12. Bouyer, *Liturgy and Architecture*, 41.

13. Hurtado, *Origins of Christian Worship*, 41.

room in which Paul engaged in a lengthy preaching/teaching sessions,[14] the available information is focused more on a description of the activities that occurred and explanations of their relevance rather than on a description of the built environment itself.

The earliest available archaeological data offers relatively meagre assistance, but one example providing some access to the nature and variety of liturgy and associated spaces required is Dura-Europos, a house excavated at a site thought to have been a Roman outpost.[15]

There are some special features that merit consideration. It appears that there were at least three distinct areas within the house dedicated to various liturgical or fellowship activities; one area seems to be where corporate worship occurred, specifically the Eucharist. The significance of this space—apparently constructed along an East-West orientation, similar to cathedrals during the centuries that followed—is an observation open to discussion. A second area provided space for teaching, perhaps similar to the synagogue environment characteristic of that period, while a third area containing what clearly resembled a baptismal font or tank was dedicated to the initiatory rite of baptism.

A number of interesting explanations are offered for the separation of spaces. One interpretation is that this separation was an intentional design feature born out of a conviction that certain activities such as preaching, the Eucharist, or baptism should not be conducted in the same venue. There is minimal early documentation available to support this conclusion apart from a baptism reference in chapter 7 of the Didache.[16] There we read that baptism should ideally take place in cold, running water, that is, in a river or a stream—an indication of a preference for the out-of-doors. In the absence of that, "other" (warm) water would suffice. If that was unavailable, then the pouring of water over the person three times, in the name of the Father, Son and Holy Spirit, was allowed. The latter two methods could be administered indoors. In chapters 9–10 of the Didache, instruction is given for the proper observation of the Eucharist, but no specific directives are provided regarding the preferred context.

14. Acts 20:7–12 indicates that there were many lamps in the upstairs room located three floors up. Numerous lamps suggest a room of substantial size.

15. Bouyer postulates that since this was largely an orthodox Jewish community, the house in question was possibly a synagogue first and a gathering place for Christians afterward.

16. Quasten and Plumpe, "The Didache," 19.7.

A second explanation is that the layout represents the congregation's attempt to utilize the space available, minimizing renovations and associated cost. The political and religious climate of the second and third centuries subjected the early Christian church to persecution from both the Jewish religious authorities and the Roman imperialistic authorities. A hostile milieu of this nature served as a strong deterrent to the construction or substantial renovation of any building dedicated to religious purposes other than those sanctioned by existing authorities. The similarity between this illustrated structure and a common design for many homes, particularly among those with greater financial means, suggests that this discovery was a private dwelling adjusted to accommodate the spatial requirements of the early church.

To suggest that the domestic contextual setting of the early church was intentional because it was an optimal reflection of the belief system of the time or because it evoked specific and desired spiritual responses is likewise difficult to sustain. A more logical and defensible conclusion suggests that the private dwelling provided the primary context for the majority of early Christian gatherings because of the hostile political, cultural, and religious climate of the first three centuries of the church's development. It was more a matter of expediency than one of a theology that considered any place intrinsically sacred. The Western church in the twenty-first century shares relatively little common ground politically, culturally, and religiously with the early church. Furthermore, as Jeanne Halgre Kilde points out,[17] early Christian worship practices and the places they occurred were widely diverse. Therefore, it is untenable to suggest that an analysis of early Christian worship centres will furnish us with a relevant template for the design of liturgical environments today.

The intimacy, sense of solidarity, familial community, and the participative quality of worship that were essential characteristics of the early church were undoubtedly more readily fostered and enhanced in the modest and smaller domestic context. Beyond intimacy, the element of exclusivity associated with the Eucharist was underscored by the privacy of the domestic environment in which it was observed.[18] Domestic gathering places continue to be used by the Christian church even today and not only in locations where Christians are few in number, living in poverty, or under the threat of persecution. Although the

---

17. Kilde, *Sacred Power*, 18.

18. Dix, *Shape of the Liturgy*, 18.

majority of early church gatherings took place in a domestic context, other venues gradually became necessary in order to facilitate its advancement and mission.

A prime function of early church corporate gatherings was clearly the building up of the community of believers as the Body of Christ, accomplished through the exercise of spiritual gifts and the mutual participatory ministry among all believers. Regular corporate gatherings were deemed necessary to this process.[19] In the absence of documented links between the beliefs of the early church and the associated spaces used for corporate gatherings at the time, it is best to understand what is known of the activity and worship that occurred when the early church gathered. Before serious consideration is given to the built environment for liturgy, the reason and rationale behind the liturgy must be firmly established.

In 1 Corinthians 14, the apostle Paul reminds his readers that the edification and strengthening of the church[20] was to be the objective of any ministry. To what extent does the liturgical context contribute to an edification ministry or strengthening of the church? The biblical text records that everyone was able to participate in some meaningful and gifted way, which indicates a greater degree of participation than was customary in other worship settings. Archaeological evidence leaves room to suggest that the house churches in Corinth probably had a membership of approximately fifty people, but the extent to which the venue affected the early church or manifested the beliefs of the church is virtually impossible to assert confidently.

Although liturgy was not as developed as it would eventually be, it nonetheless played a significant role in the early church. Early liturgy was more accessible to the average person than the more elaborate formats that evolved in subsequent centuries. There was little or no indication that some spaces architecturally limited access to a select few. It would seem that the average Christian was afforded opportunity for more direct involvement in the celebration of the Eucharist largely because the early church had smaller congregations relative to the larger gatherings developed under Constantine during the fourth century. The early church advanced numerically at an astounding rate, but there is no indication in scriptural accounts to suggest that they consistently gathered in massive groups. Some continued to attend the temple for prayer,

19. Hebrews 10:24–25.

20. 1 Corinthians 14:5, 26.

either individually or in small numbers,[21] as well as the synagogues[22] for times of teaching, but the private home best reflected the *domus ecclesia* as the venue of choice for the early church.[23] But again it must be stressed that this was not because the domestic setting was the most Christian or was the most accurate reflection of the beliefs and values of the nascent church.

The radical shift from the domestic setting to much larger contexts was not induced by intrinsic influences such as major shifts in theology but by the extrinsic dynamics of cultural and political forces impacting the church. As a result, the understanding of the corporate and more organic nature of the church, so readily evident in the domestic setting, began to be compromised as regular church gatherings moved increasingly into the public arena.[24]

THE BASILICA

One of the most notable, distinct changes in Christian sacred places emerged under the Roman Emperor Constantine during the fourth century. It is difficult to pinpoint another era when a more radical shift occurred within a relatively short time span as that following Constantine's imposition of the Edict of Milan in 313 A.D.[25] An immediate effect of the edict, introduced under Constantine's authority in the West, was the granting of official status and recognition to the Christian faith. Persecution of people of Christian faith was to cease and church buildings, previously confiscated during former times of persecution, were reestablished as legitimised places of worship, often with assistance from the Emperor's treasury.[26] This provision within the Edict of Milan implies that the early Christians were known to have corporately possessed

21. Acts 2:46; 3:1; 5:21; 21:26; 22:17.

22. Acts 9:20; 13:5; 14:1.

23. Aside from references in Acts such as 2:42, 46 indicating believers met from house to house, Paul refers to churches that met, seemingly regularly, in the homes of individuals, including Romans 16:3, 5; Philemon 2; Colossians 4:15.

24. Dix, *The Shape of the Liturgy*, 18.

25. "Bitter persecution and the almost complete disorganization of worship which it brought about were replaced by imperial patronage and state provision for worship in the space of much less than a decade. The next fifty years and more were a time of unparalleled liturgical revision all over Christendom" (Dix, *Shape of the Liturgy*, 304).

26. Cory and Landry, *Christian Theological Tradition*, 136.

places dedicated to their worship needs before the major attitudinal shift by Roman authorities, The Edict refers to these buildings as churches.[27] Constantine built numerous churches throughout the Roman Empire, including nine in Rome itself.

The design of most of the buildings dedicated to Christian worship during Constantinian rule was the basilica, a design commonly used in civic buildings as well as in large homes of the very wealthy. These basilicas bore no intrinsically Christian characteristics; they were not chosen because they best represented a Christian theology or most effectively facilitated Christian worship, at least as it had been conducted during the first three centuries. The basic basilica design was a common architectural feature of the day and became increasingly suitable as the church continued to experience significant growth, requiring more space than a private dwelling could provide.

Christian symbols, Scriptural texts, and creeds were painted on the interiors of these buildings, providing special attributes distinguishing them from basilicas used for secular purposes. The larger spaces provided by the basilica accommodated larger group gatherings and natural focal points from which those responsible could lead services. Long lines of pillars on either side of the nave created lines of vision that naturally led the eye toward the apse.

It was not simply numerical growth that precipitated the move to more spacious basilicas but an underlying belief that informed it, a belief initially residing with Constantine himself but soon common in

27. Note, from an English translation of the Edict of Milan 313, "And since these Christians are known to have possessed not only those places in which they were accustomed to assemble, but also other property, namely the churches, belonging to them as a corporation and not as individuals, all these things which we have included under the above law, you will order to be restored, without any hesitation or controversy at all, to these Christians, that is to say to the corporations and their conventicles: providing, of course, that the above arrangements be followed so that those who return the same without payment, as we have said, may hope for an indemnity from our bounty" (http://gbgm-umc.org/umw/bible/milan.stm). Louis Bouyer asserts "But it is now perfectly clear that long before the end of the persecutions the Christians, in Rome as elsewhere, had for their worship the regular use of buildings, either given to them or built especially for that purpose" (Bouyer, *Liturgy and Architecture*, 40). Dix suggests that this may have been due to the edict of the Emperor Gallienus in 260 AD, which provided the freedom for Christians to meet for corporate worship without threat of molestation. Dix states "We have already noted the important consequence of this in the erection of Christian 'churches,' building specially designed for Christian worship, which was a new feature of church life in most places in the last half or quarter of the third century" (Dix, *Shape of the Liturgy*, 306).

the church. It was Constantine's conviction that he was not only the thir-teenth apostle, the Vicar of Christ on earth, but also that he possessed divine qualities by virtue of which he had been appointed to lead the Christian church.[28] The imperialistic quality of Constantine's leader-ship fostered a significant change in the church's perception of Christ, from the "God of the humble, the miracle-worker and saviour," to the "Emperor of heaven."[29] The regal paraphernalia and the performative nature of ritual associated with emperor worship[30] soon became part of worship within the church, thus rendering the humble domestic con-texts of the first two centuries inappropriate.

One of the first basilicas to appear was St. Peter's, which is thought to have been started around 333 A.D. The magnitude of these buildings was a remarkable contrast from the modest domestic dwellings that had previously accommodated most Christian gatherings. Even though some features such as the atrium-courtyard were regular components both in the domestic setting and in the basilica, the intimacy of the *domus ecclesia* ("the house of the church") was eclipsed by a conspicuous shift to the *domus dei* ("the house of God") ostentation of church buildings, which was also associated with temple structures. This fuelled a shift from the milieu in which all were equals joined in a *koinonia* fellowship of the early decades of the Christian church. Having said that, it must be borne in mind that from its inception, the Christian church has always had order and rank; there have always been recognized leaders deemed essential to the accomplishment of the church's mission.

What we discover in reviewing the liturgy that evolved during the Constantinian era with the introduction of the basilica as the prime venue for Christian worship is that, as Kilde states, "space and ceremony impinge upon one another."[31] In other words, already the church was beginning to discover that *how* we worship and *where* we worship are mutually affective.

28. Krautheimer, *Early Christian*, 39.

29. Ibid., 40.

30. In Bouyer's mind, a significant and striking element of Roman basilica churches was the location and refurbishing of the bishop's seat. Its movement to the center of the apse and its reformation as a throne as opposed to a teacher's *cathedra* signaled the as-sociation of the role of the bishop with the role of magistrates, even the emperor himself (Bouyer, *Liturgy and Architecture*, 43–44). This enhancement was one initial harbinger of limited access spaces within church buildings.

31. Kilde, *Sacred Power*, 58.

THE CATHEDRAL

Although it appears that the basilica was borrowed or perhaps imposed on the Christian church by the Emperor for imperialistic reasons, a theology was invested in the designs that were to appear in the centuries to follow. "An English medieval church is a mysterious succession of self-contained rooms, seemingly stretching away into infinity; there is a gradual unveiling of its character till at last the high altar is reached at the east end."[32] The height of the soaring vaulted ceilings, accompanied by the distance between the worshipers and the altar, was intended to foster a sense of the transcendence and mystery of God. The congregation was not expected to see, hear or even understand the activities at the altar conducted by the priest on their behalf.

A hierarchical distinction between laity and clergy was jealously maintained and architecturally enshrined by the division of the nave from the chancel.[33] The participation and therefore power[34] of the laity was limited to passive observation. The chancel exemplified God's room and was entered only by priests in the carrying out of their liturgical duties. The size of the chancel in most medieval churches was as much as two-thirds the size of the nave but was reserved for the clergy and those assisting them in the liturgy. This disproportionate allotment of space to the very few has a history. "Thirteenth century bishops in building a cathedral like York or Lincoln were anxious to mark the distinctiveness and dignity of the clerical order, and in particular, that of the secular canons who staffed their cathedrals."[35]

This suggests that with the advent of the monumental design, a clear link between spiritual belief and spatial design became unquestionably evident. Otto von Simpson states, "The impact of ideas upon the life of artistic forms appears, I think, even more directly in architecture than it does in other arts, and the origins of Gothic, perhaps the most creative achievement in the history of Western architecture, can only be

---

32. Addleshaw, and Etchells, *Architectural Setting*, 15–16.

33. This distinction appeared with the advent of the basilica during the Constantinian era. It could be argued that the combination of the built environment and the already established ceremonies associated with emperor worship engendered the obvious distinction between those leading and those being led in corporate church gatherings.

34. See Kilde's excellent work, *Sacred Power*.

35. Addleshaw and Etchells, *Architectural Setting*, 16.

understood . . . as the singularly sensitive response of artistic form to the theological vision of the twelfth century."[36]

A challenge in the twenty-first century is that time has attenuated our capacity to fully appreciate the artistic and spiritual significance of the cathedral. The reason for this, according to Jantzen, is that we are no longer "cathedral-minded."[37] Like other architectural forms, the monumental cathedrals reflect the times and places in which they were built. Just as contextual analysis is an essential element in the interpretation of any sacred text, so must any attempt to understand the meaning of any sacred space be informed by understanding the context in which it was built as much as possible. The essence of the medieval theologian's perspective on church architecture can be summarized as, "The material church signifies the spiritual church."[38]

Thirteen centuries of minimal change to the essential structure[39] of the cathedral seems to substantiate the philosophical relationship between the material and spiritual church.[40] However, major changes from the Reformation to our present day, lead one to inquire whether theological shifts or other cultural or political forces prompted these architectural changes, or whether they have been influenced by a combination of forces. More specifically, does the change in church architecture (*ecclesia materialis*) reflect a change in Christianity's concept of the church itself (*ecclesia spiritualis*)? Evidence strongly supports an affirmative response.

Changes in liturgical practice, necessitating corresponding alterations to the worship environment, are also interpreted as indicators of shifts in the church's theology of worship and mission.[41] For instance,

36. Von Simpson, *Gothic Cathedral*, vi.

37. "Today we admire Gothic cathedrals, and yet, with our twentieth-century mentality, we lack any true basis for comprehending them. Even when they are preserved in a material sense, their spiritual significance seems completely hidden. Moreover, we have no real understanding of the standards which made them works of art, for we are not 'cathedral-minded' any more" (Jantzen, *High Gothic*, viii).

38. Jantzen, *High Gothic*, 169.

39. I refer to elements such as the cruciform layout, the high vaulted ceilings, the longitudinal orientation, and the clear separation between nave, chancel, and sanctuary in most cathedrals, which reflects a theological perception of the church during that time.

40. Jantzen notes these concepts have been identified historically as *ecclesia materialis* and *ecclesia spiritualis* (Jantzen, *High Gothic*, 169–70).

41. Architecture was not the only art form that underwent profound changes. Christian perspectives on the material and spiritual worlds did not remain constant in

the required inclusion of Revelation 21:2–5 in the medieval dedication ritual reflected the conviction that the church, both in its spiritual and material form, was a reflection or image of heaven.[42] In later Gothic structures, the emphasis on the humanity and suffering of Christ emerged as a theme more evident in cruciform church design.

Jantzen argues that the form or representation of Christ, manifested in medieval Christian symbolism including architecture, evolved. "Gothic led to a new epoch of a symbolical interpretation of everything connected with the spirit, using imagery and allegory on a vast scale."[43] This evolution in medieval art, influenced by a variety of sources including theological reflection, led to the construction of cathedrals in which nothing was void of meaning and significance. Jantzen asserts further, "In fact, the Gothic cathedral with its sumptuous display of picture and narrative can be described for this point of view as the sum of everything which man at that time needed to know and to believe."[44]

The variety of interpretations applied to the cathedral structure was sufficiently broad as to make the intended knowledge and belief specifics invested in those structures difficult to discern. Durandus[45] interprets the cruciform floor plan as an allegorical representation of the human body, which in turn was reflective of the church as the body of Christ. Other interpretations perceive the church building in an anagogical sense, symbolic of the City of God or the New Jerusalem.[46]

Did such interpretations inform the concepts and designs invested in the buildings, or did theologians superimpose the various interpretations following the buildings' construction? In what manner did spiritual belief relate to the medieval built worship environments? Jantzen asserts the latter supposition of theologians attributing symbolic meaning to the architectural structures and their various elements subsequent to

---

other art forms, "Here art history can present a clearer view than mediaeval theology, for it has at its disposal the panorama of historical evidence in chronological perspective. It recognizes, for example, that changes occurred in the forms in which the divine personality was represented, and that different facts of the godhead were symbolized at different times" (Jantzen, *High Gothic*, 170–71).

42. Von Simpson, *Gothic Cathedral*, 8.

43. Jantzen, *High Gothic*, 172.

44. Ibid., 173.

45. Ibid., 174.

46. Based on Revelation 21:2–3.

their construction.[47] By contrast, Otto von Simpson believes that the symbolic function of sacred architecture, representing the reality of the supernatural world, was the theme that informed both the experience of those who gathered and worshiped in them and the design of those who built them.[48]

Von Simpson presents a more compelling argument. Evidence to support his position is preserved in a work written by the Abbot Suger of St.-Denis[49] at the time of the dedication of the new choir in the abbey where he served. Suger's entire approach to the design and construction of the cathedral arises from his conviction that the divine may be approached only through material things.[50] His interpretation of the physical church building reflected his commitment to anagogical illumination.[51] Among many of the poetic inscriptions included throughout the Abbey's renovation at Suger's insistence, the one inscribed over the gilded doors of the main entrance illustrates the point well:

> Whoever thou art, if thou seekest to extol the glory of these doors, marvel not at the gold and the expense but at the craftsmanship of this work. Bright is the noble but, being nobly bright, the work should brighten the minds, so that they may travel, through the true lights, to the True Light where Christ is the true door. In what manner it be inherent in this world the golden door defines: The dull mind rises to truth through that which is material and, in seeing this light, is resurrected from its former submersion.[52]

The following illustration of the gilded door, over which the above inscription was written, shows a crucified, resurrected and ascended Christ. This image serves to remind those entering the Abbey that Christ is indeed resurrected and ascended and additionally that their minds and understanding is also 'resurrected from its former submersion,' through the means of the material.

---

47. Jantzen, *High Gothic*, 177.

48. Von Simpson, *Gothic Cathedral*, xiv–xv.

49. Scholars besides von Simpson associate the genesis of Gothic style with Abbot Suger of St.-Denis. See Panofsky, *Gothic Architecture*, 22. This is also demonstrated in Panofsky's translation of a number of Abbot Suger's works produced in relation to the major reconstruction of the Abbey of St.-Denis. (Panofsky, *Abbot Suger*).

50. Jones, *Hermeneutics*, 2:229.

51. Described in Panofsky, *Abbot Suger*, 21–25.

52. Ibid., 47, 49.

FIGURE 3.1 *The Central Door on the Western Façade, St.-Denis*[53]

Suger was convinced that art and architecture had the capacity to impose a magical, transforming influence on people regardless of their literacy level. The resulting transformation would ripple beyond the realm of devoted Christian spirituality to loyalty and effectiveness as a French citizen.[54] This belief in the transforming capability of artistic images, including architecture, continued well into the thirteenth century and found expression in the works of thinkers such as Aquinas[55] and his contemporary Bonaventure.[56] Foundational to the beliefs of Suger,

53. Panofsky, *Abbot Suger on the Abbey Church of St.* illustration 3. page 293. Used with permission.

54. Jones, *Hermeneutics*, 2:230.

55. One of the most influential statements on the function of images came from Thomas Aquinas: "A threefold reason for the institution of images in the Church: first, for the instruction of the unlettered, who might learn from them as if from books; second, so that the mystery of the Incarnation and the examples of the saints might remain more firmly in our memory by being daily represented to our eyes; and third, to excite the emotions which are more effectively aroused by things seen than by things hear" (cited in Freedberg, *Power of Images*, 162).

56. David Freedberg summarizes Bonaventure's position on the importance of images as follows: "He asserted that we have images (1) so that the illiterate might more clearly be able to read the sacraments of the faith in sculptures and in pictures, as if in books; (2) so that people who are not excited to devotion when they hear of Christ's deeds might at least be excited when they see them in figures and pictures, as if present

Aquinas, and Bonaventure alike was the conviction that the visual dimension of the ritual-architectural experience is more effective than the auditory for provoking an emotional response and enhancing the memory.

Von Simpson uses the work of Suger to resist a Darwinian interpretation of architecture that suggests the Gothic genre was nothing more than the natural, even inevitable, sequel to Romanesque architecture.[57] Gothic is a more subversive statement, born out of the spiritual and political realities unique to a specific time and location, rather than an improvement of or advancement over previous architectural expressions.[58]

A major challenge today is that attitudes toward sacred architecture have drifted to a more detached posture, what von Simpson calls "purely aesthetic observation."[59] I contend that in the North American context, even appreciation for the aesthetic elements of church buildings is in danger of being eclipsed by a commitment to pragmatic concerns. Currently, the value of location within or by the community is considered to be of more consequence when considering the construction of new facilities than any spiritual truth or allegorical message symbolized or conveyed through architectural design features.

REFORMED EXPERIMENTS

The Protestant Reformation introduced momentous change in theological persuasions, fostering a shift from priest-led worship to a more congregationally inclusive approach. Worship was no longer perceived as something performed by a priest on behalf of the people; rather it called for the full participation of all present based upon commitment to the priesthood of all believers.[60] The simple designation or identification

---

to our bodily eyes; and (3) so that by seeing them we might remember the benefits wrought for us by the virtuous deeds of the saints" (Freedberg, *Power of Images*, 163).

57. Von Simpson, *Gothic Cathedral*, 61.

58. Von Simpson suggests that the genesis of Gothic architecture is clearly linked to one specific location, "In short, Gothic is the style of the Isle-de-France; it is so closely tied to the destinies of the Capetian monarchy and encouraged by the latter to such an extent that we must assume that Gothic was considered the expression of ideas with which the crown wished to be associated" (ibid., 64).

59. Von Simpson, *Gothic Cathedral*, xvi.

60. Martin Luther as much as any reformer championed this concept and referred to it often in his writings and sermons. "Thus it follows that the priesthood in the New Testament is equally in all Christians, in the spirit alone without any roles or masks" (Luther, "The Misuse of the Mass," 139).

of one generalized architectural style as the Reformation motif is defied by a divergent variety of local expressions of widely accepted tenets of Reformation thought.

Reformed convictions were expressed in literary forms such as the Book of Common Prayer, implemented by the Church of England during the mid-sixteenth century. Complete with various versions, it presented major challenges for the medieval church spaces provided by the monumental Gothic structures that had dominated the religious landscape since the thirteenth century. Church buildings now failed to accommodate the new liturgical expression inherent in the prayer book, which assumed the involvement of all believers present and emphasized participatory congregational involvement as opposed to passive observation. The characteristic special demarcation of the typical medieval cathedral interior, complete with screens and/or rails, distanced the laity from key focal points such as the altar, rendering them spectators while the clergy and those assisting them continued to be the primary participants.

The acoustical and visual difficulties experienced in many parishes resulted from the length and shape of medieval buildings, for which adjustments had to be made. The conviction that it was essential for the congregation to be visually and audibly connected, able to understand what the clergy were declaring, gained wider acceptance through men like Martin Bucer.[61] He argued that clergy, operating from a space "off limits" to the laity, gave the impression they were closer to God and that the laity had need to worship. It was his conviction that the design most conducive to appropriate congregational worship was of a circular or centralized form where the priest functioned from the centre, within sight and earshot of all worshipers. Bucer's reasoning did underscore the significance of the built environment in facilitating the worship activity required by the Book of Common Prayer. Other Reformed expressions took on concrete forms in the architecture of liturgical spaces.

A strong relational alliance existed between the church and the monarchy. The result of this arrangement was that virtually all ecclesiastical decisions became political issues. John Hooper, Bishop of Gloucester and Worcester during the mid-sixteenth century, was convinced that proximity to the congregation allowed the minister to be more easily heard and understood. He attempted to persuade the government to close off all chancels, requiring clergy to conduct services within the

---

61. Greschat, *Martin Bucer*, 238.

nave; his efforts proved unsuccessful. He considered screens reminiscent of the veil of the Temple during the old dispensation, a separation rendered redundant by the completed work of Christ. Hooper ordered that screens between clergy and laity be removed and tolerated only one exception: the partition surrounding pews, which enhanced the worshipers' ability to reflect in quiet.[62]

The 1559 restoration of the Book of Common Prayer under the influence of Elizabethan authorities demanded the retention of the medieval arrangement of distinct chancel and nave. Although the removal of the rood-loft was permitted, a partition between the chancel and the nave was to be maintained; both the clergy and the laity now used the chancel during the celebration of the Eucharist.

Similarly, the Puritans complained to Elizabeth that the retention of screens between nave and chancel tainted churches with a resemblance to the Old Testament Temple, where people were separated from the Holy Place and the Holy of Holies. In response, Richard Hooker agreed that the distinction between chancel and nave did engender a separation between clergy and laity, but in practice it was not consistently observed. He stressed that the purpose of the screen was to mark off a sacred space "where the faithful might assemble for the Holy Mysteries without interruption or disturbance from intruders."[63] The Eucharist could be celebrated by communicants and celebrant alike, not only by the priest as in pre-Reformation days. The two distinct "rooms" were now used for two different services rather than by two different groups within the congregation.[64]

Prime Liturgical Focal Points

The Reformation ushered in significant theological and subsequently architectural changes. Some aspects of the medieval church building continued; focal points such as the font, the pulpit, and the altar-table were carried over into Protestant churches representing Anglican, Lutheran, and Calvinistic traditions. Within these traditions, a variety of views surfaced on the actual structure and location of these liturgical focal points.

62. Addleshaw and Etchells, *Architectural Setting*, 25.

63. Cited in ibid., 40.

64. Ibid., 43.

Altar, Table, or Both?

The most important focal point in many churches was and continues to be the altar or communion table. Universal agreement on the location, orientation, and the materials from which it should be built has never been reached within Protestantism. The placement, construction, and naming of the altar fostered robust discussion, particularly during the time immediately following the Reformation. Many were convinced the term "altar" connoted sacrificial elements incongruent with the definition of the Lord's Supper. "Holy Table" became the designation of choice among most Anglican churches. Altars in Lutheran congregations, particularly in Germany and Sweden, maintained a much stronger resemblance to Roman Catholic altars.

Through the combined efforts of John Hooper and Nicholas Ridley, the Bishop of London during the reign of Edward VI, a movement emerged to replace the high altars of stone with wooden tables. By 1552, the term "altar" was removed from the Book of Common Prayer and replaced with "the table," "the Lord's table," or "God's board." Ridley was prepared to use either "altar," since "there is offered the same sacrifice of praise and thanksgiving,"[65] or "table," since it was the place "where the Holy Communion is distributed with lauds and thanksgiving unto the Lord."[66] But his preference was "table," since altars were ordained for use in the Jewish sacrificial system that foreshadowed the work of Christ on the cross.

The table reminded communicants of their need and privilege of feeding on the living Christ. Logistically, the table had the advantage of mobility, allowing it to be positioned where more people could gather to hear and participate. In Anglican ecclesiology, the degree of accessibility for communicants became a prime consideration for proper placement of the altar or table. Ridley was specific in designating the chancel as the location for the table, whereas Hooper's only concern was that it be located where the minister could be clearly heard.[67]

One of the hallmark accomplishments of the Elizabethan era was relocating of the altar to the midst of the congregation. The table was moved to the center of the chancel, away from the east wall, and positioned as

65. Ibid., 27.
66. Cited in ibid., 27.
67. Ibid., 27–28.

a table as opposed to an altar. A perceived disadvantage of placing the table in the center of the chancel was that it often provided a surface for conducting other activities, such as the instruction of children in those churches that also served as schools. Churchwardens were known to conduct business sessions around it, which was a violation of the sacred purpose of the table in the minds of many. The challenge faced by the church was to maintain a balance between celebrant and communicant accessibility without succumbing to the temptation to utilize it as an ordinary table. Reverence for the act of celebrating the Eucharist was to be reflected in reverence for the table from which it was served.

Laud, the Dean of Gloucester and later the Archbishop of Canterbury (1633), convinced some to retain the altar on the top step close to the east wall. Those of Laudian persuasion devised wooden rails to surround the altar, finding that repositioning the altar did not entirely prevent the abuses suffered at the center of the chancel. Access to the altar was made possible through a door in the front of the rail, which provided the desired protection of the altar and generated a different method of administering and receiving Communion.[68] Those wishing to receive Communion were asked to come and kneel at the rails around the altar.

Laud's convictions were in part influenced by his commitment to tradition and history. He viewed the post-Reformation placement of the table in the nave or west end of the chancel as innovative at best but not reflective of the tradition that preceded it. He underscored the fact that the location of the altar was not primarily theologically motivated, but his insistence on the east end of the chancel reflected more a concern for liturgical order and practical convenience.[69] "As physically as it was impossible for them to go any further up the chancel, so life itself had nothing more to offer them; for Communion is the foretaste of heaven itself."[70]

Even a century after the Reformation, many considered the eastern end of the chancel to be the most sacred part of the church; placing the table there reminded worshipers of the profound and supreme significance of the Lord's Supper and provided more space, allowing more communicants to kneel at one time.[71] Laud represented those who

68. Ibid., 122.
69. Ibid., 138.
70. Cited in ibid., 140.
71. Ibid., 138.

considered the altar the most important piece of furniture in the church, even surpassing the pulpit, since it was here that the Eucharist, the climax of the liturgy, took place. Laud referred to the altar as "the greatest place of God's residence upon earth."[72] A major criticism levied against the Laudian persuasion was that it fell short of giving practical consideration to the worshiping congregation, the hallmark concern of Reformation thinking that concluded worship was best accomplished when the altar was situated in the midst of the gathered people.

The Laudian influence came to an end in 1643 largely due to John Williams and others like him. The House of Commons passed legislation banning the placement of the table on the eastern wall of the chancel and requiring the removal of all altar rails. The table was to be placed in a more convenient place in the chancel or the nave. Under the influence of Sir Christopher Wren, who designed many churches—including St. Paul's Cathedral in London following the horrific fire of 1666—the single room plan known as the auditory design became popular. His design objective was to allow the minister to be easily seen and heard by the entire congregation. It would be inaccurate to conclude that Wren's primary concern was for the congregation to be able to hear the sermon;[73] he explicitly maintained they must hear the entire service, particularly the Eucharist.[74]

However, the decline of Laudian influence was temporary. By the eighteenth century, a naked altar without rails was considered a sign of slovenliness or indifference. An altar was considered incomplete in the absence of a reredos, a painted ceiling or canopy, above it and a rail in front of it. Communion rails were important because they focused attention on the altar and added an aesthetic dimension to the east end of the church while protecting the altar from secular use.[75]

Disagreement over the process of inviting communicants to come and kneel around the table to receive the elements arose from the Puritans, who reasoned that communion should be served to them while they remained seated in the nave. Their rationale for resisting kneeling

72. Cited in ibid.

73. James White points out that in Reformed Churches, the auditory element of the preaching event was not the only consideration. Visual accessibility was to be a factor in the design of the environment in which preaching occurred (White, "From Protestant to Catholic," 462).

74. Addleshaw and Etchells, *Architectural Setting*, 54.

75. Ibid., 65.

as a posture appropriate for the reception of communion stemmed from their belief that such a position belied the belief in the real presence of Christ in the elements.[76] Bishop Matthew Wren and Ephraim Udnall, rector of St. Augustine's Charge in London, opposed this view because having the celebrants move through the congregation to administer the elements risked fostering a lack of reverence and a distracting confusion. Leaving the altar unprotected by rails and/or kneeling cushions to attempt to distribute the wine and the bread among the high box pews allowed for unnecessary upset and potential spillage.

Within the Church of England, significant differences continued to exist regarding the amount of theological weight that should be attached to the communion table. Proximity to the people involved the risk of robbing the table of its true and vital significance. For others, the only sacrifice left to offer was the sacrifice of oneself and praise and thanks to God, based on the belief that Jesus was sent "to be the last priest, which should offer the last sacrifice, upon the last altar that ever the world should have."[77]

The people's complaint was that the altar, positioned under the east wall, resulted in their inability to hear, thus limiting their participation in the Eucharist. Rather than insisting on a permanently legislated position for the altar, the bishop of the time decreed that the table should be placed in the position most accessible to the greatest number of people. The issue was not so much theological as it was practical.

The dynamic tension faced by ecclesiastical leadership was between maintaining an appropriate reverence for the communion service and respect for the table that was often lost through its random placement, and adequately facilitating a worship experience that empowered the congregation as genuine participants. Controversies related to these ecclesiastical issues centred on logistical or practical matters as much as theological concerns.

The Pulpit

Some Lutheran churches required a repositioning of the pulpit to architecturally emphasise the importance of the Word. This was accomplished by moving the pulpit to the midway point along one wall and arranging the pews to allow the people to face it. A distinct disadvantage was that

76. Finney, *Seeing beyond the Word*, 53.

77. Williams, cited in Addleshaw and Etchells, *Architectural Setting*, 144.

it cut off the altar from the main worship area, causing some churches to provide seating that faced both the pulpit and the altar. The willingness to retain a certain degree of Roman Catholic ethos within Lutheran churches was reflective of Martin Luther's own personal persuasions.

Calvinistic churches mirrored John Calvin's convictions and manifested different architectural arrangements. As Yates points out, "Calvinistic worship meant that buildings had to be fitted with a pulpit and seating and little else. A permanent altar was generally rejected."[78] The communion table placed in front of and beneath the elevated pulpit added solemnity to the preacher's sermon as it was delivered over the table.[79]

The relation between pulpit, altar, and congregation has featured prominently in many historical debates and structural decisions. Open or limited access to liturgical focal points was indicated by the absence or presence of screens and rails, and the mobility or permanence of the altar or table can be viewed as a theological statement about the centrality of the sacrament and the frequency with which it should be observed.

Why devote space to the pulpit itself when one could argue that any fixture used in preaching, as with any built or architectural form, is primarily incidental to the overall preaching event? Power, or potential for transforming influence, in and through the preaching event resides in the Word, not in the furniture used. Historically, the church held the pulpit in high esteem, evidenced by the large number of pulpits that remain prominently featured in many church naves or chancels. The pulpit's importance in Reformation thought is underscored by the particular attention it received during and after the Reformation.

Religious structures have always been invested with meaning(s) and thereby potentially provide a connection between concepts or ideas and physical expressions. As integral elements of what Victor Turner refers to as a "ritual process" and what Linsday Jones refers to as a "ritual-architectural event," religious structures possess the capability of linking "the abstraction of the divine to the physicality of human existence. . . . At once messengers and agents, mirrors and actors, they enable people to think through their ideas about religiosity and convey them to the rest of the world while, in turn, influencing those ideas and shaping religions and society."[80]

78. Yates, *Buildings, Faith and Worship*, 28.

79. Addleshaw and Etchells, *Architectural Setting*, 185.

80. Kilde, *When Church Became Theatre*, 10.

The suggestion that meaning exists within a built form begs the question that Amos Rapoport asks: meaning for whom?[81] "What meaning does the built environment or any structure have for the inhabitants and the users, or the public or, more correctly, the various publics, since meaning, like the environments that communicate them, are culture specific and hence culturally variable?"[82] Any significant meaning attached to the pulpit varies substantially from the perspective of designers, preachers, listeners, and one particular setting to another.

There are two constituencies directly influenced by the presence of a pulpit: those who preach from it and those who listen to the sermons, or what Jones refers to as the professional and public subcultures.[83] It appears that the necessity and nature of change to the pulpit or ambo has been determined largely by the clergy, but one should not assume that the capricious wielding of authority or position on the part of church leadership is solely responsible for the changes that occurred. Change has been linked to developments in the theology of preaching. Under the influence of Reformers such as Martin Luther, sixteenth-century Christianity moved away from the largely visual nature of worship, dominated by an emphasis on the Eucharist, that had characterized Christian worship for centuries and leaned more toward a linguistic, aural emphasis. The printing press and subsequent increase in literacy among the masses profoundly influenced Luther and other Reformers to embrace a view of worship that championed spoken and written language as exclusive manifestations infused with divine power. Martin Luther reputedly believed that "when the preacher speaks, God speaks."[84]

The prime purpose of worship in their view was to facilitate a clear understanding of the Word of God, rendering the largely visual and sensual Mass secondary in importance to the sermon as the pivotal focus of the worship event. During the sixteenth century, churches influenced by Zwingli and Calvin in the cities of Zurich and Strasbourg placed virtually no emphasis on the architecture or the furniture within the worship spaces, but yielded disparate convictions on what should be included in Sunday services and the frequency with which the sacraments should be observed.[85]

---

81. Rapoport, *Meaning of the Built Environment*.

82. Ibid., 21.

83. Jones, *Hermeneutics of Sacred Architecture*, 32.

84. Cited in Kilde, *Sacred Power*, 113.

85. Hageman, *Pulpit and Table*, 13–35.

Under Zwingli's influence, Sunday gatherings were designed as preaching services. The celebration of the Eucharist was removed from the preaching service and conducted only four times annually, a move based upon Zwingli's rejection of the Eucharist as a means of grace. For him there was but one means of receiving God's grace and that was through the preaching of the Word. "Since God is Spirit," Zwingli argued, "he can reveal himself only by spiritual and never physical means. There is, therefore, only one means of grace—the preaching of the Word. Then the Spirit speaks to spirit; the flesh profits nothing."[86] For Zwingli, the Lord's Supper was a meal of remembrance, "simply another form of preaching, the dramatic reenactment of what on other occasions has been said from the pulpit."[87]

The entire Sunday service was conducted from the pulpit, the one permanent piece of furniture in the church. During the "celebration" of the Lord's Supper there was no preaching and, until 1598, no singing. Rather than having people come forward to receive the elements, the congregation was served seated in their places.[88]

For many years following the Reformation, the liturgy in many Reformed churches was shackled to a conservative, inviolable order of service despite the fact that Calvin had purposefully permitted modifications and adaptations of liturgical prayers for specific needs and circumstances.[89] Hageman sees one distinct advantage:

> The worship of these congregations was undeniably corporate. The prayers of the service were common prayers in the truest sense of the word. There was no trace of that vicious practice of later years in which the prayers became the peculiar preserve of the minister, who often abused them to wrestle with his own theological problems, to scold the people from behind the Lord's back, or to summarize succinctly the points of his sermon.[90]

Despite some theological differences, Luther and Calvin both were strongly persuaded that the Word of God should be preached every time the church gathered. Part of the legacy of this belief was evident in a common attachment of the baptismal font or basin to the pulpit.

86. Cited in ibid., 19–20.
87. Ibid., 20.
88. Ibid., 21.
89. Ibid., 38.
90. Hageman, *Pulpit and Table,* 38.

The design was not motivated by a commitment to economy of space or function but was theologically informed, reflecting the conviction of both Luther and Calvin that the preaching of the Word should be conducted at all liturgical events and gatherings.[91]

The radical Reformed shift from the visual to the aural was accompanied by major architectural and spatial changes to facilitate the new emphasis on preaching. In pre-Reformation Roman Catholic services, hearing was not an essential consideration, but Reformers were intent on ensuring that every person present could hear and understand the declared message of the sermon. Pulpits were constructed and positioned to replace the altar as the prime center of focus, their size and intricacy conveying a visual statement underscoring the aural import of the preaching event.

Luther was committed to the priesthood of all believers, but the elevated, dominant position of the pulpit clearly implied a prominence of the clergy over the laity in terms of ability and authority to interpret and expound Scripture. From Luther's preferred arrangements within the liturgical environment, one could easily argue that his commitment to the priesthood of all believers did not translate into unadulterated egalitarianism, at least with respect to the ministry of preaching.

The Church at Hartenfels Castle in Torgau manifests what is believed to one of the first church designs informed by Luther's theology in which the ministry and location of the pulpit gained a place of dominance. Luther himself is believed to have preached at the dedication of this church in 1544.

The Font

Many churches believed that the font should be located at the west end of the nave, quite near the entrance, a theologically motivated reminder that one is baptized into the body of Christ. This location, however, tended to isolate it from the pulpit and table. A preferred arrangement for some, therefore, was to locate the font near the altar or table as a statement that

---

91. This was a conviction not unique to Luther and Calvin since it appears to reflect the persuasion of Augustine, who believed that the water of baptism is nothing but water in the absence of the Word. He adds, "But when the Word is joined to the element the result is a sacrament . . . where does the water get its lofty power to bathe the body and cleanse the soul if it is not through the action of the Word? And not because it is spoken, but because it is believed" (cited in Forrester et al., *Encounter*, 70).

both the Eucharist and baptism were to be honored equally.[92] It appears that since there is no directive regarding the location of the font in the 1662 edition of the Book of Common Prayer, by the seventeenth century this was a matter left open to the discretion of each congregation.

Seating Arrangements

The introduction of pews was precipitated by an insistence upon lengthy sermons as part of the liturgy. In previous eras, people had wandered about during Mass until going forward to receive the elements of the Eucharist, but Reformed worshipers were to assume what appeared to be a more passive posture as listeners. As Reformation theology became more pervasive and influential in the arrangements of liturgical focal points, provision of seating arrangements that would allow maximum involvement was required for the entire congregation.

During this time, each person was assigned a particular seat by the church wardens, which was thought to foster a sense of belonging within the community of the church. The sale or rental of pews was part of the legacy left by the Middle Ages and became "the mainstay of parochial finance."[93] Some churches financed the salaries of clergy through annual pew rental fees.

It was common to find little space in churches for those unable to afford the purchase or rental of pew space. These people were left to occupy the galleries, to bring their own stools, or to stand in the aisles. Children were tolerated at best, with the occasional provision of seating near the reading desk or, in the event that no communion was to take place, in the chancel. Most churches would provide special pews designated for churchwardens, mayors, or other civic officials. They would also reserve seats for a bride and bridegroom, or for those doing public penance.[94]

Box pews arose as a practical solution to shield worshipers from the often-present draughts in unheated churches. The arrangement of pews also allowed for the segregation of the sexes, a practice predating the Reformation and continuing in some sectors afterward. Pews were allocated according to a person's societal status. When new churches were erected, it was not uncommon for people to be allotted pews with

92. Addleshaw and Etchells, *Architectural Setting*, 65.

93. Ibid., 90.

94. Ibid., 92–93.

designs that indicated the magnitude of their contribution to the building's construction.[95]

In an age that incorporated a hierarchy and the concomitant limitation of empowerment in the functions of everyday life, it was not considered inordinate or improper to acknowledge rank and wealth by providing prestigious pews within the house of God for the local gentry and their families.[96] These pews were considered the owner's possessions and could be sold to new occupants in the event that a family moved to another parish.

Some family pews were separated by four- to five-foot wainscoted boards and included such domestic amenities as tables, chairs, sofas, and even fireplaces.[97] Another type of family pew took separation a step further by covering the pew with a canopy and inserting glass windows, giving them the appearance of miniature castles or chapels.

Yates suggests that individuals or corporate bodies purchased pews up to the seventeenth century.[98] As the population increased and the impact of the Industrial Revolution began to manifest itself across Britain and the Continent, such elaborate family seating arrangements soon proved to be inadequate. They were replaced with open seating arrangements that were available to more people, leaving churches with a more bland appearance.

THE MEETING HOUSE

The meeting house,[99] designed and built by seventeenth-century English Puritans, was meant primarily for Sabbath worship gatherings but was also available and frequently used for civic functions, such as town meetings and elections. A number of groups, including the Society of Friends (Quakers) and early Methodists, found these buildings to be most accommodating to their beliefs and purposes. Their design and function was a

95. Yates, *Buildings*, 37.

96. Addleshaw and Etchells, *Architectural Setting*, 94.

97. Ibid., 96.

98. Yates, *Buildings*, 37.

99. Harold Turner suggests that the meeting house concept is first found in the synagogue which to him represents the "desacralization of places and buildings used for religious purposes and so stands as a new type in the phenomenology and history of religion that we may call the meeting house, a house for the meeting of the people of God rather than a house for the god himself" (Turner, *Temple to Meeting House*, 101).

statement of their theological persuasions as dissenters in the Church of England who rejected the idea of sacred space while maintaining their Calvinistic commitment to the centrality of the preaching of Scripture. This attitude toward the physical worship context was enshrined:

> Neither prayer, nor any other part of religious worship, is now, under the gospel, either tied unto, or made more acceptable to, any place in which it is performed, or towards which it is direct-ed: but God is to be worshiped everywhere in spirit and in truth; as in private families daily, and in secret each one by himself, so more solemnly in the public assemblies, which are not carelessly or willfully to be neglected or forsaken, when God, by his Word or providence, calleth thereunto.[100]

Identifying these gathering places as "meeting houses" reflected the Puritan conviction that the term "church" designated the corporate gathering of believers who met for the purpose of worshiping God and was inappropriate to be applied to a building. Intentionally, the design-ers incorporated very little in their structures that would distinguish it as a "church" building from the exterior. Most were quite plain, modest in size, and bore strong similarities to other public and domestic structures in the community. The architecture the Puritans brought with them to New England was neither the Gothic style of Roman Catholic churches nor the neoclassicism that was beginning to emerge in England but an ordinary style associated with private dwellings and public buildings.[101] The intentional austerity of interior design was a statement that noth-ing, including the architectural setting, should detract from the central ministry of preaching. The altar that continued to be the dominant focal point in Gothic churches in England had devolved into a table similar to those found in private homes—in some cases, a wooden slab hinged to the pulpit or wall. Eventually, the degree to which these meetinghouses were used for civic purposes began to diminish until they were reserved almost exclusively for religious purposes, but any suggestion that they possessed an intrinsic sacred quality was still denied.[102]

The Reformed emphasis on preaching influenced an interior de-sign where the distinction between nave, chancel, and sanctuary was

---

100. *Westminster Confession of Faith* (1646) 21.6, http://www.reformed.org/docu-ments/westminster_conf_of_faith.html#chap21.

101. Williams, "Metamorphoses," 482–83.

102. Loveland and Wheeler, *Meetinghouse to Megachurch*, 7.

dissolved. The preferred design was a single, undivided space in which the dominant, central feature was the pulpit. By the eighteenth century, many meeting house pulpits were of fine design, some with elaborate carvings attached, but no image of any creature or person was permitted lest it encourage an idolatrous attachment to the fixture.[103]

MULTIPURPOSE AND MEGACHURCH PHENOMENA

Although one may consider the multipurpose church building a recent ecclesiastical emergence, there is ample evidence suggesting they were in existence long before the twentieth century. Arguably, the Puritan meeting houses of the seventeenth and eighteenth centuries could be described as multifunctional buildings employed for gatherings such as town hall assemblies and political meetings in addition to Sunday worship services. Methodist Sunday school superintendent Lewis Miller, assisted by a local architect Jacob Snyder, developed a notable design that came to be known as the Akron Plan and enjoyed impressive acceptance among evangelical churches during this time. The plan was built around a semicircular sanctuary/auditorium that was encircled by one to two tiers of boxes, similar to those found in a theatre, that could be used either as sanctuary seating or as classrooms. The following pictures depict what a multipurpose facility would look like:

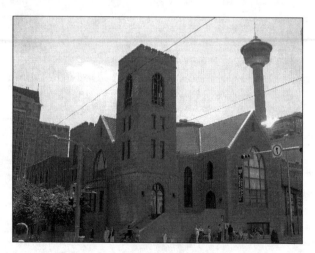

FIGURE 3.2 *Exterior of Central United Church, Calgary, Alberta, Canada; typical nineteenth-century design used in many Methodist preaching posts. Photo by William R. McAlpine.*

103. Ibid., 7–8.

FIGURE 3.3 *Interior of Central United Church showing the position of the pulpit just to the left of center and large space off to the right formerly used for classrooms in the balcony. Photo by William R. McAlpine.*

A feature commonly utilized in the vast majority of applications and adaptations of the Akron Plan was the movable doors or rolling partitions that allowed congregations to separate classroom space from the sanctuary, or expand the sanctuary when necessary. Placing the pulpit in the corner and utilizing a diagonal orientation allowed a preacher to address a gathering often double the size of the sanctuary's normal seating capacity when the portable walls were retracted. It is not surprising that this design had its origin within the Methodist tradition, as the Methodist Church was an active participant in the early Sunday School movement. The advantage of this design's versatility was quickly noticed and widely accepted by a significant number of other denominations as well.

It is difficult to find references to the term "megachurch" prior to the 1970s, yet according to some observers the number of these churches in the United States increased from ten to approximately four hundred between the early 1970s and the mid-1990s.[104] The definition of megachurch that enjoys the widest acceptance is a church consistently attended by two thousand or more people per week.[105]

104. Loveland and Wheeler, *Meetinghouse to Megachurch*, 1.
105. Thumma, "Exploring the Megachurch."

The essence and significance of the megachurch goes beyond the parameters of quantitative realities. It represents an articulate statement of mission informed by a passion to transform the world. These aspects have caused some scholars such as Os Guiness[106] to position the megachurch phenomenon in the broader church growth movement.[107] There are certain features of the megachurch that clearly distinguish it from the more traditional churches that are equally committed to the vision and passion of the church growth movement. The megachurch reflects a closer kinship with current cultural icons, particularly the shopping mall, rather than loyalty to any particular tradition. This significant shift is indicative of a deepened awareness of and sensitivity to changes that were occurring on a cultural level.[108]

Some view the megachurch building as a key instrument for mission. "The church building was an instrument of evangelism and that architecture could and should be used to make an impression on the un-churched and unsaved that would lead them to attend a worship service or become involved in some other church-sponsored program activity."[109] Megachurch builders regard "the megachurch structure and its architecture as an advertisement for the 'product' and 'services' offered by the church."[110] Pastor Ed Young expresses a sentiment shared by many: "Our culture doesn't have much to say, but it knows how to say it. The church has everything to say, but we don't know how to say it."[111]

This concept underscores an idiom that architects and builders of megachurch complexes like to associate with their contemporary designs, namely, marketing orientation. More conservative church leaders may resist or even disdain the association of the corporate business world with the church, but there are clearly many embracing the values of corporate headquarters. They are convinced that the prestige and worth of the "product" offered inside can and should be advertised through the design of the built environment as effectively as any other method. It is

106. Guiness, *Dining with the Devil*.

107. The North American expression of this movement is often associated with names such as Donald MacGavran and C. Peter Wagner as well as the Charles E. Fuller Institute of Evangelism and Church Growth.

108. See Loveland, *Meetinghouse to Megachurch*, 128.

109. Ibid.

110. Ibid., 129.

111. Ibid., 157.

also clear that some consider the megachurch design to be a statement of disassociation with the traditional church.[112]

It is intriguing that this intentional dissociation with aspects of more traditional church design has not prevented megachurches from incorporating traditional symbols into the exterior design of their modern structures. Of all such symbols, crosses are likely the most popular. There are exceptions, such as Willow Creek Community Church, which has intentionally omitted religious symbols in an effort to affect a neutral presentation believed to be more attractive to unchurched Baby Boomers.[113]

Jeanne Halgren Kilde[114] reminds us that as Protestants in the United States altered their beliefs and practices during the nineteenth century in an effort to address societal changes more effectively, they also modified their church buildings. Fred Craddock's book *As One Without Authority*, published in 1971, served as a catalyst for a major shift in the Western church's approach to preaching, particularly within the North American context. Craddock's main premise is that preachers should not assume that people listening to sermons will acknowledge the authority of the preacher or the preaching event itself as previous generations had. Although he does not suggest that Scripture itself is any less authoritative, he is convinced that preaching should not be conducted from an authoritative posture declaring scriptural truth. Rather, the preacher should present truth for the listener's careful and thoughtful consideration, inviting listeners to explore and discover truth and meaning together. The authority formerly reserved for clergy, properly trained in hermeneutics and homiletics, shifted to the listeners as much as to the preacher.

Pulpits, which had formerly dominated liturgical environments by virtue of their size and position, were now incongruent with the style of preaching advocated by Craddock. A pulpit, bearing striking similarities to a judge's bench, created a fortress-like barrier between preacher and audience. The sheer breadth or height of the "sacred desk" also proved restrictive for the preacher who preferred to "perform" a sermon, using

112. Hybels, *Rediscovering Church*.

113. Loveland, *Meetinghouse to Megachurch*, 157. In a telephone interview with Mr. Scott Troeger of Willow Creek Community Church, I was told that a cross is often used during various services although not installed as a permanent application.

114. Kilde, *When Church Became Theatre*, 9.

the majority of square footage available on the platform. The move to a portable, less obtrusive podium, adequate for holding a Bible, sermon notes, and little more, became the appropriate solution.

Transitions of this nature raise questions on the essence of the preaching event itself. What is the primary relationship in the preaching event? Is it the relationship between the preacher and listener, or between the hearer and God, through his Word? The rationale behind a move to the smaller podium is that it removes the physical barrier created by a larger pulpit, ostensibly allowing for more openness, transparency, and connectedness between preacher and listener. In other words, it "provides minimal interference to the communication process while still offering a handy place to rest their notes."[115]

Such a position grants significant importance to the "horizontal" relationship between preacher and audience. Should not the primary relational concern be that which exists between the audience and God? Should not the preacher be as inconspicuous as possible in order to avoid interfering in that vertical relation? Even Fred Craddock wisely says, "The pulpit reminds me that I am one of a long line of people whom the church has called to preach and teach. It is a humbling thing to approach the pulpit. With no pulpit, I come on stage, and I am the center."[116]

A pulpit, like the church building in which it may be located, communicates something whether a preacher is present or not. The format, size, and even location of a pulpit does provide significant, albeit inconclusive, insight into a church's theology of preaching. What was Jesus's theology of preaching, or that of the early Christian church? If the pulpit's absence did not prove detrimental to the church's effective ministry during the first three centuries, should we not aspire to replicate the same approach? If that is our conclusion, why be satisfied with just the removal of pulpits? Apart from providing shelter from the elements, why build or possess any architectural church forms or buildings at all?

The economic, political, and cultural dynamics of the first three centuries of church history affected virtually every aspect of the nascent church's development. The Western church of the twenty-first century shares little contextual similarity with the early church. Translating the experiential built forms of the early church so that they are prescriptive

---

115. Taken from an unpublished paper by Kenton C. Anderson, "The Place of the Pulpit."

116. Quoted in Anderson, "The Place of the Pulpit."

for the twenty-first century Western church will prove to be risky at best, and theologically and experientially hazardous at worst.

Having considered these various concrete expressions of the built environment, the following conclusions are offered. Historical evidence suggests that effective Christian worship is not limited to one particular kind of environment. Whether a house, a basilica, a cathedral, a meeting house or multipurpose megachurch, all types of environments have fulfilled particular needs that are unique to specific times and cultural contexts. The development of these various designs has not been strictly chronological, linear, or even evolutionary, in the sense that one design emerged only as a previous one was rendered inappropriate or dysfunctional. Many different types of spaces, including houses, tents, theatres, warehouses, community halls, and school buildings, have been adapted to accommodate the needs and theology of worshiping communities. Contrary to the long-standing belief embraced by many Christians that the cruciform footprint was the only acceptable outline for church buildings, the Christian church has actually demonstrated a wide variety of preferences. I would maintain that in the midst of diversity, the worship spaces most effective to fulfilment of church mission are those that are born out of theological reflection on what the church is and what the relevant liturgy entails.

Thomas G. Long states, "Well-planned sanctuaries communicate by their very design the kind of worship that takes place within."[117] In an increasing number of situations, spaces dedicated to worship events provide little overt or obvious indications that Christian worship occurs there. This is similar to the introduction of the basilica as the prime context for church gatherings and the shift from *domus ecclesia* to *domus dei* in the Constantinian era.[118] The large, simple design of the exterior gave little indication of the intricate and often opulent interior of the basilica church.

Visual engagement was deemed essential to proper participation in the Eucharist. "To hear without seeing was merely to be allowed to eavesdrop, to overhear. Visual participation made the difference between

117. Long, *Beyond the Worship Wars*, 67.

118. Miles points out that even after construction of many larger church buildings under Constantine's edict, many "semipublic house churches" continued to be used. She suggests there is evidence to support the existence of at least twenty-five Christian house churches in Rome itself, by the beginning of the fourth century (Miles, *Image as Insight*, 48).

outsider and member."[119] Traditions that appear to embrace similar theological convictions can give disparate concrete expression to those beliefs through the architecture in which they worship and which they leave for others to inherit. Churches committed to congregational participation in worship produce liturgical spaces that bear little or no resemblance to other churches that are equally and similarly committed, as evidenced by design particularities reflecting the convictions of Luther, Zwingli, and Calvin. Luther's commitment to the inclusion of preaching at virtually every gathering, including the celebration of the Eucharist, contrasted sharply with Zwingli's belief that these two sacred events should never be conducted in the same place.

As the Church of England learned and demonstrated from the late sixteenth to mid-seventeenth centuries, the impact of liturgy and architecture is mutually effective. A great struggle encountered by post-Reformation churches grew out of the new liturgies that developed from Reformation theology. These liturgies were not easily facilitated in the cathedrals inherited from the medieval era. Costs involved in demolishing ancient churches and constructing new ones were prohibitive, limiting many attempts to alter interior arrangements.

As separatist groups such as the Puritans developed and constructed new venues dwarfed by the magnitude of medieval churches, a radical departure from the monumental cathedral began to emerge. This involved major shifts in both exterior and interior design. The cost of constructing meeting houses and chapels in the absence of government or ecclesiastical support generally dictated a much simpler product and approach but was not indicative of a shallower theology or a conviction that the built environment was incidental to the corporate expression of the Christian faith. Notwithstanding the Puritan refusal to attribute sacredness to any built environment, church buildings characterized by austerity and simplicity were no less eloquent in conveying the theology of those who built and utilized them than were the monumental cathedrals of medieval Europe.

The momentum of the Reformation, influenced substantively by a cultural paradigm shift precipitated by an incremental increase of print and literacy, inspired many to risk advancing outside the accepted para-

---

119. Ibid., 51. Miles comments assume a congregation of people who can see, but should be taken to mean that the visually impaired are, therefore, excluded from meaning participation in the Eucharist.

digm that had been so firmly entrenched for several centuries. Shared risk-taking did not result in people agreeing on the same special design, as is evidenced by the multitude of denominations and architectural styles of church buildings today. The evidence remains that Christians during the Reformation and for several years following perceived their theology, liturgy, and sacred places as being intrinsically interwoven. This commitment has gradually surrendered to a more utilitarian, pragmatic application of the architectural experience and expression of Christianity.

From a practical theological perspective, which built environments are going to be the most conducive to the accomplishment of church mission in this present, postmodern century? The suggestion that the built environment is irrelevant, or that the context in which the church's mission and beliefs are embodied is inconsequential, is untenable. Only if symbolism is insignificant; if tradition is eclipsed by novelty; if the built environment in which mission is accomplished is nothing more than a designated space devoid of any meaning or potential for influence; and if contemporary culture is not considered a stakeholder in the accomplishment of the church's mission should the built environment be ignored.

The following chart connects the five dominant structures examined in this chapter, with my own perspective on the primary determining influences and strategic approaches to church mission evidenced during each era.

TABLE 3.2. *Historical Feature, Influence, and Strategy*

Time Frame	Prominent Feature	Prominent Influence	Mission: Strategy Utilized
First to fourth centuries	Private Home	Cultural and Political	Mission strategies organic, personal; unfolded and developed as the church grew. Early church featured 'apostolic' initiation, control and later, influence.
Fourth to twelfth centuries	Basilica	Political	Mission and citizenship within Roman Empire are closely connected, virtually synonymous. Strategy is imperialistically initiated, defined, controlled and emphasized.

Time Frame	Prominent Feature	Prominent Influence	Mission: Strategy Utilized
Twelfth to sixteenth centuries	Cathedral	Political and Theological	Mission driven through cooperative strategies and alliances between church and State. State controlled, clergy elevated, distinct and predominate. Emphasized the visual, material.
Sixteenth to twentieth centuries	Reformed Experiments	Theological	Mission strategies intentionally reflect and emphasize theological conviction. Aural, literary focus. Philosophical approach to congregation characterized as inclusive.
Twentieth century to present	Multi-purpose and Megachurch	Cultural and Theological	Mission strategies intentionally crafted to "reach out," utilizing "take-in" tactics. Reflect sensitivity to contemporary cultural trends and values, concurrent with loyalty to theological conviction.

This historical survey underscores a human tendency that appears to have surfaced in virtually every era and in the vast majority of religious movements: we are prone to attach a primordial quality to the activities and sacred spaces associated with our liturgy, as though God had dispensed an interdiction against any creative, alternative expressions of worship. As Hageman points out, "The embalming of a liturgical form, no matter how ancient or orthodox, was one of the very things against which the reformers had protested. But now their spiritual descendants were guilty of the same practice."[120] The apparent ossification of what once may have been vibrant, meaningful rituals inevitably renders them anachronistic and/or prosaic, at least from the perspective of the "uninitiated" or younger generations.

This observation does not suggest that we abandon predictability or consistency, nor call for a spontaneity that would obviate careful, thoughtful preparation for what occurs when the church gathers. Misplaced or overused novelty can easily become as mundane or monotonous as any long-established ritual or liturgical environment.

But a glance backward in time also reminds us that there are always factors that influence the design and even meaning of the sacred

120. Hageman, *Pulpit and Table*, 42.

spaces used. These factors, be they political, social, or theological, are fluid and ever changing. The architecture that grew out of liberal theology, for instance, in many respects makes sense with its emphasis on the immanence of God. Buildings were promoted as servant churches and emphasized the humanity that God loves. As Torgerson points out, "The transcendence of God was not denied (at least not by all), but was placed in subservient position as a theological construct to be pondered later in the face of chaotic political and oppressive economic circumstances of the mid-twentieth century."[121] Therefore, the benefit of historical reflection is not the recovery of methods or paradigms for reapplication in our present context. Rather it is an understanding of how important the partnership between cultural awareness and theological reflection really is in the development of authentic sacred spaces that will be relevant to the mission of the church in this present day.

Having taken a glance back in history and considering the ways in which changes have occurred within the ecclesial built environment, we need to consider the "So what?" question: how does any of this apply to our present day and age? But before engaging history to move us toward where we need to be, it is important for us to focus on a theological framework for sacred space and the missional church.

121. Torgerson, *Architecture of Immanence*, 23.

Chapter 4

A Theological Framework
for Sacred Space

HAVING ASSEMBLED A BRIEF historical survey of sacred places, we will now focus on
the particularity of sacrality and its application to place through the lens
of theological reflection. But a chapter dedicated to a theological framework for sacred places must also include a significant voice from those
outside the theological disciplines, incorporating insights from religious
studies scholars into a dialogue with theologians and biblical scholars.

We begin by establishing of a working definition of sacrality for-
mulated in dialogue with perspectives arising from within the social
sciences, followed by an examination of a theology of the built environment. A. W. Tozer wrote a small booklet that became popular particularly among evangelicals in North America[1] in which he indicts the
evangelical church for marginalizing worship. In reflecting on this critical dimension of our humanity and the corporate life of the church, I
would suggest that the neglect of worship identified by Tozer has been
influenced by the lack of that which is more fundamental, namely, a
proper grasp of the *sacred*.[2]

---

1. Tozer, *Worship*.

2. Tozer also wrote *Knowledge of the Holy*, which addresses this issue. However, he
writes more on the holiness of God himself rather than the general concept of sacrality.

DEFINING THE SACRED

The concept of sacrality is clearly and significantly interwoven through-out the fabric of the vast majority of religions, both ancient and contem-porary, and the technology of the twenty-first century also demonstrates a willingness to create space for it as well.[3] Patricia Wilson-Kastner is correct when she suggests that sacredness or holiness is something to which humanity is intrinsically drawn. The intentionality with which we construct our sacred spaces declares the degree to which we agree with this premise.

But attaching a clear and succinct definition to the word "sacred" is challenging. Although the concept is largely and typically associated with religion, it is not confined within religious parameters. The follow-ing definitions illustrate the point:[4]

1. Dedicated to or set apart for the worship of a deity.

2. Worthy of religious veneration: the sacred teachings of the Bud-dha.

3. Made or declared holy: sacred bread and wine.

4. Dedicated or devoted exclusively to a single use, purpose or per-son: sacred to the memory of her sister; a private office sacred to the President.

5. Worthy of respect; venerable.

6. Of, or relating to religious objects, rites, or practices.

Yi-Fu Tuan offers a noteworthy perspective when he suggests that in order to understand the significance of "the sacred" we must go be-yond the traditional culture-bound images of temples, shrines, or other such symbols and move to the experiential level. "At the most common level of experience, sacred phenomena are those that stand out from the commonplace and interrupt routine."[5] Tuan is careful to guard against

3. I am referring to the availability of sites on the internet. Using any number of search engines, one will find into the millions of sites dedicated to the sacred or, more specifically, sacred space.

4. Taken from *The American Heritage Dictionary of the English Language*, 3rd ed. (New York: Houghton Mifflin, 1992).

5. Yi-Fu Tuan, "Sacred Space: Explorations of an Idea," in *Dimensions of Human Geography: Essays on Some Familiar and Neglected Themes* (Chicago: University of Chicago, 1978), 84.

the suggestion that anything spatially set apart is automatically sacred space, "nor is every interruption of routine a hierophany."[6] Tuan also believes that the word "sacred" implies more than separateness or distinction; "it also suggests order, wholeness, and power."[7]

Among the many influential thinkers that could be cited with regard to the concept of the sacred, we will give brief consideration to the contributions made by Rudolph Otto, Emile Durkheim, and Mircea Eliade.

Rudolph Otto's Concept of "the Holy"

Few works have aroused more global interest in the study of religion than Rudolf Otto's *The Idea of the Holy*. Arguably the popularity of his work was fostered by his departure from the rational assessment of ideas or abstract concepts associated with religions, which was typical in his day, to an analysis of the nonrational, experiential dimension of spirituality.

In Otto's mind, any concept of holiness that was limited primarily to a moral obligation was myopic and incomplete. Although he did not exclude any ethical element from the meaning of holy, he did state, "If the ethical was present at all, at any rate it was not original and never constituted the whole meaning of the word."[8] In Otto's thinking, the New Testament description of the early disciples as "holy ones" or "saints" does not refer to moral perfection or purity but rather "it means the people who participate in the mystery of the final Day."[9] He invented the term "numinous," which he considered necessary in conveying the concept of the holy "minus its moral factor or 'moment.'"[10] "Numinous" describes the response of the one encountering the holy as much as the actual experience itself. Otto describes a numinous mental state as "perfectly *sui generis* and irreducible to any other; and therefore, like every

---

6. Tuan, "Sacred Space," 84.

7. Ibid. In his emphasis on the aspect of order and wholeness in the "sacred," he explains how an interesting departure has occurred from the view held for centuries that the wilderness or nature was considered chaotic and the city epitomized order and safety. "Raw nature, far from being chaotic, is now perceived to be a model of ecological harmony. Wild life, far from being red in tooth and claw, is a lesson in symbiotic cooperation. Order remains a characteristic of sacred space but the environments in which we discern order are reversed" (Tuan, "Sacred Space," 87).

8. Otto, *Idea of the Holy*, 5.

9. Ibid., 83.

10. Ibid., 5.

absolutely primary and elementary datum while it admits of being discussed, it cannot be strictly defined."[11] He suggests that various elements comprise the "numinous." The first he calls "creature feeling,"[12] which he takes a step beyond Schleiermacher's "feeling of dependence"[13] to refer to "the emotion of a creature, submerged and overwhelmed by its own nothingness in contrast to that which is supreme above all creatures."[14] Elaborating further, Otto describes the awesome mystery (*mysterium tremendum*) of the numinous as denoting that which is beyond comprehension or description—that which is both awful, repelling a person, and fascinating in a way that attracts (*mysterium fascinans*). It is this awesome dread, or lower stage of numinous consciousness, that Otto sees as characteristic of primitive religions.[15]

Otto suggests quite clearly that the experience of the numinous comes about only as the direct result of revelation.[16] Unlike certain aspects of religion such as dogma or rituals, the numinous aspect of religion cannot be taught. It must be awakened, induced, aroused, or incited.[17] A person is only capable of recognizing the holy when it is revealed if there is an *a priori* cognition. "And we maintain that this is only possible by an element of cognition, comprehension, and valuation in one's own inner consciousness, that goes out to meet the outward present fact, i.e., by the 'spirit within.'"[18]

To underscore his point, Otto draws analogies from the realms of aesthetics and music. A piece of music or a thing of beauty can only be appreciated and understood by a person who has received or developed a musical or aesthetic valuation. The use of these analogies points to Otto's distinction between *a priori* cognitions and innate cognitions. He delineates the difference as follows:

---

11. Ibid., 7.

12. Ibid., 10.

13. Referred to in ibid., 10.

14. Ibid.

15. Ibid., 72.

16. Revelation is a term Otto seldom uses except, for example, in referencing the work of Schleiermacher. Otto states, "In Schleiermacher's language the 'presentiment' goes out to meet the 'revelation' to which it belongs" (ibid., 160).

17. Ibid., 60.

18. Ibid., 160.

> The loftier *a priori* cognitions are such as—while everyone is indeed capable of having them—do not, as experience teaches us, occur spontaneously, but rather are "awakened" through the instrumentality of other more highly endowed natures. In relation to these the universal "predisposition" is merely a faculty of *receptivity* and a *principle of judgment and acknowledgement*, not a capacity to produce the cognitions in question for oneself independently. This latter capacity is confined to those specially "endowed."[19]

This special endowment implies an ability similar to a person's gift of creating an original piece of music or art that is distinguished from another person's capacity to appreciate or respond to such a creation. In the religious realm, Otto believes that whereas most of humanity has the capacity to receive religious truth, there is a higher stage beyond mere receptivity reserved for the prophet, the person endowed by the Spirit with "the power to hear the 'voice within' and the power of divination."[20] Implicit in Otto's belief is that not everyone experiences the holy to the same degree or on the same level. This is significant, particularly as it pertains to the variety of people's experiences of sacred places.

Otto's emphasis on the *experience* of the holy, that is, his conviction that God was more than an idea that could be explained but a power that was to be encountered and experienced, was highly influential in the development of the theology of sacred places. Other well-known and highly respected scholars, including Mircea Eliade,[21] have been influenced by Otto's work. Although there appears to be no direct correspondence between Otto and Durkheim, there are nonetheless some interesting similarities in their thinking.

Durkheim's Complete Heterogeneity: Sacred and Profane

Early in his seminal work,[22] Emile Durkheim posits that a common characteristic among all known religious belief systems is a clear distinction between the sacred and the profane.[23] He stresses that our understanding

---

19. Ibid., 177.

20. Ibid., 178.

21. Eliade refers to and builds on Otto's *Das Heilige* in two of his works in particular: *Sacred and the Profane*, 8–10 and *Myths, Dreams, and Mysteries*, 123–54.

22. Durkheim, *Elementary Forms*.

23. Ibid., 37–38.

of sacrality must not be limited to deities or spirits. Virtually any object, location, or rite can be considered sacred. A site could be considered sacred, for instance, by virtue of a deity manifesting itself there and/or declaring such a place sacred. Likewise the burial site of a saint or the location of a miraculous occurrence were often identified as sacred sites. He also observed that in some cultures, an object would be considered sacred if an ancestor had selected it as a posthumous residence just before his or her death.[24]

Designating an object or location as sacred is not determined by a hierarchical scheme in which one item or site is deemed superior either in power or dignity. A hierarchy can exist between things that share a common heritage or are of the same species, but the distinction between the sacred and the profane is, in Durkheim's words, absolute; "the sacred and the profane have always and everywhere been conceived by the human mind as two distinct classes, as two worlds between which there is nothing in common."[25] The relation between the sacred and the profane is characterized by intense heterogeneity, which according to Durkheim is "even so complete that it frequently degenerates into a veritable antagonism."[26]

This complete heterogeneity does not preclude any movement between the two worlds, but the nature of such a change "implies a veritable metamorphosis."[27] He concludes that the possibility of a person, place or thing residing in both worlds at the same time is untenable.[28] All religious beliefs assume "a bipartite division of the whole universe, known and knowable, into two classes which embrace all that exists, but which radically exclude each other."[29] The sacred, in Durkheim's observation, is that which is isolated from the profane and is protected by prohibitions.

24. Ibid., 169.

25. Ibid., 38.

26. Ibid., 39.

27. Ibid.

28. It is this, he argues, which precipitated the ascetic lifestyle of religious monasteries. "From that come all forms of religious suicide, the logical working-out of this asceticism; for the only manner of fully escaping the profane life is, after all to forsake all life" (ibid., 40).

29. Durkheim, *Elementary Forms*, 40.

Eliade's Sacred Centre

In Mircea Eliade's thought, sacrality varies from time to time and place to place. He believed that anything in the world has the capability of becoming sacred. Until a certain "irruption"[30] occurs in what previously was "homogeneous space," a place remains profane. "Every sacred space implies a hierophany, an irruption of the sacred that results in detaching a territory from the surrounding cosmic milieu and making it qualitatively different."[31] For Eliade, what makes a sacred place so significant is that it provides a breakthrough, or an opening, from one ontological level to another.[32] Thus he refers to sanctuaries as "doors of the gods."[33]

For Eliade, it is only in this heterogeneous space, this space that has been detached from "the surrounding cosmic milieu and making it qualitatively different,"[34] that humanity can participate in Reality.[35] However, when an object does become sacred, it does not cease to be itself. A rock considered sacred continues to be a rock.[36] A location or object might be considered sacred only when certain activities take place or when certain people, such as a group of worshipers, gather there. A place would be sacred in a *derivative* sense.

The common ground shared between Mircea Eliade and Durkheim is evident in Eliade's statement, "The first possible definition of the *sacred* is that it is *the opposite of the profane*."[37] Although this distinction between the sacred and profane is woven throughout his work, Eliade

---

30. This appears to be a favorite expression for Eliade along with "repetition." Jonathan Z. Smith suggests, "However, we may note that when Eliade speaks of sacred space, it is the irruptive element which predominates; when he speaks of sacred time, it is the repetitive" (Smith, *Map Is Not Territory*, 94).

31. Ibid., 26.

32. Eliade states that a hierophany "makes it open above—that is, in communication with heaven, the paradoxical point of passage from one mode of being to another" (Eliade, *Sacred and the Profane*, 26). He uses the term "paradoxical" to describe how the extraordinary manifests itself through the ordinary, or the heterogeneous irrupts through the homogeneous.

33. Eliade, *Sacred and the Profane*, 27.

34. Ibid., 26.

35. "When the sacred manifests itself in any hierophany, there is not only a break in the homogeneity of space; there is also a revelation of an absolute reality, opposed to the nonreality of the vast surrounding expanse. The manifestation of the sacred ontologically founds the world" (Eliade, *Sacred and the Profane*, 21).

36. Ibid., 12.

37. Ibid., 10. This parallels Durkheim's "bipartite division of the whole universe."

also suggests that archaic societies did not have the category of "profane." Instead, "Every act which has a definite meaning—hunting, fishing, agriculture; fames, conflicts, sexuality—in some way participates in the sacred."[38] He posits a double relationship in which the sacred is both transcendent and exemplary[39]—the sacred is both completely *other* than humanity[40] while at the same time "it establishes patterns to be followed."[41]

One of the most distinguishing features of the Eliadean approach to sacrality is the concept of the "center." This concept received significant attention in many of his major works[42] and is often found described in strikingly similar language from one work to another. One cannot appreciate Eliade's concept of sacred places without attending to this pivotal element. In his own words, "The Center, then, is pre-eminently the zone of the sacred, the zone of absolute reality."[43]

Eliade draws the following conclusions with respect to the symbolic expressions of the Center:

1. The Sacred Mountain—where heaven and earth meet—is situated at the center of the world.
2. Every temple or palace—and by extension, every sacred city or royal residence—is a Sacred Mountain, thus becoming a Center.
3. Being *axis mundi*, the sacred city or temple is regarded as the meeting point of heaven, earth, and hell.[44]

---

38. Eliade, *Myth of the Eternal Return*, 27–28.

39. Eliade, *Myths*, 18.

40. Perhaps this is a reflection of the "wholly other" (*ganz andere*) aspect of Otto's "numinous." See Eliade, *Myths*, 124.

41. Ibid., 18.

42. This is a concept to which Eliade dedicates more than a passing mention in at least four of his major works: *Images and Symbols*, 27–56; *Patterns in Comparative Religion*, 374–81; *Myth of the Eternal Return*, 12–21; *Sacred and the Profane*, 36–47. One of his other major works, *Myths, Dreams, and Mysteries,* basically omits any mention of the "centre."

43. Eliade, *Myth of the Eternal Return*, 17. See also his statement in *Images and Symbols*, 51: "We have seen that it was not only temples that were thought to be situated at the 'Center of the World,' but that every holy place, every place that bore witness to an incursion of the sacred into profane space, was also regarded as a 'center.'"

44. This list is found both in *Myth of the Eternal Return*, 12, and *Patterns in Comparative Religion*, 375.

The "center" for Eliade consisted of a break[45] in the homogeneity of profane space through which communication from one cosmic level to another was made possible. This break was disclosed through a symbol of the *axis mundi* (be that a ladder, a pillar, or a bridge) around which our world is located, thus designating the axis as the center, or navel, of the earth.[46]

Eliade deemed the construction of "sacred places" as completely plausible since such an effort represented a cosmogony—"a creation of the world."[47] This was based upon the following significant propositions in his thinking:

1. Every creation repeats the preeminent cosmogonic act, the creation of the world.

2. Consequently, whatever is founded has its foundation at the center of the world (since, as we know, the creation itself took place from a center).[48]

Timothy Gorringe questions the precision with which Eliade claims sacred space can be located.[49] He argues convincingly that many people's actual experience of sacred space refuses to conform to the constraints of Eliade's formalized categories. Yet there are those who believe that the need for sacred places is an inherent trait of our humanity. Patricia Wilson-Kastner has argued that intrinsic to human nature is a "fundamental instinct to respect sacred places."[50] Citing the work of Mircea Eliade, she suggests that sacred space is a "connecting point between the divine and the world . . . it is a place where either the divine has made itself known or a manifestation of the sacred has been provoked."[51]

Although the dichotomy between the sacred and the profane enjoyed a hegemonic influence among anthropologists and theologians for many years, more recently this distinction has been called into question if not jettisoned altogether. William H. Swatos Jr. considers the two

---

45. Or to use another of his favorite terms, an "irruption."

46. Eliade, *Sacred and the Profane*, 37.

47. Eliade, *Images and Symbols*, 52.

48. Eliade, *Myth of the Eternal Return*, 18.

49. Gorringe, *Theology of the Built Environment*, 37.

50. Wilson-Kastner, *Sacred Drama*, 43.

51. Ibid.

concepts of the sacred and profane as incapable of being synthetically melded into a unity yet at the same time so interrelated as to take their meaning from each other.[52] In Swatos's mind, not separation but penetration designates the essence of the sacred. "The sacred takes meaning precisely as it runs in and through everyday life in constant dialogue with the mundane demands of everyday existence."[53] In this way, the sacred has a transformational capability that would be rendered impossible as long as the separation of the sacred and the profane is maintained.

Application and Terminology

The concept of the sacred has variegated implications in different societies. In many Western societies the concept of the sacred has a limited application to one aspect of life, namely religious activity, whereas in other societies it is much more pervasive, touching all facets of life.[54] In many indigenous societies, the quality of sacredness is extended to the land of an entire nation. Although translating the concept of the sacred from one culture to another is often linguistically challenging, certain elements consistently appear to accompany sacred sites regardless of the culture in which they are found. For instance, one will often find the sacred demarcated from the mundane or ordinary out of respect or honor.

Historically, the terms "sacred" and "religious" have been used interchangeably, but some are of the opinion that doing so fosters an inaccurate conception of the sacred. A. T. Mann resists the application of the term "sacred" in the architectural realm if it "is defined as a building or monument which has a religious function or uses the vocabulary of forms consistent with religious practice."[55] For Mann, architecture is sacred if it has "a common root in the life of the soul and spiritual vision, rather than merely in forms, which qualify as being religious."[56] The concept of the sacred has become detached from that which is

52. Swatos, "Revisiting the Sacred," 34–35.

53. Ibid., 34.

54. On April 27, 2001, I was privileged to participate in a field trip to Findhorn, a New Age community on the north shore of Scotland. In a conversation with one of the staff members I was told that the motto of business for the community was "Business Is Sacred." The membrane between the visible and invisible worlds is considered very thin, to the point that the Eliadean distinction between sacred and profane finds little or no acceptance at Findhorn.

55. Mann, *Sacred Architecture*, 13.

56. Ibid.

religious, even though the two are indeed related. I agree that the sacred transcends and overwhelms the religious.

Sacrality, while often associated and sometimes equated with religion, is also closely linked with other concepts such as holiness, liturgy, and ritual. Don S. Browning suggests that each concept, whether sacred, holy, religious, ritual, or ritualistic, not only has its horizon and periphery but also has a focus or center.[57] The conceptual horizons may indeed converge or overlap but at the center, or focus, the concepts are distinct. The indiscriminate and interchangeable use of these terms is likely to inhibit clarity of communication between people embracing divergent traditions and perspectives.

DESIGNATING THE SACRED

There has been an intriguing and recent resurgence of interest in Celtic spirituality. Philip Sheldrake has provided some helpful insights into how sacrality was attributed to various locations within early Celtic tradition. He posits three elements that were reflected in the selection of religious or sacred sites. First was the existence of "the creative tension between the desire for seclusion and the wish to be accessible and open to society at large,"[58] reflecting the theological tension between God's transcendence and immanence in Celtic Christian spirituality. Second was the unusual meshing of the monastic lifestyle with the traditional social structures of the day. "Speaking more broadly, spirituality was not something detached from social values and organization, but was intimately entwined with them."[59] Third was the fascination with borderlands, or frontiers and liminality, particularly associated with a pervasive sense that the "other" world was extremely proximate to the world of everyday experience. "To an extent, all places were points of access, or doorways to the sacred. But certain places or points were marked off as special or particular, for example cemeteries, monastic enclosures or certain natural features with a long spiritual history."[60]

In dramatic contrast, at a public lecture, in an almost arbitrary manner, Canadian photographer Courtney Milne stated, "A place is holy

---

57. Browning, *Fundamental Practical Theology*, 91.

58. Sheldrake, *Life Between Two Worlds*, 31–32.

59. Ibid., 32.

60. Ibid.

because I said so!"[61] Deity of any sort is virtually nonexistent or irrelevant in Milne's concept of sacred or holy places. "Mother Earth" features more prominently in his thinking and often informs the kind of photography he produces. One gets the impression that his concept of the sacred is rooted in a pantheistic or a panentheistic persuasion, notwithstanding his avoidance of direct reference to "deity."

Mircea Eliade would strongly disagree with Milne's persuasion that the designation of a place or object as sacred resides squarely within the realm of human prerogative. He believes instead that the actual indication of a sacred site is dependent upon the manifestation of the sacred either through a divine presence or miracle, or through the actions of animals that serve to direct one to a sacred place. He writes, "This is as much as to say that men are not free to *choose* the sacred site, that they only seek for it and find it by the help of mysterious signs."[62]

Eliade's approach is somewhat similar to the manner in which the sacrality of a location is determined among the Native American tribe, the Navajo Indians. Types of Navajo sacred places include the following:

1. A location mentioned in oral tradition.
2. A place where something supernatural has happened in oral tradition.
3. A site from which plants, herbs, minerals, and waters possessing healing powers may be taken.
4. A place where individuals communicate with the supernatural world by means of prayers and offerings.[63]

A. T. Mann advocates a belief that the actual shape, geometry of design, and orientation of a given space are influential in determining its sacrality. He cites the Muslim belief that all sacred places must face toward Mecca since that is where, according to their convictions, heaven and earth meet.[64] He points out how the circle has featured prominently in the architecture of several different traditions, including Native American, Buddhist, Hindu, Islamic, and Christian. He then develops at

---

61. Courtney Milne, "The Sacred Earth," public lecture held at the Museum of Natural History, Regina, Saskatchewan, on October 22, 1991.

62. Eliade, *Sacred and Profane*, 28.

63. Warshall, "Liturgy of Place?" 52.

64. Mann, *Sacred Architecture*, 123.

length the relationship between the square and the circle; the square is created by the human mind, nonexistent in nature, while the circle, symbolizing deity and wholeness, is found throughout the natural world. Thus when a dome, representing the heavenly realm, is situated upon a square base, representing the earthly realm (as is the case with most mosques), it is a sacred representation of "the perfect meeting of heaven and earth."[65]

The aspect of spatial reference or separation is common throughout many suggested concepts of the sacred. It may be applied to numerous divergent spaces and shapes, including single stones, stones in a circle, rivers, seas, mountains, trees, shrines, sanctuaries, temples, synagogues, churches, mosques, and burial plots.[66]

Scott Peck states that "consensual validation"[67] is an essential element to determine whether a place is in reality holy or sacred. In other words, the element of group or social construction is involved in the determination and designation of the sacred. He is careful, insisting that such consensus is inadequate by itself. In designating actual sites as "holy," Peck thinks in terms of "conjunction: a mysterious conjunction of natural beauty, past human construction, *and* a present beholder."[68] Holiness, or sacrality, is intimately linked with *wholeness*.

An important question that remains is *who* decides whether or not a particular rock, river, or sea is sacred while others, which may be endowed with even more striking beauty, are not. Turner believes that a common misconception is that the designation of the sacred is a human choice, sanctioned by an act or some ritual whereby that space is consecrated.[69] Reflecting the thought of Mircea Eliade, Turner believes that deity must ultimately determine the location of the sacred, whether that is through an actual manifestation of the god or by some miracle brought about by divine intervention in human space-time history. "Neither natural nor human agency makes a place sacred, but only the action of the gods."[70] Referring to the fact that the earliest known sacred sites were quite independent of any buildings or structures, he

65. Ibid., 129.

66. Turner, *Temple to Meeting House*, 14.

67. Peck, *In Search of Stones*, 75.

68. Ibid.

69. Turner, *Temple to Meeting House*, 17.

70. Ibid.

concludes, "The essentials of a sacred place for worship are location and spatial demarcation rather than buildings or other elaborations that come first to our own minds."[71]

Peck takes a different tack, suggesting that a place need not be a site of worship in order to be considered holy or sacred, at least not as we would typically think about worship. Instead, every moment, location, and person has the potential for being holy. Referring to a belief held by some Catholics, "the sacrament of the present moment," he believes that "every moment of our lives is sacred, and that we should make of each moment a sacrament."[72] For Peck, a place becomes holy to him when he *experiences* something, whether that is the presence of God or a palpable sense of a spirit of peace.[73] Similar to A. T. Mann, Peck opposes the notion that sacrality or holiness must be linked to religion. Spirituality, however, *is* a crucial element of the sacred.[74]

THE FUNCTION OF THE SACRED

If Patricia Wilson-Kastner is correct and the need to respect the sacred is an inherent, integral part of our humanity, then one could argue that one of the functions of the sacred is to contribute to the fulfillment of our humanness. Though in slightly different terms, Harold Turner arrives at the same conclusion, suggesting that a prime function of the sacred is the provision of a center of reference that establishes meaning and direction for our actions.[75] Turner's explicit connection of the center of reference with the sacred has significant Eliadean overtones:

> Such a center of reference is found in the sacred place where contact may be made with a much more real and solid world than that of everyday uncertain and changing experience. The transient and vulnerable affairs of men then have "an anchor in the ultimate." To the sanctuary all human needs may be brought, here every failure may be confessed, guidance sought in every problem and power invoked against every threat of danger.

71. Ibid., 15.

72. Peck, *In Search of Stones*, 71.

73. Ibid., 73.

74. Ibid., 76.

75. Turner, *Temple to Meeting House*, 21.

From this center man can face his environment and find his way
through life's hazards and problems.[76]

It is particularly significant that he sees the sacred as equipping
people to live effectively in their world rather than as a means of with-
drawal or escape from it. In my mind, the sacred is an essential ingredient to the effective resistance of all that is dehumanizing. Unfortunately,
when the distinction between the sacred and the religious is blurred or
minimized, and activities are deemed sacred automatically because of
their religious character, the realization of the fullness of a person's humanity may be hindered as much as it would be under the bureaucratic
"irrationality of rationality" described so eloquently by George Ritzer.[77]

One of the ways in which this potential danger can manifest itself
has been effectively underscored by Richard Giles.[78] Legitimate need for
and commitment to sacred space can unfortunately devolve into what
Giles refers to as "a consuming interest in the built environment."[79] He
suggests that eventually we fall victim "to this irrepressible urge to possess a holy place of one's own."[80] I wonder if this "irrepressible urge" is
not partially due to the unfortunate experience of too many people who
have not been permitted, let alone encouraged, to express their humanity in the presence of the sacred. The sacred space—or perhaps better
described in this present discussion as *religious* space—in which many
people gather from week to week is prescriptive by design. It allows for
little kinaesthetic participation, that is, embodiment or enactment, on
the part of those gathered to worship.[81]

THE IMPACT OF THE SACRED

Any attempt at analyzing the emotional experiences of people who
entered sacred spaces during the early days of the church must be left
to conjecture since data from biblical records and rabbinic writings are
insufficient to sustain much beyond an educated guess. Such existential

---

76. Turner, *Temple to Meeting House*, 19–20.

77. Ritzer, *McDonaldization of Society*, 24, 136–39.

78. Giles, *Re-Pitching the Tent*.

79. Ibid., 37.

80. Ibid., 50.

81. Sample, *Spectacle of Worship*, 82–84.

details, according to Seth Kunin,[82] must be viewed as secondary to the manner in which the sacred was in fact conceptualized. Kunin does see sufficient evidence in biblical accounts to support the suggestion that divine communication—and, more important, transformation—takes place in sacred space. In Exodus 19–32, the account of Moses's venture up Mount Sinai, a permanent covenant is established between God and Israel in which they are transformed into the covenant people of God.[83]

Victor Turner sees time spent in journeying to a sacred space as a merging, or a threshold, between two categories or worlds. He refers to this as "liminality."[84] Kunin states that Jewish pilgrimage does not include a liminal element; rather, liminality is to be experienced in the sacred space itself.[85] It is in these liminal spaces that direct communication with the divine and the resultant transformation takes place.[86] Such locations do not intrinsically possess this liminality, but the potential for this "can be actualized by a particular narrative or cultural context."[87] Accordingly, virtually any location has the potential to provide the liminal experience of the sacred.

SACRED PLACES IN THE OLD TESTAMENT

The Old Testament provides numerous examples of places designated as holy or sacred. In some instances, including Exodus 3:5, God declares the site holy. In others, such as Genesis 28: 22, the declaration is the result of human initiative. Likewise, the construction of a dwelling place for God is described both as a human endeavor[88] and as something for which God himself is responsible.[89] From Scripture, it appears that the designation of a place as sacred can be the result of human or divine initiative or a combination of both. One consistent pattern does not emerge in which locations or objects are identified as being endowed with sacral

82. Kunin, *God's Place in the World*, 2.

83. Ibid., 32.

84. See Turner, *Ritual Process*, and Kunin, *God's Place in the World*, 30–36.

85. Kunin, *God's Place in the World*, 82–83.

86. Ibid., 30.

87. Ibid.

88. See 1 Kings 8:13: "I have indeed built a magnificent temple for you, a place for you to dwell forever."

89. See Exodus 15:17: "The place, O Lord, you made for your dwelling, the sanctuary, O Lord, your hands established."

qualities. From Eliade's perspective, Jacob was able to designate Bethel as a sacred site only because God had chosen to reveal himself in that place and at that time.

Scholars have offered other means of categorizing sacred places in biblical literature. Seth Kunin suggests two conflicting models of sacred space appear in the Old Testament: multiple sacred spaces and a single sacred space,[90] also described as decentralized and centralized sacred space.

Decentralized Sacred Space

Old Testament texts provide numerous examples of places that are designated or established as holy or distinct from surrounding places. Genesis 28:12–22 records the experience of Jacob's dream in which he saw a stairway connecting heaven and earth with angels ascending and descending; at the top of the stairway stood the Lord and he spoke promises to Jacob regarding himself and his descendants. Upon awaking, Jacob declared, "Surely the Lord is in this place, and I was not aware of it. . . . How awesome is this place! This is none other than the house of God; this is the gate of heaven." This very ordinary location, selected the night before as a suitable place to sleep, was now perceived as sacred, the very house of God. Jacob's expression "Surely the Lord is in this place, and I was not aware of it" suggests the reason, a vivid example of Eliade's principle, "Every sacred space implies a hierophany, an irruption of the sacred that results in detaching a territory from the surrounding cosmic milieu and making it qualitatively different."[91]

It is clear from this passage that the terms "house" and "gate" are not used in the same sense as they would be used in reference to a place where a person made his or her abode, nor as a means of access into a walled city. In verse 22, Jacob vows, "And this stone that I have set up as a pillar will be God's house." It is not likely that Jacob had in mind the establishment of the one and only place where a person could meet God. The symbolic metaphor of a gate or gateway as a means of passage from one space or world to another—or as Eliade suggests, from one mode of being to another[92]—is rich.

---

90. Kunin, "Judaism," 127–28.

91. Eliade, *Sacred and the Profane*, 26.

92. Ibid.

Inherent in various perspectives of the sacred is the concept of a sacred site being the point of intersection between two worlds. Jacob's dream is a dynamic manifestation of this intersection. By saying "this is the gate of heaven," Jacob declares this place to be a site at which access to another world, heaven, was temporarily provided. Although Jacob does not use the terms "sacred" or "holy" in his consecration of this place, his actions of setting up a monument, pouring oil over it and designating the place Bethel ("house of God"), clearly indicate that this was no longer a profane or ordinary space.

Similarly, David describes the threshing floor of Ornan as "the house of the Lord God and this is the altar of the burnt offering for Israel."[93] Based on numerous Old Testament examples, it is clear that this term "house of God" or "house of the Lord God" was not applied exclusively to one specific location. One possible exception to this was Ornan's threshing floor, which eventually did become the Temple site—a more fixed sacred location. The supernatural intersection of human space-time history that took place at Ornan's threshing floor, with the accompanying promise of God to end a plague upon the land, does seem to provide some justification for designating this specific place as the location for the Temple site.

In Exodus 3–4, another specific site is declared holy at the place of encounter between Moses and God at the burning bush. God directs Moses to "take off your sandals, for the place where you are standing is holy ground." God declares the sacrality of the place.

One difference between the holy places experienced by Moses and Jacob is that there appears to be no indication that Moses left any kind of monument marking the location of the burning bush for posterity's sake. Yet the encounter of divine presence that Moses experienced at this site is of the sort that typically would inspire the construction of a memorial separating it from its ordinary, profane surroundings. A prescriptive template of universal applicability to determine whether a site deserves to be designated as sacred is elusive, with one exception: in all the instances cited here, a personal encounter with the living God occurred.

93. See 1 Chronicles 21:14—22:1, and 2 Samuel 24:15–25.

Centralized Sacred Space: The Tabernacle

One of the realities of the wilderness wanderings of the ancient nation of Israel was that for approximately forty years, they were not led to places previously designated as sacred. In order to create any place of sacred significance, it was necessary to carry a portable sacred place designed an approved by God himself. Although rustic, even primitive in comparison to the magnificent Temple structure that eventually became central to ancient Israel's world, the tabernacle nonetheless provided the sacred space where God revealed himself and could be encountered by his people. It served as a visual reminder of both God's immanence and transcendence. Donald Bruggink and Carl Droppers suggest that "the tabernacle and its arrangements are to tell the people something about God. The structure in which Israel is to worship is to serve as an aid to God's message. It is to be, in fact, a part of that message."[94]

Before ancient Israel's establishment in the land of Canaan and the construction of the Jerusalem Temple in particular, sacred space functioned under the rubric of what Seth Kunin refers to as the dynamic model of sacred space.[95] This model has its prime focus on not only the tabernacle or Tent of Meeting but also includes the entire camp of ancient Israel. In the Song of Moses and Miriam (Exod. 15:1–8), reference is made to the land into which God was going to bring the nation of Israel. Terms typically used in reference to specific places of worship, such as "the mountain of your inheritance" and "the place, O Lord, you made for your dwelling" and "the sanctuary," are applied to the land as a whole.

Sacred space was not tied to one particular location but was to be found in a variety of places. In contrast to the gods of the Canaanites, who were believed to dwell and rule from specific mountains,[96] Yahweh moved with the nation of Israel. "The tabernacle therefore represents the dynamic and eschatological nature of existence as God's people, over against more static conceptions of a consummation indicated by the building of temples where the gods may dwell with men."[97] Kunin's description of this dynamic model of sacred space is helpful:

---

94. Bruggink and Hoppers, *Christ and Architecture*, 3.

95. Kunin, *God's Place*, 11–12.

96. Peterson, *Engaging with God*, 24–25.

97. Turner, *Temple to Meeting House*, 94–95.

> By definition, dynamic sacred place is not confined to any particular location or even kind of location. There is, for example, no reason to assume that the camp was always built on one type of geographic feature rather than any other. This distinguishes the model from other variations developed in the text in which sacred places were associated, for example, with hills or groves. Nor is sacred place associated with a historical or mythological experience of the divine. Sacred place is directly tied to the people and moves with them through the wilderness. . . . Dynamic sacred place is temporary and disassociated from physical space. It is based on the conjunction of other significant categories, objects, people, and activities, rather than locations.[98]

Kunin's comment regarding the connection between the people and their wilderness movement with sacred space resonates with the convictions of those who embrace similar views in reference to the New Testament church. The tabernacle was dynamic sacred space in that it was not tied to one particular location, but it did maintain a centralized quality by virtue of its presence wherever the camp of Israel was temporarily established. "In a real sense it served as the center of reference in the life of Israel, even if it was not placed in the center of the encampment."[99]

Centralized Sacred Space: The Temple

A Place of Encounter

Historically, a common function attributed to temples has been their provision of a place facilitating experiential encounters between humanity and deity, often mediated through the service of a priest or priests. The actual space designated as the dwelling place of the deity, or place in which the deity was to be encountered, was commonly small and dark relative to the rest of the temple area. By design, the vast majority who gathered to worship were excluded from being physically present in the space in which the encounter or manifestation occurred. Their divine encounter was vicarious in nature, or as Forrester and others have suggested, "Only in a secondary and derivative sense, and that only by attending from afar,"[100] since it was the high priest alone who was permitted to enter the holy of holies on behalf of the people. The Temple

---

98. Kunin, *God's Place*, 21.

99. Turner, *Temple to Meeting House*, 91.

100. Forrester et al., *Encounter with God*, 17.

was not designed to allow great masses of people to meet in the presence of God. Thus, in a manner very similar to the function of the Tabernacle, ancient Israel was reminded of the fact that God was both immanent and transcendent; he was present among them while at the same time unapproachable for almost everyone but the priests.

The emphasis on the Temple as the worship center, a place of encounter between God and his people, does not preclude the possibility of worshiping him beyond the confines of the Temple area. One of the dangers David had to be warned about by the prophet Nathan prior to the construction of the magnificent Temple in Jerusalem was the propensity, like the nations surrounding Israel, to believe that his God could be contained in this one specific place.[101] Several texts remind us that Israel's devotion to Yahweh was to be evidenced in the discharge of daily routine;[102] "the whole of the chosen People understands itself as called to become the place where the glory of the Lord dwells: a holy, royal nation of priests spreading God's Word not by means of sacred ceremonies, but by their lives."[103]

A Statement of Distinction

The distinction between the sacred and the profane, highlighted in the writing of scholars such as Durkheim and Eliade and found in many ancient sacred environments, was also clearly manifest in Israel's Temple in Jerusalem. Access to the various spaces became increasingly limited as one moved from the outer courts through to the holy of holies. The arrangement was based on what Kunin refers to as a segmentary opposition model, in which each smaller unit of distinction was considered "qualitatively more positive than the previous level."[104] This progressive distinction was not only symbolic of the horizontal plane but the vertical as well. Each successive court or section of the Temple approaching the holy of holies was elevated so that "the ascent to the Temple is not only the ascent to the Temple Mount, it is also the ascent, starting from the outer enclosure of the Temple, from one level of sacredness to the other."[105] With each successive court leading toward the holy of holies,

101. See 2 Samuel 7.

102. See, for example, Exodus 19:5–6; Isaiah 56:6–8; Micah 6:6–8.

103. Forrester et al., *Encounter with God*, 18.

104. Seth Kunin, "Judaism," 120.

105. Schmidt, *How the Temple Thinks*, 84.

the most sacred space within the Temple, the number of people granted entry was significantly reduced. Ultimately only one person from the entire nation of Israel, the high priest, was permitted into that space.

This demarcation of the pure and impure, this prohibition against intermingling, was not only to be manifest in the design and construction of the temple; it was to be a part of daily living as well.[106] Clothing was not to be made from mixed materials.[107] The only possible exceptions were the garments worn by the priests while ministering in the Temple. According to Leviticus 19:19, fabric that was a hybrid of wool and linen was to be reserved for the priests at such times. Agricultural directives forbidding the mixture of various seeds within the same field and the crossbreeding of animals were also clearly delineated.[108] Dietary restrictions forbade the mixture of certain kinds of animal flesh.[109] The bias toward endogamy underscored the importance of maintaining distinction even from tribe to tribe.

All of these distinctions provided consistent symbolic reminders of the essential order so that, as Schmidt suggests, "Through this symbolic system, the Temple as an institution organizes the natural and supernatural world. It controls the factors of uncertainty. It reduces those of disorder and of confusion."[110] One of the primary functions of the Temple was to model and maintain the distinction between the sacred and the profane, the pure and the impure. It served as a concrete reminder of God's immanence and transcendence; God was clearly present in the midst of the nation Israel, but direct access to his presence was limited in terms of both time and space.

The incrementally limited access to the altar built into most ancient cathedrals is a clear reflection of the Temple design and metaphor. It was this limited accessibility to the altar that Reformers such as Martin Luther resisted. The Temple was a symbolic statement of Israel's identity, providing a reminder that Israel was to be distinct from all other nations.

Forrester, McDonald, and Tellini posit the view that in some ways no distinction exists between the sacred and the profane. Worship was

---

106. Deuteronomy 23:10–15.

107. Leviticus 19:19; Deuteronomy 22:11.

108. Leviticus 19:19; Deuteronomy 22:9, 10.

109. See Leviticus 11:1–19.

110. Schmidt, *How the Temple Thinks*, 95.

to influence all of life, having "immediate and practical consequences."[111] The entire camp of Israel was considered pure and inaccessible to those from other nations. "It is set into structural opposition with the world, which is the realm of the profane and the impure."[112] Outside the camp was the designated location for those who suffered from more permanent impurities such as leprosy. It is difficult to contest the fact that within the camp itself there were also varying degrees of purity or holiness ascribed to various spaces and people.

A Statement of Community

Although the Temple provided a venue for certain important functions and rituals, it was also intended to be a concrete visual aid illustrating some aspects of the nature of Israel's God as well as the unique spiritual identity of Israel as a nation. As Francis Schmidt has stated, "The Temple, even in its architecture, is an image of the Jewish community, with its classifications, its hierarchies, its procedures for advancement through the interplay of alliances of the social scale, its rites of passages as well, and its exclusion."[113]

Within the Temple, physical boundaries created various areas accessible only to the Jewish people. Allowing foreigners into courts from which they had been excluded previously ran the risk of profaning the sacred and even of obscuring Israel's national identity. But refusing access to foreigners wishing to enter various courts ran the risk of offending them to the point of retaliation, perhaps even war.

The Land and Landedness

In order to do justice to the consideration of sacred space and places in the Old Testament, one must broaden the scope beyond the specifics of the Tabernacle, the Temple, and other locations in which a divine-human encounter occurred. John Inge argues that it was the land more than anything which featured prominently in Jehovah's promise to ancient Israel. "The anticipation, the promise, is of landedness, a place which is rooted in the Word of God."[114] The story of ancient Israel can be read as

---

111. Forrester et al., *Encounter with God*, 18.

112. Kunin, *God's Place*, 14.

113. Schmidt, *How the Temple Thinks*, 85.

114. Inge, *Christian Theology of Place*, 37.

a threefold relationship between Israel, God, and the land (or place).[115] The Promised Land was not simply the location or the receptacle in which Israel lived out her relationship with God but a vital aspect of that relationship. As Inge states, "God relates *to* people *in* places, and the places are not irrelevant to that relationship but, rather, are integral to divine human encounter."[116]

This is not to suggest that Israel had no relationship with God before their entry into the land of promise. But Egypt and the wilderness where they wandered for nearly forty years were not the places they belonged. Their identity and their sense of belonging were not to be found in those places. They could not enjoy the rest there that had been promised to them through the Abrahamic covenant. Their identity and their relationship to God were directly linked to the land he had promised them.

The promise God made to Israel regarding the possession of a land underscores the need for belonging or rootedness as an essential element of our humanness. Walter Brueggemann posits the view that "our humanness is always about historical placement in the earth."[117] Torrance's summation of Aristotle's perspective on space and place is helpful at this point. Aristotle did embrace a receptacle notion of space, but one in which "there is a relation of interdependence between the container and its contents. The normal vessel is a moveable place, but place is an immovable vessel."[118] Torrance believes that this view of place is not surprising since it is consistent with Aristotle's insistence on a "point of absolute rest as the center of reference for the understanding of change and transition."[119] This commitment to a point of absolute rest resonates with Aristotle's doctrine of the "unmoved Mover."

Summary: Characteristics of Sacred Space in the Old Testament

The Old Testament provides a variety of examples of sacred space reflective of both the dynamic and the static model, of centralized and decentralized sacred space. Kunin argues convincingly that although both models of sacred space are represented in various portions of the

115. Ibid., 46.
116. Ibid., 58.
117. Brueggemann, *The Land*, 3.
118. Torrance, *Space, Time, and Incarnation*, 7–8.
119. Ibid., 8.

Old Testament, the centralized model features more prominently.[120] Applying a synthesis of Mircea Eliade's principles of sacred space, we can summarize the essential characteristics of Old Testament sacred spaces. At the risk of oversimplifying his seminal works, four principles emerge from Eliade's perspective on sacred space.

First, sacred space creates a differentiation of space. Many spaces are significantly and qualitatively different from others. In contrast to sacred space, profane space tends to be without reference point or order, a principle evident in Old Testament literature. During the wilderness pilgrimage, the entire camp of the nation of Israel was clearly marked off from its surrounding areas. Those outside the camp were considered impure and were thus restricted from entering various spaces. Once settled within the land of Canaan, the city of Jerusalem and the Temple within it were significantly different from surrounding spaces. Within the Temple itself, spaces representing varying degrees of sacredness were clearly differentiated physically.

Second, sacred space creates meaning by providing a center around which the everyday world revolved. This is what Eliade and others have referred to as the "navel" of the world or an *axis mundi*, or what Aristotle considered to be a point of absolute rest. This applied particularly to the centralized models of sacred space such as the tabernacle, the Temple, and the land itself as opposed to the altar set up by Jacob at Bethel. When the sacred manifests itself, there is a break in what Eliade refers to as the "homogeneity of space."[121] He believes that there is more than a mere break; "there is also a revelation of an absolute reality, opposed to the non-reality of the vast surrounding expanse. . . . In the homogeneous and infinite expanse, in which no point of reference is possible and hence no orientation can be established, the hierophany reveals an absolute fixed point, a center."[122]

Eliade's conviction was that "religious man has always sought to fix his abode at the center of the world."[123] Although one does not find lengthy or explicit references in the Old Testament to Jerusalem or to the Temple itself as being the center of the earth, the concept is there is a broad sense. At least three times a year, a pilgrimage that revolved

120. Kunin, *God's Place*, 41.

121. Eliade, *Sacred and the Profane*, 21.

122. Ibid.

123. Ibid., 22.

around the temple in Jerusalem was required of ancient Israel, which seems to reflect a similar perspective on the centrality of that particular location in the life and world of the nation.

Third, sacred space provided a point of intersection between two worlds. As in Eliade's conviction, humans encountered the divine in sacred places. Because of this, the location of these sites was not left to the arbitrary whim of human decision. In Deuteronomy 12:13–14, the divine directive is unquestionably clear: "Be careful not to sacrifice your burnt offerings anywhere you please. Offer them only at the place the Lord will choose in one of your tribes, and there observe everything I command you." This biblical text represents a significant contradiction to van der Leeuw's position: "We cannot make shrines and cannot select their 'positions,' but can never do more than merely find them."[124] In the Old Testament, the location of sacred spaces and places was never incidental or coincidental but was instead the result of God's intentional intersection with human history.

Fourth, sacred spaces serve as a reminder of the original act of creation. Eliade believes that every act of construction replicates primordial time, "every construction or fabrication has the cosmogony as paradigmatic model."[125] Any act of consecrating a place or space was considered reminiscent of the original creative activity of the gods. Despite the absence of any direct link between Jerusalem, the Temple, or any other sacred place and the creation accounts of Genesis 1–3, some have argued that the poetic language of the Psalms comes close to providing that kind of connection.[126] Reference to a river "whose streams make glad the city of God, the holy place where the Most High dwells" (Psalm 46:4) has been interpreted as a look back to the river in the Garden of Eden mentioned in Genesis 2:10. Jerusalem has no river running through it. The same fruitfulness and pleasure associated with the Garden of Eden has been connected with Zion, the city of God. "God's house is poetically parallel with the river of pleasure, where the very name of Eden is the term used for 'pleasure'; through Zion, evidently, flows the primordial Edenic river of fruitfulness."[127]

---

124. Van der Leeuw, *Religion in Essence*, 398.

125. Eliade, *Sacred and the Profane*, 45.

126. Clines, "Sacred Space," 4.

127. Ibid.

When applying Eliade's principles of sacred space to Old Testament texts, it must be remembered that although God showed himself to be genuinely present in specific places, other passages underscore that God will not be bound to any one location. A tension then exists between the assurance of his immanence and his freedom to be absent or transcendent. As Belden Lane states, "A theology of transcendence will never be comfortable with place."[128] Solomon expresses these two divergent concepts in the very same prayer, at one point stating, "I have built a magnificent temple for you, a place for you to dwell forever."[129] Yet in his public prayer of dedication in front of the assembly of Israel, he declares, "But will God really dwell on earth? The heavens, even the highest heaven, cannot contain you. How much less this temple I have built."[130] God does dwell on earth, but he cannot and will not be contained therein. The association of God's presence with the particularity of specific locations and his apparently random manifestations in places that might be considered mundane does not create an irreconcilable tension in the designation of sacred spaces.

One final observation regarding specific sacred spaces in the Old Testament merits mention. There is compelling evidence to suggest that the sacred nature of a site, including one as significant as the Temple, is not permanent or inalienable. In Jeremiah 7, the prophet is instructed to declare a prophecy indicating that inappropriate action on the part of the people who frequent the Temple has the capacity to render that site no longer sacred. Similar prophetic action is evidenced in the life of Jesus, as recorded in John 2:12–16 when he castigates those who had turned the temple into a marketplace.

SACRED PLACES IN THE NEW TESTAMENT

A Sacred Background to the Church

The quality of sacredness, implying a clear distinction between the divine and the earthly and limiting access to a particular shrine or specific space, was not foreign to the history and experience of the people of ancient Israel. Prohibitions such as those found in Exodus 24:1–4 and

128. Lane, *Landscapes of the Sacred*, 243.

129. 1 Kings 8:13.

130. 1 Kings 8:27.

Leviticus 16:16–17 were clearly associated with the manifest presence of God. The concept of sacredness or holiness that was so often associated with specific locations or physical objects in the Old Testament makes an interesting shift in New Testament thinking. As Harold Turner points out, "It is plain that for the New Testament holiness applies to persons and actions and not to things and places."[131]

A key passage often used in support of this position is the rather intriguing statement Jesus makes in John 4:21, 23: "Jesus said to her, 'Woman, believe me, the hour is coming when you will worship the Father neither on this mountain nor in Jerusalem. . . . The hour is coming and is now here, when the true worshipers will worship the Father in spirit and truth." Jesus was not implying in this text that significant spaces would be rendered unimportant. I concur with Karl Barth when he states, "God does not cease to dwell in the world in definite and distinct ways. . . . He does not cease to be in special places."[132]

However, there is clearly a New Testament shift in emphasis from the actual physical temple structure to the corporate reality of the body of Christ in addition to the physical body of the individual believer as the temple of the Holy Spirit. The temple is no longer considered the primary or only place where God dwells or manifests himself. The temple could no longer be described as theologically necessary. Rather, "The church in the New Testament is never the place or the building where it may be meeting, but always the community where Christ is with his people."[133] Church then was not a location as much as it was a corporate identity. However, it must be borne in mind that all of the letters written by the apostles preserved for us in Scripture were written to churches that were identified by location, their particular context.

One of the significant impacts of this shift in focus is a diminishing of the distinct and rather wide chasm between the sacred and the profane. Since the presence of God is no longer considered to be available exclusively or primarily in a consecrated built environment but rather wherever two or three or more believers meet in the name of Jesus, the mundane need no longer be considered unholy, nor should legitimate worship be limited by location.

---

131. Turner, *Temple to Meeting House*, 152.

132. Barth, *Church Dogmatics* II/1, 481.

133. Turner, *Temple to Meeting House*, 129.

Specificity of place continued to hold significance both in the Old and New Testaments, but Philip Sheldrake's point is insightful: "In a sense, it seems that the marginal ground *between* fixed places is where God is most often encountered."[134] Consider Moses's encounter with God in the wilderness[135] or Jacob's encounter through a dream[136] or Jesus's conversation with the two disciples, on the road to Emmaus[137] or Saul's encounter with Christ on the road to Damascus.[138] These places of liminality,[139] or nonplaces,[140] have been invested with enormous significance resulting from the divine intersection of human space-time history. God may be experienced in the transitional place, a sacred place of encounter, which can lead to transformation, depending on a person's response.

An Incarnational Perspective

From a New Testament perspective, the quintessence of the sacred is embodied in the incarnation of Christ. The incarnational insights illuminated in the Gospels allow for a diversification of centers without loss of meaning or potential for discord. Tod Swanson argues, "Appearances of the sacred across the globe could finally be recognized as cumulative rather than competitive."[141] The Old Testament furnishes examples of decentralized sacred places, but nothing else brings the dynamic nature of sacred places into such stark relief from the previous hegemonic influence of static sacred sites as the incarnation of Christ. Eliade's argument

---

134. Sheldrake, *Spaces for the Sacred*, 34.

135. Exodus 3.

136. Genesis 28:10–22.

137. Luke 24:13–35.

138. Acts 9:1–9.

139. Turner and Turner, *Image and Pilgrimage*, 249–50. The Turners describe those in this transitional state as follows: "During the liminal period, the characteristics of the *liminars* (the ritual subjects in this phase) are ambiguous, for they pass through a cultural realm that has few or none of the attributes of the past or coming state. Liminars are betwixt and between. The liminal state has frequently been likened to death: to being in the womb; to invisibility, darkness, bisexuality, and the wilderness. . . . Liminars are stripped of status and authority, removed from a social structure maintained and sanctioned by power and force, and leveled to a homogeneous social state through discipline and ordeal."

140. Augé, *Non-Places*.

141. Swanson, "To Prepare a Place," 243.

for the potential sacrality of any location is soundly reinforced by the Gospel accounts of the incarnation.

One of the characteristics of preincarnational culture was the ethnic territorialism often associated with various sacred places. Jesus's conversation with the Samaritan woman at Jacob's well[142] addresses the ethnic identity of certain locations in a manner that appears to render such particularity no longer germane to the worship of the true God. When faced with her own moral failure, this woman's employment of the contentious issue of Samaritan-Jewish sites of worship as a diversion tactic suggests that this issue prevailed in many people's thinking at that time.

This issue concerned Jesus himself, based upon his statement in John 10:16: "I have other sheep that are not of this sheep pen. I must bring them also. They too will listen to my voice, and there shall be one flock and one shepherd."[143] Jesus's statements to the Samaritan woman in John 4 do not indicate a desire to denigrate either the mountain of Samaritan worship or the Jewish Temple in Jerusalem but rather to emphasize his concern over the inordinate human attachment of ethnic identity to those places. The worship that the Father desires is to be anchored in a loyalty to the Son, the Logos, a worship that is unencumbered by territorialism in the placeless space of "spirit and truth."[144]

The same could be said of the well where this scenario unfolded, to which the Samaritan woman attached profound ancestral significance.[145] The memory of Jacob providing this well, plus its utilization by his progeny for years to follow, rendered it a sacred place in the woman's mind. By drinking water from this well, the Samaritans connected themselves to their ancestral heritage and their founder Jacob in particular.[146] By asking for a drink from this well, Jesus was challenging its character as an exclusive reserve only for Samaritan use. Jesus was not advocating the inconsequential nature of places.

142. John 4:1–26.

143. Swanson, "To Prepare a Place," 245.

144. John 4:23–24.

145. In John 4:12 the woman asks Jesus, "Are you greater than our father Jacob, who gave us the well and drank from it himself, as did also his sons and his flocks and herds?"

146. Swanson suggests that "According to a tradition . . . the well was believed to be located at the very center of the world, and its waters were the primordial waters of creation" (Swanson, "To Prepare a Place," 249). This is an interesting possibility, but Swanson provides no insight as to its source.

In the prologue to his Gospel John states that by becoming flesh, the Logos "made his dwelling among us,"[147] alerting us to the consequential significance of space and place, of particularity of presence. The significance of Jesus's teaching and miracles cannot be abstracted from the places in which they occurred. The incarnation does not demand that the world be purged of sacred places. Rather while maintaining an appreciation for their meaning and significance, we must not allow our loyalty and devotion to sacred places eclipse our commitment to the God worshiped there.

One is hard pressed to find convincing evidence for an adamantly hostile posture against the temple in the teachings or actions of Jesus. J. G. Davies would disagree: "There is no record that Jesus ever took part in the Temple cultus. Indeed, he seems to have adopted a position of steady and determined hostility to it. . . . It is also apparent that Jesus was charged with wanting to destroy the Temple."[148] These comments represent an "eisegetical" hermeneutic and an unwarranted extrapolation of scriptural fact. He also believes that the death of Jesus ended the need for the Temple and its associated cultus. I concur, but contend that the most one can legitimately suggest is that Jesus did intentionally work outside the bounds of the accepted sacred space of the Temple confines. To interpret these actions as representative of "steady and determined hostility" is, in my mind, unjustifiable.

One other consideration drawn out from the incarnation of Christ is the point of view that the incarnation underscores the need for manifest humility and servanthood in our buildings. Such argumentation is compelling, but only to a point. The point is that the incarnation is not the only manifestation of God. The Psalmist and the writer to the Hebrews remind us that God has spoken and manifested himself in many ways—some of which are not entirely humble! Even in the person and ministry of Christ we find greatness, indeed majesty. His resurrection from the dead, his ascension into heaven, and his ultimate glorification into which John's Apocalypse give us but a glimpse all speak of power and grandeur.

It is difficult to substantiate Davies's linear logic that leads him from Jesus's statement, "the hour cometh, when neither in this mountain, nor in Jerusalem, shall ye worship the Father . . . the hour cometh, and now is,

147. John 1:14.
148. Davies, *Secular Use*, 2.

when the true worshipers shall worship the Father in Spirit and truth"[149] directly to the explicit rejection of any kind of holy place.[150] His choice to place the Temple under the same rubric as pagan temples, "erected on the false premise of sacrifice and specially holy places,"[151] oversteps the bounds of allowing Scripture to speak for itself. The Jerusalem Temple was no longer a theological necessity for Jesus's followers, and the sacrificial cultus was fulfilled in the completed work of Jesus. But the sacred significance of certain places, times, and rituals are not rendered unnecessary or inconsequential.

The incarnation provides a beautiful redemptive analogy of the sacred-profane relationship in the hypostatic union of divinity and humanity. Both natures mutually interact, each nature mutually vital but united and cooperating together, honoring one another in the accomplishment of God's redemptive purposes in this world. Both natures are distinctively maintained without devolving into adversarial tension, although there are times when one nature appears to take precedence over the other without attenuating the significance or reality of the other.[152]

I discern a similar analogous truth in relation to the sacred and profane. A blurring of the two must be resisted[153] since there is a function to be fulfilled by both. The mission of the church does not permit the church to exist perpetually and exclusively in the realm of the sacred but requires it to be engaged in that mission largely in the realm of the mundane.[154] However, there are occasions when a designated, consecrated, sacred place functions as a pivotal contributor to the rituals and events that occur there, facilitating the achievement of her mission.[155]

149. John 4:21, 23.

150. Davies, *Secular Use*, 3.

151. Ibid.

152. Jesus experienced pangs of human hunger (Matthew 4) and the pain of human suffering, but there were other times when His divine nature was more dominant than his human nature (Matthew 17) leading John to describe the incarnation as: "The Word became flesh and made his dwelling among. We have seen his glory, the glory of the One and Only, who came from the Father full of grace and truth" (John 1:14).

153. For example, to suggest that everything is sacred, is to render nothing sacred, which is incongruous with the description of "sacred" espoused by Otto, Durkheim, and Eliade, and as adopted in this project.

154. It is here that Swato's suggestion is particularly significant; the essence of the sacred is seen in the penetration of the ordinary by the sacred, not the separation of the two.

155. I readily acknowledge that in many contexts in which the Church has been

The significance of the sacred is often underscored by its distinctive and sometimes transversal relation with the profane rather than by the subsumption of the profane by the sacred.

Historically, sacred places have consistently fulfilled an important role in the lives of God's covenant people and in the mission of the church, though varying according to covenant, time, and context. Sacred places are not only influenced by theology but inevitably they convey the theology of those who construct and use them. Significant changes in the role, shape, and nature of sacred places can be influenced by major shifts in the realm of theology as well as major shifts in politics and culture. Such changes could also be precipitated by a broader understanding and appreciation of the significance of the sacred, fostered through dialogue with disciplines outside the realm of theology. The following chapter examines the significance of place through the lens of representative social science research.

---

forced underground;the luxury of such consecrated places such as churches or synagogues is not feasible. In these cases, the mundane or profane spaces emerge as sacred in a derivative sense by virtue of the nature of the people who gather and by the nature of the activities in which they engage.

Chapter 5

The Significance of Place
in Fulfilling the Mission
of the Church

INTRODUCTION TO PLACE:
DIALOGUE WITH SOCIAL SCIENCE

Aᴸᴛʜᴏᴜɢʜ ʜᴜᴍᴀɴ ɢᴇᴏɢʀᴀᴘʜʏ ʜᴀs existed
virtually as long as humanity has inhabited
the earth, it is nonetheless relatively nascent as an academic discipline.
But it offers much to the understanding of our humanness. Perhaps one
of its most significant and helpful contributions has been the realization
that built environments represent more than a response to the need for
privacy or shelter from the elements. Amos Rapoport suggests such environments are "physical expressions of ordering systems, of the attempt
to make the world meaningful by imposing an order on it—a process
which, I would argue, seems to be a basic property of the human mind."[1]
Arguably, it is humanity's intrinsic need for order and meaning as much
as any other fundamental human need that has influenced the construction of built environments.

The intent of this chapter is to demonstrate how spatial particularities, including built environments, both reflect the human need for

1. Rapoport, "Sacred Places," 77.

order and meaning and affect people, specifically their emotional and behavioral responses. As Winston Churchill commented regarding the rebuilding of the parliament buildings, "We shape our buildings, and afterwards our building shape us."[2]

Rapoport and other scholars[3] believe that although the precise expressions invested in built environments are culturally specific, "they all involve the re-creation of a divine order on earth, a reflection, however imperfect, of a divine, higher harmony and order."[4] Rapoport suggests that settings or environments, which are a more perfect reflection of that divine ideal, are those that are considered sacred.

This chapter focuses on a variety of historical and contemporary theories on space and place in an effort to gain insight into the ways in which people attach meaning to, or derive meaning from, such environments. In an attempt to test the conviction that there are certain dynamics of the human experience of space and place that are transcultural and transtemporal, the approach adopted here will emphasize the similarities of various architectural eras and developments, although significant distinctive features will be referenced as well. An attempt to compare spatial dynamics solely or primarily on cultural grounds, or primarily on areas of distinctiveness, is in danger of overlooking what Yi-Fu Tuan identifies as "the problem of shared traits that transcend cultural particularities and may therefore reflect the general human condition."[5]

THE PLACE FOR PLACE

Although the term "place" is often used interchangeably with "space," after considering a variety of theories and practices related to the concept it becomes evident that theorists have maintained a distinction for significant reasons. Consideration should be given to the pivotal role that "place" or "a sense of place" plays in human expression and experience, and to the resulting implications for the mission of the church in the twenty-first century. The insights of notable representatives of the

2. Cited in Turner, *Temple to Meeting House*, 3.

3. See, for example Eliade, *Sacred and the Profane*, and Durkheim, *Elementary Forms*.

4. Rapoport, "Sacred Places," 77.

5. Tuan, *Space and Place*, 5.

disciplines of theology, biblical studies, church architecture, and the social sciences have been examined in this process.

It is both interesting and disconcerting to reflect on the relatively minor attention paid by theologians to the study of "space" or "sense of place" and its role in the expression of our humanity—the search for identity and meaning—and to the mission of the church, particularly when compared with the effort invested by scholars in the social sciences. This is not to suggest that Christian scholarship has nothing to offer to the discussion. Three excellent works included in this research are by Richard Giles,[6] Philip Sheldrake,[7] and Timothy Gorringe.[8] The work of Bruce Malina,[9] although not directly focused on space or place, provides understanding, principles, and insights from cultural anthropology that are applicable to the study of sacred space.

Part of the challenge of attempting to define or attach any degree of significance to the concept of place is that the term may designate something as large as an entire nation, or as specific as a single building, or even a space within a building. Social theorists are studying the impact of globalization and computer-mediated communication (CMC), particularly as they pertain to the role and significance of locality and "place" in everyday lives. The influence of globalization has challenged the credibility and importance of place and, according to Mahyr Arefi, has created two divergent scholarly persuasions: one proposing a minimization of the significance of place and another convinced that there is a place for "place."[10] Technological advances likewise have had the profound effect of contesting the notion that place is static or fixed.

Articles on topics such as "space" or "sense of place" or "place attachment" can be located in journals dedicated to behavioral science,[11] environmental psychology,[12] education,[13] architecture,[14] society and

6. Giles, *Re-Pitching the Tent.*

7. Sheldrake, *Spaces for the Sacred.*

8. Gorringe, *Theology of the Built Environment.*

9. Malina, *Christian Origins.*

10 Arefi, "Non-Place and Placelessness," 180.

11. Pred, "Structuration," 45–68.

12. See articles by Gustafson et al. referred to below.

13. Hall et al., "Self, Space, and Place," 501–13.

14. Rapaport, "Sacred Places."

natural resources,[15] and even landscape design.[16] Considering the volume of research conducted and consequently the subsequent material available, there is substantial opportunity to gain insights and perspective from the dialogue of those involved in disciplines beyond the parameters of theology and biblical studies.[17]

THE MEANING OF PLACE

Architect Daniel Libeskind comments in an interview for *Time* magazine, "People won't be settling for the clichés of form and function. They will want to integrate many more desires into whatever they build, to create architecture responsible to the environment. It's not the old modernist world anymore. Buildings won't just look pretty but will have meaning to people's everyday lives."[18] Libeskind's suggestion that buildings will give meaning to people's lives merits consideration and resonates with Heinrich Klotz's sentiment: "Whether architects like it or not, a building acts as a vehicle of meaning even if it is supposed to be meaningless."[19] Timothy Gorringe adds that buildings have the inherent capability to make moral statements.[20] From the perspectives of architects, philosophers, or theologians, one finds ample support for an important underlying presupposition that place and built environments impart meaning.

David Canter offers a succinct definition of "places": "places . . . are units of environment."[21] He is careful to distinguish between "place" and the objects that reside in an environment. He believes that theories and methods used in the study of objects cannot properly be applied to research and the design of places even though geographers, architects, and planners have all, unfortunately, succumbed to the temptation to do so.[22]

15. Eisenhauer et al., "Attachments," 421–41.

16. Hull et al., "Place Identity," 109–20.

17. For an excellent work addressing the globalization issue from the vantage point of practical theology see Ballard and Couture, *Globalization and Difference*.

18. Libeskind, cited in *Time*, September 8, 2003, 68.

19. Klotz cited in Jones, *Monumental*, 21.

20. "For good or ill buildings, from the humblest garden shed to the grandest cathedral, make moral statements" (Gorringe, *Theology of the Built Environment*, 1).

21. Canter, *Psychology of Place*, 2.

22. Ibid., 2.

A significant number of scholars contributing to and influencing the discussion on "space" and "place" have maintained a clear demarcation between the two. According to Philip Sheldrake, philosophers have shifted away from a position that had earlier found wide acceptance, in which "space" was considered fundamental and prior to "place." Although "place" was viewed as a necessary human construct that provided meaning to space, it nonetheless occupied a position of secondary importance.[23] The current inclination among theorists is that "a sense of place actually precedes and creates a sense of space. Space is an abstract, analytical concept, whereas place is always tangible, physical, specific and relational."[24]

French anthropologist Marc Augé[25] offers valuable insights on "place" by contrasting it with what he terms "non-place."[26] His descriptions of "place" and "non-place" are set against the suggestion that one of the main characteristics of the present situation of "supermodern" is the quality of *excess*. He suggests that time is overburdened with events "that encumber the present along with the recent past . . . it is our need to understand the whole of the present that makes it difficult for us to give meaning to the recent past."[27] He also implies that with the proliferation of satellite transmissions, the whole realm of space has become available in excess. The reason for this is not that the world we live in is one that has little or no meaning, rather it is "that we seem to feel an explicit and intense daily need to give it meaning: to give meaning to the world, not just some village or lineage."[28]

Rapoport and Tuan echo such comments with respect to the human need to relate humanity, nature, and the cosmos in a meaningful way.[29] A new surplus of space, indeed new types of space,[30] unknown to

23. Sheldrake, *Spaces for the Sacred*, 6.

24. Ibid., 7.

25. Augé, *Non-Places*.

26. Mahyar Arefi believes this term first appeared in M. M. Webber's chapter entitled "The Urban Place and the Non-place Urban Realm," in Webber et al., *Explorations into Urban Structure*, 79–153. See Arefi, "Non-Place," 180. In Arefi's mind, the essence of non-place resides in "freedom from the constraints of proximity."

27. Augé, *Non-Places*, 29–30.

28. Ibid., 29.

29. See specifically Rapoport, "Sacred Places," 77.

30. For example, cyber-space is a concept unknown to most grandparents of the average baby-boomer today. This topic will be considered in the next chapter.

previous generations is available through the advancement of technology, and humanity is driven to attach meaning to it.

With the advance of supermodernity and the rapidity and magnitude of resulting change, Augé postulates that the world we *believe* we live in does not necessarily coincide with or parallel the world that we do in fact inhabit. We need to learn how to look at this world and to "relearn to think about space."[31] Augé suggests that this incongruity that exists between the world we think we live in and the one we actually inhabit is fostered by the amount of time that many live much in what he calls "non-places." These would include waiting rooms, airports, bus or train stations, as well as the cars, trains, or planes in which we travel from one "place" to another.

The major difference between "non-place" and "place," in Augé's mind, is that "place" has a significant locale, a full historical and symbolic element as well as a relational or social aspect, whereas "non-place" "creates neither singular identity nor relations; only solitude and similitude."[32] It is Augé's conviction that the absence of "collective contractual obligations"[33] founded on shared values and beliefs renders non-place more conducive to solitude than to community. Augé's concept of "place" has less to do with the "where" and more to do with the "whom" and the "what" associated with a given location.

Three main aspects Augé envisages as essential to "place" are identity, relations, and history.[34] I contend that referencing history as an ingredient of place does not shackle one to past, possibly outdated traditions. Rather historical awareness inducts one into a stream of continuity, freeing one to more fully experience and appreciate the present reality while envisioning future possibilities and anticipating glorious hopes. History serves to promote understanding and appreciation of the fullness, or wholeness of meaning, of our human existence.

Relph believes that places have less to do with geography and more to do with what occurs in a given location; places are "fusions of human and natural order and are the significant centers of our immediate experience of the world. They are defined less by unique locations, landscape,

31. Augé, *Non-Places*, 36.
32. Ibid., 103.
33. Ibid., 94.
34. Ibid., 52.

and communities than by the focusing of experiences and intentions onto particular settings."[35]

Both Augé and Relph are less concerned with the tangible, physical setting, focusing more on the personal, experiential elements of "place." "Places" are not necessarily static; they are in process. Relph states, "Place is not a simple undifferentiated phenomenon of experience that is constant in all situations, but instead has a range of subtleties and significances as great as the range of human experiences and intentions."[36] It is on the suggestion that specificity of location is unimportant that I depart slightly from Relph's and Augé's point. Such a view permits too much latitude. "Place" in the sense used in this book insists on the inclusion of the physical environment in which persons are immersed, activities are carried out, and relationships are established and nurtured. Place contributes to the establishment of a memory, similar to Augé's's historical element; an increased discovery, awareness, and development of one's identity; and a testing or challenging of previous experiences and past conceptions.

People immerse themselves in settings that may vary significantly, or they may frequent places such as churches, shrines, or other favorite locations. The activities that occur may be corporate, lively, or even playful nature, or individuals may be engaged in a more subdued manner. Although I concede that there is a relational element inherent in most significant or sacred places, I am convinced that sacred places can exist in the absence of the company of others. Sacred places dedicated to personal solitude can offer as much to humanity's search for meaning, to the expression of our humanness, and to the mission of the church, as do places designated for corporate or communal activity.

I would emphasize that a location can only become a "place" if or when a person is present and immersed in that environment, and if a cognitive memory emerges for them. Implicit in this perspective of "place" is that interpretation of sacred space cannot be based solely on an analysis of the physical setting, even if it includes meticulous detailed descriptions of the multifarious components of the place in question. Likewise, a lone, careful assessment of the participants and the rituals in which they engage cannot provide full access to an understanding of the meaning of any given place. The assessment must include an analysis

35. Relph, *Place and Placelessness*, 141.
36. Ibid., 26.

of those who immerse themselves in the environment, the activities in which they participate, and the actual physical setting to fully comprehend the meaning or significance of a sacred place.

An emphasis on one or more of these components at the exclusion of another influences the criteria utilized to assess and understand the significance and meaning of any place. Focusing only on the physical dimensions of the built environment fosters a quantitative assessment, endangering the identification and appreciation of the other existing qualitative aspects. Two-dimensional images and carefully crafted descriptions are inadequate to give a true sense of place; the people who use the space are omitted. Many photographs or artists' representations of interior church spaces display areas void of any human presence. Interpretation of the meaning of sacred places based primarily on these types of images is limited, akin to interpreting a passage of Scripture solely based on syntax and morphology while neglecting to incorporate an understanding of the cultural context in which it originated and the resulting perspectives of the people originally involved.

A casual walk through any number of typical, unoccupied church structures provides significant evidence to suggest that the Western evangelical church has permitted the importance of the symbolic to be subsumed by the imperatives of the functional. In many churches, apart from an occasional centrally located tapestry, banner, or cross, there is little that is inherently symbolic in the design or the layout of the space dedicated to the assembly of worshipers. Typically, spatial dimensions and arrangements are manifest responses to the question "What do we want or need this space to allow us to do?" The focus for the design decision has been on the perceived *functionality* of the space.

My suggestion is not that functional concerns are superfluous or even unspiritual but that another equally important question exists and requires consideration: "What do we want or need this space to *say*?" What should the structure communicate, what *meaning* should this space impart? In particular, how is the meaning that is conveyed by the architecture relevant to the mission of the church?

For centuries, language was the assumed prerequisite to accessing meaning, whether from a historical or anthropological perspective. Lindsay Jones argues convincingly that the hegemony of linguistic evidence must be balanced with an appreciation for the built environment as a repository of meaning.[37] In order for any text to convey meaning, certain assumptions must be in place. There must be some common perceptions upon which people can discern understanding or meaning. The same principle can be applied to the built environment.

The spatial arrangement of a Gothic cathedral, in which apse, sanctuary, chancel, and nave are clearly differentiated, would convey something very different to a person brought up in that church than it would to an aboriginal person from the Australian outback entering that cathedral for the first time. One could certainly understand the Aborigine's unintentional violation of appropriate demeanor and conduct were they to wander up to the sanctuary and examine the various implements placed on the altar. What the Aborigine would lack is a grasp of the underlying rules, which not only give meaning to the various spaces but determine access and govern appropriate responses.

Clifford Geertz's emphasis on semiotics in the transmission of culture reminds us that symbols exist as tangible metaphors that facilitate an understanding of life and reality. I contend that the use of space can provide similar and equally effective metaphors. Philip Sheldrake believes that such metaphors are not options or embellishments of our normal modes of communication but are essential in the construction of our concept of reality.[38] He is convinced that "physical places are vital sources of metaphors for our social constructions of reality."[39] I would take Sheldrake's comment a step further, suggesting that rather than simply being the place in which such metaphors can be found and symbols are housed or presented, space and the physical attributes of place can be significant symbols in themselves. Both have intrinsic narrative qualities, and their design elements often evoke emotional responses as profound as those fostered by other compelling cultural texts.

THE FUNCTION OF PLACE

I have suggested that "place" features prominently in the expression and experience of our humanness, but what role or function does it fulfill? Relph views places as vital repositories of "individual and communal

---

37. Margaret R. Miles likewise addresses the problems of constructing a history of ideas solely on a linguistic basis (Miles, *Image as Insight*, 15–27).

38. Sheldrake, *Spaces for the Sacred*, 4.

39. Ibid.

identity, and [they] are often profound centres of human existence to which people have deep emotional psychological ties."[40] According to Lyndon and Moore, ideas can be memorialized by situating them in space. "Places could bring emotions, recollections, people, and even ideas to mind; their qualities were a part of a culture's intellectual equipment."[41] I propose that there are five primary functions of "place."

Place and Memory

Virtually without exception, sacred places are rooted in history or have an essential historical dimension. Sacred places are informed by or are designated to establish a memory of some significant event or divine provision. Walter Brueggemann says, "Place is space which has historical meanings, where some things have happened which are now remembered and which provide continuity and identity across generations."[42] Philip Sheldrake concurs: "Place is space that has the capacity to be remembered and to evoke what is most precious."[43]

The Old Testament provides numerous examples of places that were designated, either on the basis of what appears to be human initiative or as a result of a divine directive, as a means to establish and maintain a reminder of some significant event. The human propensity to forget is consistently taken into account throughout the history of the ancient people of Israel. In many such instances, the purpose of such memorials superseded the mere retention of historical fact and served to remind a people of their own identity. The history they are to remember is either their own or that of their ancestors—without which their present identity would be radically altered, perhaps to the point of nonexistence. In essence, sacred space or places can impart a narrative.

Place and Identity

A central tenet found within existing identity theories is that identity is separate or disembodied from physical environments.[44] However, Twigger-Ross and Uzzell's research conducted in the community of Docklands

---

40. Relph, *Place and Placelessness*, 141.

41. Lyndon, *Chambers for a Memory Palace*, xi.

42. Brueggemann, *The Land*, 5.

43. Sheldrake, *Spaces for the Sacred*, 1.

44. Twigger-Ross, "Place and Identity Processes," 218.

in London supports the premise that rather than serving as a backdrop in which experience arises, place plays a significant role in the construction of identity. They state, "We suggest that all identifications have location implications, place is part of the content of an identification."[45] Using the framework of Breakwell's identity process theory, which is made up of distinctiveness, continuity, self-efficacy, and self-esteem, they demonstrate that place features prominently in all four aspects. They determine, "The environment becomes a salient part of identity as opposed to merely setting a context in which identity can be established and developed."[46]

Twigger-Ross and Uzzell clarified that the degree to which the relationship between place and identity can be applied may vary and that "there may be life stages when attachment to place and identity become more salient."[47] For some, the attachment is strengthened over time; the longer they have lived in a location, the more prominent that place becomes in the construction of their identity. For others history, specifically the memory of a loved one, is what fosters a strong attachment to a specific place. Another discovery resulting from their research is that the disruption of place often poses a threat to identity, particularly for those people who have developed a strong attachment to a specific location.[48]

Although the focus of Twigger-Ross and Uzzell's research is a residential environment, certain principles present themselves as useful for serious reflection with respect to application in an ecclesiastical or liturgical environment. Generational, cultural, and personal factors vary from place to place; one particular framework does not provide adequate means to interpret every person's experience of and relation to "place." However, research literature, particularly in the area of environmental psychology, demands that careful attention be given to the relation between "place" and identity processes. Place is not merely space in which experience occurs. It is not peripheral to the human experiences of constructing identity, worshiping God, or making love; rather it constitutes a significant facet of the wholeness of that experience. Life occurs "somewhere," and the "where" is of substantial significance.

I allege, based on the biblical account of creation in Genesis 1–3, that if God invested five days in creating the cosmos prior to the final

45. Ibid.
46. Ibid.
47. Ibid.
48. Ibid., 18–19.

day on which he created humanity, then "place" was his design, meant to play a vital role in the experience and expression of our humanness. It would seem like an extravagant waste of creational activity on God's part if the prime purpose of the cosmos were to merely provide a contextual container in which humans participate relationally with one another and God. Jesus's assurance to his disciples in John 14 that his departure was necessary in order for him to prepare a "place" for them likewise underscores the significance and centrality of place—not only in this present earthly life but in the post-resurrection life yet to come.

Place and Healing

Place, or environment, has also been presented as a major contributor within the recent advance of Attention Restoration Theory.[49] Kaplan and Kaplan[50] suggest that directed attention, which requires incremental mental effort due to the unattractive or uninteresting nature of the material, can become fatigued if overused. The fallout of such fatigue may range from an inability to concentrate or solve problems to an increased tendency to accidents or mistakes.[51] Certain types of environments have been discovered to emit a restorative influence on those suffering from directed attention fatigue. Four features of restorative environments are

> being away, which implies a setting that is physically or conceptually different from one's everyday environment; extent, which implies a setting sufficiently rich and coherent that it can engage the mind and promote exploration; fascination (or effortless attention), which can come from content (animals, people, water, fire) or process (story telling, gambling, problem solving); and compatibility, which implies a setting that fits with and supports one's inclinations or purposes.[52]

From their research in Attention Recovery Theory (ART), the Kaplans have observed four benefits of restorative environments: clearing of the mind from residual cognitive noise associated with one's everyday environment; the ability to re-engage in directed attention; space to reflect on one's immediate and perhaps unresolved problems;

---

49. See Herzog et al, "Reflection and Attentional Recovery," 165–70.

50. Cited in ibid., 165.

51. Ibid.

52. Herzog, "Reflection and Attentional Recovery," 165.

and opportunity to reflect on one's life in general—goals, priorities, and place in this world.[53] Herzog and others condense these four benefits into two: "attention recovery . . . and reflection."[54]

Obviously, certain types of environments are more conducive to attention recovery while others are more conducive to reflection. From their research they discovered that places such as sports arenas, amusement parks, rock concerts, and bars proved effective in restoring directed attention but were ineffective in facilitating reflection. ART suggests that the environmental factor most likely to foster quality reflection is based on the type of fascination it fosters.

Kaplan[55] posits a fascination continuum ranging from "hard" to "soft" fascination. Hard fascination is characterized by a high degree of intensity monopolizing one's attention, leaving little room for reflection. Such settings could include front row seats at a major sporting event, a place in the mosh pit at a rock concert, watching television, or playing video games. Soft fascination, by contrast, is marked by moderate intensity and does not impinge on a person's mental capacity to reflect. The probability of its occurrence is greater in aesthetically pleasing, natural, outdoor places, such as a quiet garden or a forest trail.

Researchers have concluded that environments and activities that facilitate the recovery of both direct attention and reflection are more beneficial than those not permitting quality reflection. This was acutely evident among AIDS caregivers, who understandably have "a strong need to reflect on questions of life and death as part of their mental coping."[56]

It needs to be underscored that the individual's personality enters into the equation, as Twigger-Ross and Uzzell discovered. Some people prefer a busy location like London over a more serene pastoral setting in the country. Two research participants commented, "I just like the hustle and bustle of London. I like to go to the country and stay, but I like to get back to London—more to do" and "I think it [the country] would be too quiet; I like it like this with things going on."[57]

Some of the principles proposed by ART theorists have much to offer the church when contemplating both the design and functional

53. Ibid., 166.

54. Ibid.

55. Cited in ibid., 166–67.

56. Herzog et al., "Reflection and Attentional Recovery," 166.

57. Twigger-Ross and Uzzell, "Place and Identity Processes," 212.

implications of the liturgical places we build. Our intent to present a holistically redemptive, foundationally biblical message needs to be evident not only in our activities or praxis but also in the sacred spaces and places in which they take place. Effective response to the human needs of both attention recovery and reflection, as well as to the mission requirement for declaration of biblical truth, requires intentionality and thoughtfulness in the design of our sacred environments.

Place and Action

Canter believes that "place," or people's perception of place, and action are intrinsically linked. His argument is essentially that "any act is made in relation to the context within which the individual thinks himself to be. In other words, the organism recognizes, acknowledges or in some way takes account of its context, failing which, action is difficult and appropriate action is impossible."[58] A number of studies substantiate the idea that different environments or settings have the capacity to induce a variety of emotional responses and mental states.[59] Conduct, ranging from serious to playful and planned to spontaneous, can be influenced by the context in which people find themselves.

Contrast the difference in the emotional atmosphere and behavioral conduct of a crowd of people entering a stadium in anticipation of a football match in Britain or a playoff game in any major sport in North America with a group of people entering a cathedral. The former are generally characterized by a somewhat "playful" disposition while the latter exhibit a more serious or subdued demeanor. Such moods and behavioral norms are primarily attributable to personal histories and experiences in similar settings, but people's emotional responses and conduct are not irresistibly imposed by the "place" itself; a personal response of self-regulation, has typically been acquired.

Place and Narrative

A primary element of the mission of the church is the communication of the story of God's redemptive activity in the world through the incarnation of Jesus. Michael Riddell believes, "Our world is weary of sermons,

---

58. Canter, *Psychology of Place*, 1.

59. See, for instance, Kerr and Tacon, "Psychological Responses," 287.

but hungry for stories."[60] Marketing and entertainment industries have understood the appeal of narrative and have utilized story with formidable success. Marketers understand that people are captivated by story because it invites the viewer's emotional participation, enhancing the probability of gaining a desired commitment. What can the church, particularly in the global north, learn from this?

I do not suggest that the church should engage in similar marketing methodologies to accomplish her mission. It has less to do with understanding method and much more to do with understanding the postmodern individual who is impacted, directly and profoundly, by narrative. Narrative has the capacity to influence a broad spectrum of life activities, from viewing to spending habits, often directly influencing one's value system and the construction of one's perceptions of reality.

Narrative can be communicated through a wide array of media and forms that include drama and other artistic expression such as sketches, sculpture, or paintings. But spatial design or layout must also be recognized as effective conveyors of story. Architecture and design have their own rhetoric, which are never silent. Richard Giles states, "The church's building is a commanding preacher and no one should underestimate its power to communicate. Its message can linger on long after our own words have died away. Buildings, no less than people, have a body language."[61]

It is unfortunate that on many occasions, a narrative worth hearing has often been drowned out by the cacophony of the space in which it is told. Such dissonance between message and context can be caused by a venue's blandness or, alternately, by gaudy detail. The place or space needs to inconspicuously support the narration of the story. This will not occur if commitment to the functional role of space is allowed to impinge on our conviction that the built environment can and does speak with clarity.

Amos Rapoport argues similarly, "Meanings are clearest and strongest when there is redundancy, when spatial organization and meaning systems are congruent and therefore reinforce each other."[62] Supportive redundancy, or congruity between setting, meaning, and action, is crucial in reducing ambiguity. As Rapoport insists, "The greater the redundancy,

60. Riddell, *Threshold of the Future*, 156.
61. Giles, *Re-Pitching the Tent*, 103.
62. Rapoport, "Sacred Places," 79.

the more likely the message is to get across."[63] He believes this has particular significance relative to sacred environments and the cohesion of groups engaged in common rituals. All environments convey meaning, and the stronger the integration between that meaning and the setting itself—as well as the activities that occur in that environment—the more effective the mnemonic impact will be.

Lyndon and Moore draw a strong parallel between the work of an architect and that of a writer or composer. "Playing with variations in openings to establish a basic underlying rhythm, adjust sizes, and create incidents of special interest—tracing on the building's surface a story of the life within—can be a great pleasure, bringing the architect close to the spirit of a composer or writer of narrative."[64] Their suggestion is developed further by designating certain human functions to various architectural features: "If the openings are the eyes of the building, then the portal is the mouth, the aperture most able to tell us about what is beyond."[65]

THE EXPERIENCE OF PLACE

Hans-Georg Gadamer developed a concept of experience that provides an excellent platform from which to consider the experience of place. He identifies Georg Simmel as the person responsible for endowing the concept of "experience" with the quality of adventure.[66] Augmenting Simmel's perspective, he distinguishes an adventure from an episode:

> Episodes are a succession of details, which have no inner coherence and for that very reason have no permanent significance. An adventure, however, interrupts the customary course of events, but is positively and significantly related to the context, which it interrupts. Thus an adventure lets life be felt as a whole, in its breadth and in its strength. Here lies the fascination of an adventure. It removes the conditions and obligations of everyday life. It ventures out into the uncertain.[67]

Gadamer insists on the integration of an experience with life as a whole. The vitality and significance of any experience is realized only

63. Ibid., 80.

64. Lyndon and Moore, *Chambers for a Memory Palace*, 110.

65. Ibid., 120.

66. Gadamer, *Truth and Method*, 69.

67. Ibid.

as it is "worked into the whole of life consciousness. . . . Because it is within the whole of life, the whole of life is present in it too."[68] Based on Gadamerian thought, no individual will repeat the same identical experience in the same location. Gauging experiences solely on the basis of results[69] ignores that experience is fundamentally a process that is essentially negative or inverse to a previous experience. The objective or result of experience is not the generation of acceptable universals; rather genuine experience challenges, indeed refutes, that which is "typical." An experience that merely confirms or conforms to our previous expectations is not genuine experience. As Gadamer states, "Every experience worthy of the name thwarts an expectation."[70] The ability to achieve a "determinate negation"[71] is what gives genuine experience a dialectical quality.

An intentional openness to the dialectical nature of experience and a willingness to be receptive to new experiences prevents a person's perspective from becoming skewed by dogmatism.

> The experienced person proves to be, on the contrary, someone who is radically undogmatic; who, because of the many experiences he has had and the knowledge he has drawn from them, is particularly well equipped to have new experiences and to learn from them. The dialectic of experience has its proper fulfillment not in definitive knowledge but in the openness to experience that is made possible by experience itself.[72]

Gadamer's perspective on experience seems particularly pertinent to the experience of space and place.

Two or more people immersed in the same environment do not necessarily enjoy or endure the same experience. "Place" as described to this point is incapable of imposing a particular experience common to all that are present. Different people have different experiences within the same setting, suggesting that each person brings something to the setting that is equally influential in determining the nature and quality of their experiences.

---

68. Ibid.

69. For example, did a person feel, hear, see, or do the same thing in separate events?

70. Gadamer, *Truth and Method*, 356.

71. Ibid., 353.

72. Ibid., 355.

The effect of proportion on a person entering an ancient, large cathedral is close to being universal; the vast majority of people will be moved to a hushed stillness, with a profound awareness of their smallness in comparison to the dimension of the building itself. Some prefer to think that the awe experienced and sometimes expressed is directed toward divinity, that a person stands in reverential awe of the God who is worshiped there. It could be argued that such a response is simply an understandable psychological response akin to a sensation one might experience while standing in or in front of any other impressive monument to humanity's ingenuity and technological prowess.[73] The decisive factor likely to determine which response it is resides within the person experiencing the given environment rather than in some quality intrinsic to that built environment.

Amos Rapoport developed a model used to conceptualize the design of various environments that includes the four variables of space, time, meaning, and communication.[74] I suggest a slightly different combination of five components that directly shape the nature and quality of a person's experience of any given place. The first two components are what a person brings to a place: an awareness of one's identity and an awareness of one's preunderstandings or preconceptions. The degree to which these are understood or developed varies, but they nonetheless influence a person's experience of "place." The other three components are an appreciation of others present, an appreciation of the setting itself, and an appreciation of the activities that transpire in any given place.

An Awareness of One's Personal Identity

A person's self-understanding relative to place will be determined by the setting itself. A person may feel intimidated or lack confidence if they enter as an "outsider." First-time appearances in a church, a faculty meeting, or a pub will commonly foster a degree of angst for most people. Personal awareness and a degree of comforting familiarity will affect the manner in which a person relates to or appreciates others that

---

73. For example, standing on the top observation deck of the Eiffel Tower or at the base of an Egyptian pyramid can leave one impressed, inducing an awe-filled silence, when realizing the limitations of the technology that was available at the time of its construction. In our present day similar experiences are common among those who visit any gravity-defying, towering edifices that pierce the atmosphere, which formerly were the domain only of small aircrafts.

74. Rapoport, "Sacred Places," 79.

are present as well as the degree to which a person initially appreciates the environment itself.

By contrast, a person entering a place as an insider with an established identity in the context enjoys a sense of belonging that Sheldrake suggests "involves both a connection to specific places and also our existence within networks of stable relationships."[75] They will be much freer to relate to others and to appreciate the setting. A comforting familiarity does not guarantee the person will experience greater freedom but the encumbrance of not belonging will not mitigate their enjoyment of the experience.

This principle is not limited to a "place" that is shared by others. Choosing to engage in a time of solitude in the bush of northern Saskatchewan, an experience of place I have enjoyed on a number of occasions, is more enjoyable if an aspect of one's personal identity includes a working knowledge of the bush, wilderness survival, and the route to the desired destination.

An Awareness of One's Preunderstandings

The work of Hans-Georg Gadamer addresses the impact of one's preconceptions and preunderstandings. Gadamer built a compelling argument postulating that it is virtually impossible to enter into a search for meaning while bracketing one's "pre-arguments" or "pre-understandings," referred to as "fore-understandings" or "fore-concepts."[76] His contention is that the best approach is to intentionally bring such assumptions to the dialogue. Gadamer's insight is essential to understanding and benefiting from our experience of "place."

No one enters a place carte blanche but instead approaches with theory-laden assumptions informed by their previous experiences of other places—some remarkably similar, others distinctively different. A place may represent a radical departure from previous experiences in terms of aesthetics or dimensions, but a redolence characteristic of previously visited places may generate a parade of images that either enhance or intrude upon the present experience.

Cultural predilections or religious persuasions are likewise capable of directly shaping one's experience of places. The preunderstandings that we bring to any place are products of our own personal histories,

75. Sheldrake, *Spaces for the Sacred*, 10.

76. Cited in Browning, *Fundamental Practical Theology*, 38.

our cultural and religious formation. Relph states, "All places and land-scapes are individually experienced for we alone see them through the lens of *our* attitudes, experiences, and intentions and from our own unique circumstances."[77] The degree to which we are able to harness our preconceptions and preunderstandings without suppressing or denying their existence, or without allowing them to predominate or infringe on the moment, will determine the degree of success in establishing a location appreciated as a place of meaning.

An Appreciation for Others Present

Herbert Anderson reminds us that "encounters with diversity that once were the province of missionaries, the adventurous, the open-minded, or those too poor to live where they wished are an unavoidable and ir-reversible dimension of daily living for more and more people."[78] Since our mission as the church goes, or should go, beyond the conversion and transformation of others, "learning how to live with the Other as neigh-bor and partner is an inescapable agenda because diversity is nearby and domination is undesirable."[79]

Anderson offers three ways of understanding "the Other." One is seeing the other or others as *not me*, a recognition and acceptance of the distinction between others and ourselves. A second is to consider the other as *not like me,* with the underlying assumption that I represent the norm and the Other, who is not like me, is abnormal or subnormal—an outsider, perhaps a stranger, and therefore less likely to be considered as one who belongs. The third, Anderson suggests, is to consider the Other as proximate: *"like me and yet different from me."*[80] This perspective can become rather unsettling when we recognize ourselves in someone who appears to be different.

Adopting Anderson's approach to the "other," or others, suggests that our experience of "place" will be directly impacted by the manner in which we allow ourselves to relate to others who share the same "place." Any lingering angst or resentment over the presence of the "other" that we view as an outsider will hinder our freedom to experience and our

---

77. Relph, *Place and Placelessness,* 36.
78. Anderson, "Seeing the Other Whole," 3.
79. Ibid.
80. Ibid., 4.

propensity to enjoy any given place. Two or more people may simultaneously share the same geographical space, but that does not guarantee they share similar intentions for being there or that they will depart having shared a similar experience. It is imperative that we free ourselves from the tyranny of unreasonable expectations and false or unfounded assumptions. Appreciation for others requires recognition and acceptance that other people's histories and experiences are different from our own and may be unique from those experienced by many. It also permits people to come to the "place" and not enjoy a similar experience or share our same sense of appreciation for the place.

Appreciation for others is evidenced in openness to the probability that others have something to contribute to our own experience in and of the place. Noragh Jones addresses this issue well:

> The first tenet of our spirituality of place is this necessary relating of diversities, because the places where we live now are diverse and multicultural, fragmented and privatized. We need to think incarnationally and act locally to make a difference, to render our "here-and-now" a more hospitable place. We begin to do that when we acknowledge the richness of diversity, when we attend to the particular rights and responsibilities of all the people who dwell in our place, and when we do our best to enter into dialogue with people not like us.[81]

The need for us to think incarnationally is a relevant point; it emphasizes that we must not allow our "spirituality of place," as Jones refers to it, to remain in the realm of the conceptual or ethereal. We must weave it into the tactile, physical present. The manner in which we relate to others, particularly those who share and shape our experience of a given place, significantly demonstrates the extent to which we are, in fact, thinking incarnationally.

An Appreciation for the Setting

Research has established that whether intended or not, built environments evoke responses from those immersed in them. Qualitative design factors including color, lighting,[82] spatial dimension (soaring vaulted ceilings, the intimacy of a small room with a lit fireplace), and the nature

---

81. Jones, "A Spirituality of Place," 47.
82. Knez, "Effects of Indoor Lighting."

and arrangement of objects within a place exert significant and some-times subtle influences on people. Restaurant owners have realized these efficacious factors and manipulate the built environment in ways that influence the duration and frequency of customers' visits.

The recent trend among numerous mothers in North America opt-ing for domestic settings instead of the sterile environment of a hospital delivery room for the birth of their children strongly suggests an appre-ciation and preference for one particular setting over another. Meyrowitz, however, would not be comfortable with attributing that degree of influ-ence to the setting. He questions, "Is it actually place that is a large deter-minant of behavior, or is it something else that has traditionally been tied to and therefore confused with place?"[83] Rather than the physical setting determining the nature of interaction and activity occurring in a place, he suggests it is what he terms "the patterns of information flow,"[84] the divergent methods through which mediated encounters occur. With the advancement of electronic media, semi-social encounters are now pos-sible and are commonly experienced in the absence of face-to-face meet-ings. Physical presence is no longer a prerequisite to the flow or exchange of information, or even for the initial development of relationships.

Interestingly, he suggests that the information age, significantly enlarged by electronic media, has actually fostered a reversion to more primitive social forms characteristic of the hunting and gathering soci-ety. Loyalty to specific localities and "sense of place" became virtually nonexistent since specific events and behaviors are not intimately linked to specially designated locations.[85] "Electronic media destroy the spe-cialness of place and time."[86]

I perceive the emergence of a phenomenon I would call "para-place" resulting from postmodern electronic sophistication in which the distinction between private and public places has effectively been blurred. Televised media and the Internet now provide access to places formally recognized as private, whereas personal, portable sound sys-tems, such as MP3 players or iPods, have converted public places into private ones.[87]

83. Meyrowitz, *No Sense of Place*, 36.

84. Ibid., 37.

85. Ibid., 315.

86. Ibid., 125

87. Ibid.

Meyrowitz would agree that the setting does have inclusive and exclusive powers. "The walls of a room simultaneously permit focused interaction among some people while isolating the participants from other people."[88] The rigidity of these boundaries may vary from place to place. Mircea Eliade draws attention to the important role of doors or gates: "The threshold concentrates not only the boundary between inside and outside but also the possibility of passage from one to the other."[89]

An Appreciation for the Activities

Many of the activities that occur in "places," particularly sacred places, are designed and exercised as a means of acting out a myth, custom, or rite deemed essential by those participating. The place cannot be separated from the activity but is integral to it. Even though there is the possibility of allowing what we are doing to overshadow where we are doing it, another potential effect underscores the important relation between "place" and activity. Relph describes it as follows:

> Much ritual and custom and myth has the incidental if not deliberate effect of strengthening attachment to place by reaffirming not only the sanctity and unchanging significance of it, but also the enduring relationships between a people and their place. When the rituals and myths lose their significance and the people cease to participate fully in them the places themselves become changeable and ephemeral.[90]

Attachment to place can result from the activities that occur within the place. In the performance of ritual or in the acting out of myth, meaning is expressed and attached (or perhaps initially discovered for some). Churches should ensure that such attachments not devolve into an idolatrous commitment to the place itself.

The other four elements mentioned, personal identity, preunderstandings, appreciation of others, and appreciation for the setting will affect the nature of activities that occur in a given place. However, the activities themselves influence a person's self-awareness, challenge their preconceptions, or influence appreciation for others who are also present. The relevant point is that all five components of "place" described

88. Ibid., 36.

89. Eliade, *Sacred and the Profane*, 18.

90. Relph, *Place and Placelessness*, 33.

here are mutually influential. A valid understanding of the meaning or significance of a place must incorporate all of these mutually interacting aspects. Place, then, is more than mere location. It is a meaningful integration of activity and persons with location.

A place that is going to be a significant center of meaning will reflect and incorporate the physical, aesthetic, social, spiritual, and personal elements and needs of the culture in which it is located.[91] It will provide for, indeed encourage, a full expression of our humanness as all of these significantly influential components are intentionally considered and cohesively coordinated. The following diagram illustrates how these various components function interdependently and influence an experience of place.

The Experience of Place

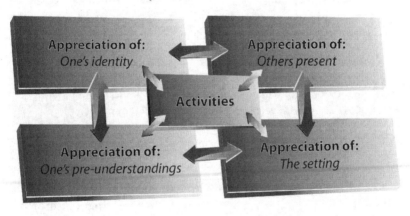

FIGURE 5.1. *The Experience of Place (Graphics by George Toth)*

"Place" or "sense of place" plays a pivotal role in the experience and expression of our humanness. Failure to consider "place" appropriately in our efforts to connect with humanity in a meaningful way will inevitably lead to well intentioned but dehumanizing efforts. Sinclair Gauldie says, "To live in an environment which has to be endured or ignored rather than enjoyed is to be diminished as a human being."[92]

If the intent of the Western church was to extend the redemptive message of the gospel to humanity in a holistic manner, attention must

91. Ibid., 67.

92. Cited in Relph, *Place and Placelessness*, 147.

be given to the pivotal role place plays in the human experience, particularly human spirituality. To excuse our apparent lack of intentional concern for "places" and "sense of place" on the grounds that such endeavors are less than spiritual is demonstrative more of a postmodern version of Gnosticism rather than a commitment to biblical truth.

WHEN SPACE BECOMES PLACE: LESSONS FROM OTHER DISCIPLINES

In the minds of some scholars, including Walter Brueggemann, it is best to maintain a clear distinction between the terms "space" and "place." He considers space as "an arena of freedom without coercion or accountability, free of pressures and void of authority."[93] By contrast, he states that "place"

> is space which has historical meanings, where some things have happened which are now remembered and which provide continuity and identity across generations. Place is space in which important words have been spoken which have established identity, defined vocation, and envisioned destiny. Place is space in which vows have been exchanged, promises have been made, and demands have been issued. Place is indeed a protest against the unpromising pursuit of space. It is a declaration that our humanness cannot be found in escape, detachment, absence of commitment, and undefined freedom.[94]

Over the past few decades there has been an intriguing increase in interest in an area known as "a sense of space," which has manifested itself in a number of divergent disciplines. Recent developments and publications produced by a number of major contributing theorists are referenced by Robert Hay.[95] Although written from a geographical and anthropological perspective, the insights and observations of Hays's study can be easily applied to the focus of this project.

Hays believes that a place, which provides a sense of belonging, helps to establish a feeling of dwelling or settledness and provides a "repository of meaning."[96] If a group shares the place, they can share that

---

93. Brueggemann, *The Land*, 5.
94. Ibid.
95. Hay, "Sense of Place."
96. Ibid., 5–6.

sense of meaning. Hays notes that unless there is daily or regular physical contact with a given location, the sense of place will be lost and devolve into nostalgia rather than a sense of rootedness. Eisenhauer, Krannich, and Blahna offer similar beneficial insights in a coauthored article.[97]

Place as a Nonnegotiable

Far beyond the notion of a receptacle, the significance of place is foundational to the vast majority of what I have been arguing thus far and is supported by numerous scholars from a variety of disciplines. Theologian John Inge alleges that because ours is an embodied existence, place is as essential as our capacity to breathe.More specifically, it has the capacity to shape our human experience.[98] Inge contends that minimizing the significance of place inevitably fosters effects that are dehumanizing.

It is difficult to argue against the opinion that for the past three centuries, the West has been living under the shadow of the twin towers of modernity, time and space. The West has relegated place to the position of "an impoverished second cousin of Time and Space."[99] An increasing number of architects are convinced of the importance of places and of the power of buildings to "transform undifferentiated *space* into marked and delimited *place*,"[100] whether theologians and church builders are prepared to acknowledge it or not. Social theorist E. V. Walker provides the following "theological" observation:

> We take for granted ritual and doctrine as theological subjects, but we tend to overlook the theology of building, settling, and dwelling. As expressions of religious experience, sacred places are as important as doctrine and ritual. They energise and shape religious meaning. They help to make religious experience intelligible. Sacred place is not only an environment of sensory phenomena, but a moral environment as well.[101]

Walker restates what theologian John Inge and philosopher Henri Lefebvre[102] have argued convincingly: places are not inert containers.

---

97. Eisenhauer et al., "Attachments to Special Places."

98. Inge, *Christian Theology of Place*, ix.

99. Casey, cited in Inge, *Christian Theology of Place*, 11.

100. Inge, *Christian Theology of Place*, 19.

101. Walker cited in Inge, *Christian Theology of Place*, 31.

102. Lefebvre, *Production of Space*.

They have cultural relevance and historical specificity; they result from human effort and activity; and they manifesting power to influence. Marchita Mauck would be uncomfortable attributing power to places; she believes that buildings seldom have the power to change or impact people although they do invoke the kind of experiences that bring about transformation.[103]

The implications of place are profound for church buildings. The construction or renovation of a church structure has far more consequence than the mere provision of a space in which people gather to engage in rituals. "It is rather about translating a liturgical theology (i.e., what we believe about what we do in ritual actions) and beauty into three dimensions. It is about forming a holy people whose lives are transformed, motivated, formed and sustained by their experiences in that place."[104] Thomas Torrance argues convincingly that it is impossible to conceive of any relationship with God in the absence of places.[105] Inge reminds us that God relates to people in specific places, and the places in which humanity encounters God are not irrelevant but pivotal to that relationship.[106] For Inge, a high view of place is the inevitable outflow of a proper view of the incarnation.[107]

A wide spectrum of perspectives and approaches exists with respect to the significance and function of place and space. I observe that the Western evangelical church, of which I have been a part all of my life, has substantially underestimated both the significance of sacred space and the potential for achieving a profound impact for the kingdom through reflective and thoughtful design and creative uses of sacred spaces in our postmodern culture.

It seems sacred space is winning the interest and commitment of an ever-increasing number of people in our post-Christian era. Unfortunately, many of the church buildings of our day are constructed or renovated primarily for today's Christians, with relatively little consideration given to another key stakeholder group comprised of future Christians and today's unchurched. The elements of mystery and beauty that contribute to a sacred ethos are so often eclipsed by financial and

103. Mauck, *Places for Worship*, 9.

104. Ibid., 7.

105. Torrance, *Space, Time, and Incarnation*.

106. Inge, *Christian Theology of Place*, 58.

107. Ibid.

other pragmatic considerations. I do not advocate that the church engage in reckless abandon, ignoring sound stewardship principles by erecting opulent monuments to human achievement. However, I am convinced that it is crucial for the church to listen heedfully to those who are drawn more and more to sacred spaces.

Harold Turner suggests that there is an inverse relationship between the vitality of a "distinctively Christian position" and the movement from *domus ecclesia* to *domus dei*.[108] I am not convinced that the issue is that simple or that one must decide solely upon one or the other, as Turner implies. The concept of a church being a place where the gathered church meets and ministers coincides well with scriptural mandate and example. There is a place for the *domus ecclesia,* but our neglect or minimization of the *domus dei* aspect of our sacred spaces has contributed to disenchantment with the church felt by many in our culture. In so doing we have surrendered a pearl of great price.

108. Turner, *Temple to Meeting House,* 335.

Chapter 6

Missional Challenges and Opportunities in the Twenty-first Century

FEW PEOPLE WOULD QUESTION that a well-documented general religious malaise and disenchantment with the church exists today. The church's popularity appears to be waning and its previously enjoyed position of respect, authority, and influence can no longer be assumed within Western culture. There is an inherent danger when looking at this present state of affairs, which is a tendency to be preoccupied with the negative to the point of failing to see that there are good things occurring within and because of the church today.

The church has typically and historically represented the place where God could be met. Then why are people not flocking weekly to fill church buildings? William Hendricks catalogues case studies of people who, for a variety of reasons, have chosen to leave the church. He uses the term "back-door believers" to describe those who initially entered the church through the front door yet are slipping quietly out the back door, and observes that the majority have not given up on their faith.

> On the contrary, they may be quite articulate regarding spiritual matters. Indeed, some have remarkably vibrant spiritual lives and touchingly close friendships with a kindred spirit or two. But in

the main, they tend to nurture their relationship with God apart from traditional means of church and parachurch.[1]

People continue to need community, worship, instruction, and accountability, things generally associated with participation in a church community, but they seem to be finding other sources more accessible or palatable. Some now question the attribution of a pivotal role to the church or to religion, or even to the divine, in their spiritual experience. In light of this apparent trajectory, it behooves us to listen carefully and respond to those who question the relevance of the church's existence in the twenty-first century, and, subsequently the need for sacred spaces called churches. What I have found interesting in my own journey and conversations is that the greatest resistance to the need or the very existence of sacred space has come from people who share my own evangelical Protestant heritage.

In this chapter we will address a number of realities that could represent potentially significant arguments against the need for buildings dedicated to the twenty-first-century ministry of the church. Two phenomena in particular that deserve our consideration are the resurgence of the house church movement, particularly in North America, and the technological advancements of cyberspace. A third underlying question that must be addressed relates to the ever-present and increasing concern over the legitimization of costs associated with the construction of numerous, ambitious church building projects.

But before moving into these matters it would serve us well to be mindful of two fortuitous realities that have the potential to underscore the place of sacred space in the mission of the church, namely, an apparent increased openness to ecumenical dialogue and an openness to, and even longing for, spiritual experience that transcends denominational or traditional boundaries.

AN OPENNESS TO ECUMENICAL DIALOGUE

A trend over the past few decades that has significant implications for the praxis of sacred space within the broader Christian community is a move toward more porous walls between divergent religious groups. Before this movement toward a more open theological exchange and dialogue, many religious traditions operated from a posture of isolation

---

1. Hendricks, *Exit Interviews*, 17.

from other religious groups. The status quo enjoyed a deep and long influence; change was not expected or sought; a loyalty to tradition rendered innovation unnecessary and undesirable. During the late 1960s, this mindset began to lose its stranglehold on the Western church.

A number of Roman Catholic scholars[2] have documented the pivotal role of Vatican II in opening avenues of dialogue between the Roman Catholic Church and the World Council of Churches. Louis J. Luzbetak states, "One of the most remarkable and at the same time most welcome developments in more recent times, especially since Vatican II, has been the growing *ecumenical understanding and cooperation* among the different Christian traditions."[3] Roman Catholic scholars have demonstrated a freedom to highlight and criticize pre-Vatican II positions and procedures relative to evangelization. Whether this freedom was fostered by or merely accompanied the increased openness to ecumenical dialogue is certainly open for debate.

There is evidence of a residual reticence to engage in ecumenical dialogue within some sectors of evangelicalism based on a conviction that it adds little to the overall purpose of world evangelization. This reservation arises in part from the perspective that all relevant necessities for salvation have been finally, completely, and authoritatively revealed. An isolated position that refuses to communicate with others is destined, according to Peter Berger, to immediate irrelevance and ultimate extinction.[4] Max Stackhouse is representative of evangelicals who recognize a need for openness to interdenominational dialogue, and is concerned that "the present fragmentation of the church is a stumbling block to those who do not have a saving knowledge of the gospel, and it is an impediment to effective witness against the classism, racism, sexism, ideologism, and militarization that divide and threaten our world."[5]

Ecumenical dialogue over global concerns has contributed to a long overdue attenuation of many barriers between various religious groups that in turn has encouraged a willingness to observe, listen, and learn from others outside our own traditions. One area in which this

2. Authors cited in this book are Schreiter, *Constructing Local Theologies*; Bevans, *Models of Contextual Theology*; Arbuckle, *Earthing the Gospel*; Arbuckle, *Refounding the Church*; and Gallagher, *Clashing Symbols*.

3. Luzbetak, *Church and Cultures*, 176.

4. See Berger, *Heretical Imperative*, 125–56.

5. Stackhouse, *Apologia*, 32.

is particularly significant is sacred space. The experience of worship in an environment different than one is accustomed to should not be hindered because of mere difference. The investment of time and effort to understanding the rationale and theology that informs the structure of another tradition's sacred space not only equips us with an appreciation for that built environment and those to whom it is important but also can and does enhances our appreciation for our own preferred worship environments.

SPIRITUALITY IN THE TWENTY-FIRST CENTURY

According to George Gallup, one of the top three reasons people leave the church is that they are looking for a deeper spiritual meaning than organized religion has been able to deliver.[6] A plethora of published materials indicate that although religion appears to be losing its prominence in today's Western society,[7] spirituality is increasingly popular. To understand and appreciate the significance of sacred space within contemporary spirituality, it is important to clarify how the term "spirituality" is used here. Walter Principe suggests that there were times when the term "spirituality" was used in a more pejorative way, particularly during the eighteenth and nineteenth centuries.[8] Spirituality has always been popular, but it is crucial to recognize its significance in present day Western culture. According to one leading social observer and analyst, "Failure to understand the role of spirituality in our culture renders a social analyst incapable of completely comprehending the dynamics of American life."[9]

Defining Spirituality

Landing upon a widely accepted definition of spirituality is by no means an easy or straightforward task. As Philip Sheldrake puts it so well, "It appears that spirituality is one of those subjects whose meaning everyone claims to know until they have to define it."[10] With respect to Christian

6. Cited in Collins, *Exploring Christian Spirituality*, 9.

7. Reginald Bibby presents interesting and compelling evidence that suggests a contrary view (Bibby, *Restless Gods*).

8. Walter Principe, "Toward Defining Spirituality," in Collins, *Exploring Christian Spirituality*, 45–46.

9. Collins, *Exploring Christian Spirituality*, 10.

10. Sheldrake, *Spirituality and History*, 32.

spirituality, the term is typically used in reference to the theory and praxis of the Christian life. The ascetic, mystical theology that for centuries enjoyed a hegemonic influence on Christian spirituality has held relatively little appeal for current generations.[11] The way humans think about the divine, about the church, or about what it means to be human has morphed almost rhythmically over the past hundred years or so. There have been seasons, for instance, when the human body and experience, and nature itself, have been marginalized if not alienated altogether from any theology or theory of the spiritual life. In recent decades, however, a major shift has occurred that has legitimized human experience as an authoritative source of revelation as well without negating the concrete revelation of God in Jesus.

The apparent resurgence of interest in spirituality, particularly within the global north, underscores the fact that people have not lost interest or belief in the transcendent divine nor spirituality itself. Rather they have become disenfranchised from the institutional church and the intrusive manner in which the church has, in many people's minds, meddled with personal spirituality.

A significant result of this shift is that there is no transcultural, transtemporal concept of spirituality that can be applied universally. In fact, spirituality is deemed more fluid and inclusive than previous, conceptually-oriented approaches to spiritual theology. Contemporary spirituality is less exclusive, not associated with any one particular tradition. In fact, when any organization or institution attempts to define or set the parameters for legitimate spirituality, it is bound to meet resistance. Because contemporary expressions of spirituality are not only concerned with the interior life but with the whole human experience—body, soul, and spirit—there seems to be less of an emphasis on the application of prescriptive dogmatic principles. However, as Sheldrake states, "Without specific points of reference, it is difficult to say precisely what is spirituality and what is not, and what is appropriate or not."[12] Furthermore, spirituality is profoundly relational, informed by a concern to engage and connect with that which is beyond us—that is, the transcendent.

11. That is, until recently. One of the interesting tendencies among a number of Emergent leaders particularly has been a manifest interest in and return to the mysticism and spiritual disciplines of early church fathers.

12. Sheldrake, *Spirituality and History*, 52.

To summarize, then, spirituality, as used in this chapter is understood in terms of the following assumptions:

1. Spirituality, that desire and capacity to reach beyond ourselves to that which is transcendent, is an essential element of our humanness. It is this element, I would argue, that distinguishes humanity from other creatures.

2. Spirituality is profoundly experiential. Rather than being solely or primarily rooted in abstract ideas or dogma, as was the tendency historically, spirituality has become more and more embodied and embedded in human experience.

3. Spirituality is concerned with the delicate blend between transcendence and integration, that is, the interweaving the transcendent with the mundane, ordinary aspects of life.

4. Spirituality is both an individual and a corporate reality. Despite the propensity toward a robust individualism in our day, there is an interesting, concomitant, and increasing desire to live that connection out in community with others who share similar desires and commitments.

Ritual and Spirituality

No attempt at understanding contemporary spirituality will be complete without an appreciation for the nature of and need for ritual and sacred space and their combined potential for dynamic impact on authentic spiritual experience. Unfortunately for many, the term "ritual" has rather negative connotations suggesting vain or empty repetition, formalism, or meaningless activity. Mary Douglas describes a "ritualist" as "one who performs external gestures without inner commitment to the ideas beings expressed."[13]

The term "ritual" is not limited to the religious realm: rituals are conducted without religious connotation, such as blowing out candles on a birthday cake, kissing someone under a sprig of mistletoe, or even shaking hands as a form of greeting. Robert Fulghum presents intriguing approaches to a number of significant rites of passage, such as birth, marriage, and death. He considers other activities of varying degrees of significance, such as family meals, resolving personal conflict, and

13. Douglas, *Natural Symbols*, 20.

getting ready for each new day as rituals. [14] He explains, "I began seeing much of my life and the life around me as ritualized. I realized that the important rituals were not stored in books and service manuals but were being lived daily by all of us."[15] Interpreting Fulghum in the extreme, one may conclude that virtually any activity can potentially function as ritual. The experience of ritual(s) is an essential referent within spirituality.

Some distinguish between ritual and ceremony, suggesting that ritual refers to repetitious behavior that has explicit religious connotations or significance whereas ceremony refers to activity which is primarily if not exclusively social. Although usage can infer a close or overlapping meaning, the term "ritual" seems more widely associated with the religious or spiritual realm. For the purposes of maintaining consistency, this association is assumed throughout this book.

Margaret Mead argues for the continuing place of ritual in society: "I do not think ritual can be relegated to the past—to antiquity, to barbarism, or to the life of early man. Ritual is an exceedingly important part of all culture, all the cultures we know about and, hopefully, all cultures that we will know about."[16] Others do not agree, believing instead that "if Christianity is to be saved for future generations, ritualism must be rooted out, as if it were a weed choking the life of the spirit."[17]

Whether we are worshiping God or loving our children, it is virtually impossible to do either without ritual, without some type of outward expression of an inward reality. The focus of much of the controversy surrounding this issue relates to the viability of using historical rituals carried on from previous generations and to the need for discovering or creating alternate ones. The same could be said of sacred spaces that have been passed on and inherited by younger generations. If we believe we must get beyond the continuation of historical rituals, we must suggest rituals to replace those that are no longer relevant. We must not allow the anachronistic nature of some rituals or sacred spaces to persuade us that there is no need for any at all. The propensity toward ritualistic activity is an inherent quality of humanness, and to frustrate or minimize the exercise of rituals is to court significant problems.

14. Fulghum, *Beginning to End*.

15. Ibid., viii.

16. Mead cited in Mitchell, *Meaning of Ritual*, xiii.

17. See Mitchell, *Meaning of Ritual*, 116.

Consider the circumstances that appear to prompt ritualistic action: dark or perplexing times, even tragedies such as an untimely death of a princess or the shocking assassination of a president, can move people to act out their feelings. Emile Durkheim refers to this spontaneous response as "collective effervescence," which surfaces "under the influence of some great collective shock."[18]

Sometimes words prove woefully inadequate to express deep or intense feelings or to process various life events. Silence accompanied by symbolic gestures, such as the lighting of candles or the placing of flowers or gifts of remembrance at a specific location, is frequently a spontaneous means of corporate coping. Ritualistic activity is born out of a human need to physically express deep emotions or convictions, to cope with or celebrate the realities of life. In all of these instances, the particularity of place and space becomes important.

Rituals are not necessarily or inevitably religious in nature, despite some Christians' preference to insist they are an indication of humanity's need for God. Virginia Hine effectively demonstrates that the basic human need for meaning is "usually codified in myth and ritual."[19] The need for ritual, even in the most neutral sense, is an inherent quality of being human.

The relevant question is not whether humans need to engage in ritualistic activity but rather why, how, when, and where ritual should be engaged in.[20] People require a mechanism to give meaning and shape beyond the superficial; rituals often impart and extract deep meaning. Hine suggests that with the secularization and demythologization of Western society, the need for ritual and myth was distorted if not suppressed altogether.[21] Evidence in the twenty-first century strongly suggests that such suppression or distortion has been relatively short lived.

When we consider phenomena such as liturgical reform, Christian charismatic renewal, and other similar movements within Judaism, we discover that attempts to jettison ritual and myth through secularization have proven less than convincing in the end. Rejection of rituals is primarily a Western tendency, a residual effect of the modern, post-Enlightenment persuasion to distance society from rituals, or to dimin-

---

18. Durkheim, *Elementary Forms*, 210.
19. Hine, "Self-Generated Ritual," 404.
20. Driver, *Magic of Ritual*, 6.
21. Hine, "Self-Generated Ritual," 405.

ish their significance.[22] Rituals associated with significant rites of passage including funerals, weddings, and state ceremonies are tolerated but there is a resistance to identify any aspect of the mundane as a ritual.

The felt need for such outward expression is evidenced in the re-emergence of time honored tradition and in an interesting eruption of ritual innovation.[23] People starved for ritual forms who fail to find meaningful expression in church gatherings are now creating personal modes of ritualistic expression. One should not downplay the significance of these rituals, as Hine states:

> The very act of putting together a personally meaningful ritual seems to tap the transpersonal layers of consciousness. I am always amazed at the sense of authenticity that pervades these kinds of rituals and the capacity for poetic expression that seems to take hold of even the most inarticulate participant.[24]

Notwithstanding the recent resurgence of interest in spirituality in general and rituals in particular, the need for ritual is not universally accepted. When assessing an apparent disenchantment with ritual, one needs to examine the factors that lie beyond the ritual itself. A major complaint about rituals relates to their lack of connection with life in our contemporary culture.

Whereas some contend that ritual functions as nothing more than corporate symbolic action,[25] Lundquist suggests, "Ritual is the primary means that makes communication possible between humans and the powers beyond immediate human life—the transcendent. Ritual is the process through which contact with the world of the numinous powers is activated."[26] This understanding is born out of the conviction that one cannot approach the divine (or the numinous, transcendent powers) casually. Limited access, appropriate personal preparation, and even designated attire have been incorporated into ritualistic protocol in a variety of religions, from ancient Judaism to contemporary Roman Catholicism. Ritual appears in virtually all religions and societies, even those claiming no need for it.

---

22. Driver, *Magic of Ritual*, 12.

23. Hine, "Self-Generated Ritual," 405.

24. Ibid., 407.

25. Mitchell, *Meaning of Ritual*, xiv.

26. Lundquist, *The Temple*, 20.

Zuesse deduces, "Ritual centres on the body, and if we would understand ritual we shall have to take the body seriously as a vehicle for religious experience."[27] Others believe that rituals have the power "to alter psychic patternings and restructure basic attitudes."[28] Rituals common among many cultures outside North America occur when a child passes into adulthood; the transition is marked by a rite of passage in which the young person is typically thoroughly prepared for the event or series of events. Subsequently, they are expected to demonstrate attitudes and behaviors that are qualitatively different. Equally significant is the change in the accompanying response of their culture to them. Hine concludes that the most similar North America rituals might include significant milestones such as the acquisition of a driver's license or graduation from high school.[29] She believes that when the primary participants in a rite of passage contribute to its design and execution, the subsequent change and impact is more likely to remain. By implication, then, rituals that are imposed are far less likely to remain meaningful and subsequently passed on to future generations.

Ritual cannot be relegated to the realm of the optional or the peripheral. Rather it reflects a fundamental human quality, which I believe relates to the image of God invested in all humanity. Ritual provides an experiential focus of the sacred or holy, a process through which humanity connects with and approaches the divine. It serves as a reminder and, in many instances, allows us to re-enact significant realities or divine interventions in human space-time history—including the creation itself.[30]

Eclectic Spirituality

One of the hallmarks of many postmodern expressions of spirituality is a willingness to borrow the language and even engage in an eclectic collection of cultic expressions from a variety of traditions while declaring allegiance or commitment to none. An example of this is found in the life of a thirty-eight year old woman who was raised as a Roman Catholic but now attend Mass only a few times annually. The following

27. Zuesse, "Ritual," 406.

28. Hine, "Self-Generated Ritual," 409.

29. Ibid., 406–7.

30. Eliade, *Myth of the Eternal Return*, 99.

description of her spiritual journey likely resonates with that of many North Americans:

> Despite her spotty church attendance, she considers herself a deeply spiritual person. She daily sets aside at least an hour for meditation. She has a home altar that symbolizes her personal spiritual beliefs. On this altar are eighteen candles, an amulet attached to a photo of grandmother, amethyst crystals used in healing meditations, oriental incense, a Tibetan prayer bell, a representation of the Virgin of Guadalupe and some other traditional Catholic items.[31]

Eclectic spiritual practices are not unique to any specific location or to one gender in particular. Spirituality for more and more people resides in the realm of private experience and reflection and not in the religious ritual of the public domain. Consequently, as Barna states, "We must wisely and purposefully target different groups through different forms of ministry. Penetrating the unchurched world requires us to be creative and savvy. Good intentions alone will not get us too far."[32]

What has fostered this? I would argue that the residual impact of Aristotle's insistence on sensory access to God and subsequent modernistic spirituality informed by Enlightenment thinking has minimized or removed altogether two key elements of from religious experience, namely, mystery and imagination. As a result, many people have removed themselves from the influence of leadership that is not comfortable with the concept of direct experience of or with God through the Holy Spirit, that is, experience that cannot be explained and contained rationally. Aristotelian rational spirituality simply does not carry the same currency it once enjoyed. As will be demonstrated in what follows, the internet provides a context highly conducive to such an approach to spirituality.

LIVING IN TWO WORLDS: THE IMPACT OF CYBERSPACE ON SACRED SPACE

One cannot seriously consider the phenomenon of "space" or "place" without reflecting on the technological developments influencing our culture with redoubtable force. Few enjoying the benefits of technology wish that such advances had never occurred. Despite the benefits we

---

31. Ibid., 2.

32. Barna, *Grow Your Church*, 47.

enjoy and may even now consider essential, there are downsides to humanity's remarkable technological achievements. Arguably the degree to which these advances ultimately may impinge on the church's attempts to fulfill our mission, and on our fundamental approach to sacred space, is yet to be assessed and understood.

The rapidity with which technological advances have arrived leaves the average person hopelessly behind in the relentless challenge to stay current. Advances in the new frontier of cyberspace far outstrip the ability of Western lawmakers to regulate and set legal parameters within which such technology needs to operate. It is becoming increasingly evident that technology, particularly computer-mediated communication (CMC), is profoundly affecting what it means to be human both at the individual and the collective level. It seems humanity is moving toward an existence in which people live in two realms: offline and online. Steven Jones questions, "What is it about life offline that makes us so intent on living online?"[33]

The origin of the term "cyberspace" has been credited to science fiction author William Gibson who, in his 1984 novel *Neuromancer*, imagines a digital incarnation in which human flesh becomes data. Generally, however, and for our purposes, the term "cyberspace" refers to what Doug Groothuis calls "the information interface between computers and humans. It is the place or space where human consciousness and computer systems meet."[34]

With the advent of the internet has come a new, ever-expanding vernacular with which a person must become conversant in order to exist and navigate through cyberspace. The amount of redefinition that has occurred during the past few decades is not only quite astounding but also presents a major challenge to theoretician and practitioner alike. For example, concepts such as community, religion, spirituality, church, believer, seeker, the sacred, space, sacred space, and even time, to name a few, have all been adapted in the way they are used within this new possibility of being called cyberspace.

Henry L. Carrigan Jr. suggests, "Certainly the internet is the logical extension of our quest for individualism."[35] He speaks to the trend toward a more "anonymous form of community" among religious or

33. Jones, *Virtual Culture*, ix.

34. Groothuis, "Christian Scholarship," 632.

35. Carrigan, "Seeking God," 61.

spiritual seekers. By former definitions of community, the expression "anonymous community" is nothing short of oxymoronic. And yet such apparent contradiction is far from incongruous within the postmodern world of cyberspace. Although cyberspace is often used to facilitate human interaction, its fundamental meaning or essence does not require it. One can engage in cyberspace activities with or without the involvement of other humans. The entire ethos of internet culture is informed by an implicit individualism.

Rheingold enthusiastically endorses the recent emergence of "virtual communities," believing that the reason for their phenomenal growth is born out of a deep human need; "the hunger for community grows in the breasts of people around the world as more and more informal public spaces disappear from our real lives."[36] For many people, virtual communities provide an answer to their search for meaningful community that has apparently eluded them in the real world. He defines them as "social aggregations that emerge from the Net when enough people carry on those public discussions long enough, with sufficient human feeling, to form webs of personal relationships in cyberspace."[37]

I believe that all humanity is born with an intrinsic mystical tendency of varying degrees. Residual modernistic influences in Western cultures from time to time have rendered mysticism an inappropriate approach to spirituality that must be kept in check through the careful scrutiny of revered texts, scientific or scriptural. It is logical that some might look to venues in cyberspace as a place to connect with some reality beyond themselves, virtually real or otherwise. The limitation of such a mystical search to a spiritual need or dilemma tends to be reductionistic. The results can be dehumanizing, often ignoring or marginalizing the essential physical, psychological, and cultural dimensions of what it means to be human created in the image of God.

Although the advent of cyber technology may appear to herald what Karsten Harries refers to as "the increasing emancipation of the individual from the rule of the accident of place,"[38] one must not lose sight of the fact that disembodied freedom does not represent or allow for

36. Rheingold, *Virtual Community*, 6.
37. Ibid., 5.
38. Harries, *Ethical Function*, 169.

true human freedom. A human being comprises both body and spirit, and the role and necessity of both must be recognized at all times.[39]

One may hypothesize that a consequence of the advent of cyber technology will be an attenuated sense of the need for community in the more traditional form. But Peter Drucker notes that there is a stabilizing function of communities: "Society, community, family are all conserving institutions. They try to maintain stability and to prevent, or at least slow down, change."[40] By contrast, David Brown suggests that virtual communities, which thrive on the fluidity of the constantly changing world of cyberspace, have more to offer humanity than traditional communities, which are more committed to maintenance of the status quo.

With CMC, distance no longer represents the challenge it once did. A person is capable of traversing distance more quickly on the information highway than virtually any mode of transportation on earth humanity has developed to date. Mark Nunes declares:

> The technology that aims at containing distance eventually creates a virtual world, which destroys the conceptual possibility of distance. In this vertiginous moment of physical stasis and virtual travel, the "Voyeur-Voyager" experiences an immediacy which dissolves space and time: . . . Internet collapses space into one "hyperpotential point" which implodes all concept of distance, spacing, and separation.[41]

The very nature of communication is the experience of a metamorphosis. The similarity between communication methods of even one to two decades ago and this present day is all but lost. The landscape for social interaction has morphed radically in the past century, although the inherent human need for the tactile, personal dimension of communication remains. We continue to need what Jones terms "collective experiences."[42]

Much under the rubric of cyberspace contributes significantly to a radical split between our minds and bodies.[43] As people enter the two-dimensional world via a computer screen, they function primarily with the mind, relegating the body to limited engagement. The consequences

39. Ibid., 175.

40. Cited in Brown, *Cybertrends*, 111–12.

41. Nunes, "Baudrillard in Cyberspace," 314.

42. Jones, *Virtual Culture*, 4.

43. Cobb, "Spiritual Experience," 393–407.

of a dichotomy that minimizes the significance and effect of physical experience and separates humanity from its physical environment have yet to be assessed and fully understood. I would argue that Christian spirituality is an embodied experience and incorporates the whole of our humanness—body, soul, and spirit. It is difficult, therefore, to imagine this dichotomous trajectory not having any adverse impact.

Cobb describes her own experience inside "Osmose," the powerful virtual reality artwork of Char Davies, explaining how it torpedoed her previous perceptions of this type of medium and how she emerged with a far greater appreciation for the physical world in which she lives. The motivation behind Davies's work is the desire to somehow breach the Cartesian gap between mind and body and between subject and object. She does not intend to cater to some kind of Platonic wish to remove oneself from the cumbersome reality of embodied experiences and move into the pristine world of ideal forms. Yet this desire to "re-create our reality in a realistic and yet oddly sanitized form"[44] has influenced much of virtual reality technology.

Long before this kind of technology became available, Mircea Eliade believed that reality existed in the realm of the sacred. For him, the discovery of a sacred place is equivalent to the creation of the world; nothing begins or culminates in the absence of a fixed point, a center, found in the sacred place.[45]

> There is also a revelation of an absolute reality, opposed to the nonreality of the vast surrounding expanse. . . . In the homogeneous and infinite expanse, in which no point of reference is possible and hence no orientation can be established, the hierophany reveals an absolute fixed point, a center.[46]

If Eliade considers the pre-cyberspace world of his day an "infinite expanse," one has to wonder what his response would be to the ever-expanding world of cyberspace.

The experience of cyberspace advocated by Cobb is different from the one that crams increasing amounts of information into our minds but leaves us bereft of "connection, depth and spiritual meaning."[47]

---

44. Ibid., 399.
45. Eliade, *Sacred and the Profane*, 22.
46. Ibid., 21.
47. Cobb, "Spiritual Experience," 400.

The interactivity promised by much of cyberspace is seen by Cobb as counterfeit to what humanity desperately requires, namely "deep participation."[48] "Deep participation" cannot be limited to cognitive activity but must include the physical, the imaginative, and the experience of the physical environment in which we live. Cobb is convinced that people return to the reality of the organic world transformed because of technological offerings such as the "Osmose" cyber experience.

After reflecting on her article, it seems to me that the transformation fostered by Cobb's virtual reality experience is somehow similar to the outcome Christians would like our worship experiences, our personal and corporate encounters with the sacred, to generate. Similarities seem to exist between the linear experiences characteristic of many church gatherings, which primarily engage the minds of worshipers, and the types of limiting and dehumanizing interaction offered presently in cyberspace.

The term "virtual reality" belies a significant admission; the reality experienced through computer technology has the effect but not the form of reality. Our bodies and minds may respond to the magnificent images cast before us as though we were engaged in movement through time and space. Yet we know that our physical bodies have remained stationary. Rheingold sees no need for concern. "People in virtual communities do just about everything people do in real life, but we leave our bodies behind. You can't kiss anybody and nobody can punch you in the nose, but a lot can happen within those boundaries."[49] Mark Nunes suggests, "No longer does technology encompass the world; now it replaces it with a "more real than real" simulation."[50] I would argue that this phenomenon is more accurately designated as an "alternative reality."

What can we discern from people's desire or need for these types of experiences? Is this a mere techno-gimmick, taking us to another level of entertainment, or do such experiences deeply and fundamentally resonate with who we are as human beings? One positive result of the phenomenon is that we are compelled to address some fundamental issues. New forms of human brokenness for the church to address will be born from these technological experiences for both the participants and those physically proximate to them. The church must consistently

48. Ibid., 402.
49. Rheingold, *Virtual Community*, 3.
50. Nunes, "Baudrillard in Cyberspace," 3.

consider the essence of who we are and what we do as human beings, discerning the appropriate role and praxis for community in terms of our humanity, ministry, and the mission of the church.

With the advancement of "smart space,"[51] some are now providing church "gatherings" on the internet.[52] Some churches will consider incorporating "smart spaces" in future architecture, providing the transmission of services to those unable or unwilling to attend in person. Numerous churches broadcast Sunday morning services live via television, and there are indications that cyber connections will eventually replace these broadcasts.

Whereas the industrial revolution engendered a separation of home and the work place, it is increasingly evident that a return to shared space is emerging with the digital revolution[53] as telecommuters "go to work" without leaving home. Some observers, including Mitchell, are not convinced that this lifestyle will prove to be dominant in the near future.[54] Multiple movements toward flexible work schedules and spatial organization both at home and in the workplace are already operational. Mitchell believes that digital telecommunication will allow more people to spend more time in places that are particularly meaningful to them.[55] The challenge of maintaining clearly distinct working and living spaces in the domestic dwelling requires attention since the full impact of failing to do so has yet to be adequately assessed and documented.

A study conducted by the Barna Research Group[56] out of Ventura, California, demonstrates that millions of Americans are turning to cyberspace to get in touch with God and connect with other people who share similar faith interests. I find it interesting that 8 percent of the adults surveyed used the internet for religious purposes in comparison to 12 percent of teenagers. The project suggests that by the end of this current decade, up to fifty million people are likely to rely solely on the

51. See Mitchell, *e-Topia*, 52–68.

52. A popular one sponsored by the Methodist Church of England is called Church of Fools and is found at http://www.shipoffools.com/church.

53. Mitchell, *e-Topia*, 72.

54. Ibid., 73.

55. Ibid.

56. Barna Group, "More Americans Are Seeking Net-Based Faith Experiences," Barna.org, March 31, 2010, http://www.barna.org/barna-update/article/5-barna-update/48-more-americans-are-seeking-net-based-faith-experiences.

internet as their prime provider for what they call "faith-based experiences." The researchers also found that this trend cuts a wide swath
across denominational and traditional lines. Catholics and mainline
Protestants were found to be slightly more frequent users than Baptists
and other Protestants. Barna also found that people who identify themselves as born again Christians spend twice as much money annually on
electronic consumer items as they donate to their local church.

In contrast to Barna's suggestion that young people who are presently involved in some religious affiliation will eventually leave their
churches in favor of online religious activities. In her Pew Internet &
American Life Project study *CyberFaith: How Americans Pursue Religion
Online*, Elena Larson found that the most frequent users of online religious sites were also the most active in their offline religious activities.
Her conclusion is that for the time being, those using online sites for
spiritual purposes do so as a means of augmenting the religious activities offline, not as a replacement for them.

Scott Thumma from the Hartford Institute for Religion Research
found that in the approximately four-year period between 1998 and 2001,
the percentage of churches that had their own websites had grown from
11 percent to 45 percent. He predicted that within the following five years
that would increase to 90 percent. Size and depth of financial resources
appeared to influence this phenomenon as well: all megachurches (2,000
or more attendees on a consistent basis from week to week) had their
own web sites. But he also found that nearly half of the churches with
average weekly attendance of 100 or less also have websites.

Thumma makes the insightful observation that some congregations may find themselves with an appealing online image that exceeds
their ability to produce, maintain, and live up to in the offline world.
Cyberspace has the capacity to provide a sanitized simulation of reality.

It is not difficult to demonstrate that one of the benefits of the internet at the local church level is improved communication within the
membership. Emails and website postings are gaining greater popularity
due to their positive impact. A legitimate concern, however, is whether
this kind of communication will reduce the amount of face-to-face encounters, including pastoral counseling.

It would seem that ecumenical dialogue, both intentional and ac-
cidental, is bound to be one of the beneficiaries of the internet. I see this
as a good thing. People are free to explore other faiths and dialogue with

members of other traditions without the proselytizing pressure that can occur in face-to-face encounters. Interestingly enough, however, Lorne Lawson suggests that many of those who had joined new religious groups are also primary users of the internet.

On a visit to the highly popular site Beliefnet.com, I discovered an effectively designed presentation of a vast array of information and opportunities. On the main page under the tab "Community," for instance, one finds instructions on how to join the Beliefnet community as well as a list of forum topics that includes "Does the soul exist after death or not?" and "Ban the Burka in the US?" A list of over 1,700 groups, including a C. S. Lewis group and a Sufi Seeker group, was also provided. Other items included discussion groups on human rights and child obesity, galleries of pictures of Hindu deities, and galleries of images of Jesus. But on the same page were two advertisements, one providing two tips to a "flat, sexy stomach" and another inviting visitors to discover how to earn $8,795 per month by working two hours a day at home!

With an apparent resonance between New Age philosophy and developments in virtual reality, it is particularly important with respect to the mission of the church to give careful attention to physical environments. New Age philosophers and technology entrepreneurs are both attempting to overcome the limitations of embodiment. Some see the body as "an infinitely malleable fluid object, able to be thoroughly reshaped in line with any self-transformative project,"[57] a position that challenges what it means to be human.

Ziguras contends that the New Age movement has

> acted to facilitate rather than counter the contemporary techno-scientific redefinition of what it means to be human. . . . By stripping away the outer socialized layers of the self, the New Age encourages the abandonment of those older and deeper forms of social meanings constituted within communities and across generations, in favor of the commodified pop-psychological packages peddled by the slick and soft-focused Aquarian salesperson.[58]

Some might come to similar conclusions with respect to the church and other religious organizations.

It is dangerous, perhaps foolhardy, to plunge headlong into the world that technology opens up before us without carefully considering

---

57. Ziguras, "Technologization of the Sacred," 208.

58. Ibid., 209.

the liabilities. When traveling the information highway we minimize, if not relinquish altogether, some physical aspects of our humanity; communicative expressions such as eye contact or physical touch are rendered nonessential. We are embodied beings, and the spatial dimensions of our existence and interaction cannot be ignored or marginalized without some degree of dehumanizing impact. Can we really expect virtual reality and RL (internet terminology for "real life") to exist in a symbiotic relationship, or will they inevitably operate in an adversarial manner?

David Brown is convinced that experiences fostered through virtual communities will enrich our lives in the real world.[59] The same sentiment was clearly expressed in a number of conversations I had with people in a chat room at the virtual church site Church of Fools.[60] However, Brown does admit that it is too early to assess the effect such virtual meeting places will generate on society as a whole. Similarly optimistic, Howard Rheingold states:

> Not only do I inhabit my virtual communities; to the degree that I carry around their conversations in my head and begin to mix it up with them in real life, my virtual communities also inhabit my life. I've been colonized; *my sense of family at the most fundamental level has been virtualized.*[61]

Others do not share equal optimism. Michel Foucault considered worldwide communication network technology as veiled panopticons, prisons designed to both allow one guard to survey every prisoner and prevent each prisoner from seeing anyone else. He believed that the cables and connections bringing information were also capable of extracting information from our homes for the purposes of others. We have brought a vast new world of information into our homes as well as the prying ears of the state.[62] Some may consider Foucault's assessment too reactionary, perhaps even a bit apocalyptic. His reasoning does not

---

59. Brown, *Cybertrends*, 240. Brown fails to provide convincing examples of how this enrichment will occur or what it will look like.

60. http://www.shipoffools.com/church. The vast majority of those I chatted with, who are regular attendees at the Church of Fools, do not consider their experience as a substitute to "real" church attendance but rather as a complement to it. Nonetheless, I view the need for such complimentary experiences as indicative of a felt deficiency in the real world church experience of many who attend.

61. Rheingold, *Virtual Community*, 10 (emphasis added).

62. Cited in ibid., 15.

convince me, but I am equally reticent to embrace the views of Rheingold and Brown.

Brown overstates his case, suggesting that the human and natural references formerly characterizing or informing the pursuit of our goals are in the process of being replaced by what he terms "placeless abstraction."[63] He declares, "For the first time in human history, humankind is trying to evolve without the disciplines and inspirations of physical space."[64] Brown does not suggest that virtual reality will completely replace real life or that real life is eventually to be lived in front of a computer monitor. He cites the university as a context requiring personal, real-time connection:

> The university experience, like that of the church, the family, and the community, rests fundamentally on the communication of meanings situated in their human context, and not on the mere exchange of useful signals. "Education is based on mentoring . . . role modeling . . . socialization . . . processes [in which] physical proximity plays an important role. Thus the strength of the future physical university lies less in pure information and more in *college as a community*."[65]

Brown's last statement suggests community cannot exist in the absence of a shared spatial reality, at least not in the realm of education. There are certain dimensions that virtual reality cannot supply and without which community cannot exist. One can only dispute the enormous impact of telecommunications on community by engaging in serious denial. However, this should not cause one to despair that the Orwellian predictions of "Big Brother" have engulfed us.

The degree to which the technological advances of cyberspace affect human community, or the concept of what it means to be human, has yet to be fully determined, but that ambiguity does not justify a "wait and see" attitude on the part of the Christian community. Had the church done so when the printing press made its debut, it is likely that the church we know would have faded into oblivion. The church had to decide what to do with the printed page: resist, surrender or harness it. It appears we are once again at such a juncture.

63. Brown, *Cybertrends,* 134.
64. Ibid.
65. Ibid., 157–58 (emphasis added).

HOUSE CHURCHES: THE ANCIENT WAY OF THE FUTURE?

A second phenomenon that appears to counter the need for non-domestic environments dedicated to church gatherings is the house church movement. From the time of its birth, the church has always met in houses. However, it is important to make a clear distinction between the house church and the small group, which has become a vital part more and more churches. In many if not most cases, people who are involved in a small group are also likely to be involved in other ministries, including weekly worship gatherings. Robert and Julia Banks provide an excellent resource for understanding the home/house church phenomenon in their book *The Church Comes Home*.[66] According to the Bankses, a home church is distinguished from cell churches or other interest groups by "a much stronger emphasis on becoming a Christian family by building a common life with God and one another over a long period of time."[67] Wolfgang Simson describes the house church as "a way of living the Christian life communally in ordinary homes through supernatural power."[68]

The increased presence of house churches and networks associated with the house church movement in North America in particular is quite astounding. This represents something more than a desire to engage in what could appear to be self-inflicted exile as the underground church in the West. The house church is, in essence, an invisible church in the sense that there are no obvious indicators as to where and when a local fellowship gathers. One of the downsides of this is that the church then automatically becomes a "by invitation only" community. There is little or no accommodation for spontaneous walk-ins. The whole ethos of the domestic setting precludes that. There is little question that the home provides a context more conducive to fellowship on a more intimate level than a space that can accommodate several hundred people. However, that intimacy is available only to those who are "insiders" or invited by insiders.

It is not safe to assume that every person is looking for the kind of intimacy offered in a house church context. Some people are more threatened in a small gathering than in a larger group in which their

66. Banks and Banks, *Church Comes Home*.

67. See ibid., 99–108 for a good description of the ways in which home churches differ from other kinds of groups, including cell churches.

68. Simson, *Houses That Change the World*.

anonymity can be preserved. This may be a reflection of a person's natural preferences as an introvert, not a gauge of one's spiritual depth. For others, various seasons of life leave them in need of the presence of other people but drained of the capacity or desire to interact with others. Thus the legitimate safety of a crowd becomes more of a refuge than the closeness and expected interaction of a small group. The house church is not for everyone any more than the megachurch. People can thrive or shrivel in both.

It is interesting to consider indications that the two fastest growing expressions of the church in North America today are the megachurch and the house church; two opposite ends of the ecclesiological spectrum. The congregations that are suffering demise the most are those between the two. The average congregation is hemorrhaging into one of the two: the megachurch that offers a proliferation of programs and ministries as well as large corporate worship experiences, or the house church that welcomes people into the intimacy of a small number of likeminded believers.

Many conclude that the increased presence of the house church is a long-awaited return to the *modus operandi* of the nascent New Testament church. They would argue that since the church grew at an astounding rate for the first three centuries of its existence in the absence of dedicated buildings, we should approach ministry today in like manner. In response I would first offer a question: Did the early church grow at a phenomenal rate *because* they had no buildings or *in spite of the fact* that they had no buildings? One could argue convincingly on both sides of that question. Ray Bowman and Eddy Hall, for instance, argue that the lack of buildings was a major contributing factor to the early church's growth. "Actually, its lack of buildings was probably one of the secrets to its growth."[69] This amounts to little more than conjecture with no definitive scriptural or historical backing. Second, the twenty-first century church in the global north is not living in the same political, economic, social, or religious milieu as the early church. To suggest that the absence of buildings during those first few centuries was the result of an intentional, theologically informed decision on the part of church leadership is at best an argument from silence. No explicit scriptural statement to that effect exists.

---

69. Bowman and Hall, *When Not to Build*, 113.

At some point the house church is going to prove inadequate for the full expression and ministry of the local church. The same must be said for virtually any of the buildings we erect for gathering, worship, and ministry. Neither the house church nor the megachurch provide the ideal built environment for a missional church in all contexts. I would argue, therefore, that there is a place and a need for both as well as a wide array of other expressions between.

There is no redemptive value in pitting dedicated buildings and home churches against each other. The mission of the church does not demand us to choose. But more important than all the compelling arguments that anyone could assemble on either side of this issue is the scriptural foundation that the church does not belong to any of us. It is Christ's church, and he promised that he would build it with or without church buildings and in such a way that the gates of hell itself stand helpless against it (Matt. 16:18). One of the potential downsides of owning church buildings is the tendency to lose sight of that fact and the subsequent propensity toward ownership that devolves into an idolatry in which buildings are embraced with unwarranted reverence. But that potential in itself provides no more convincing rationale for the exclusion of church buildings than the potential of gluttony does for the cessation of eating food altogether.

The house church, therefore, does not present a compelling reason to do away with church buildings, nor does the megachurch phenomenon render the house church anachronistic. My contention is that in either scenario, careful, prayerful theological reflection must be allowed to inform the design and construction of the spaces that are dedicated to the accomplishment of the church's mission.

ALL ARE WELCOME . . . ALMOST

More and more churches are confronted with difficult decisions regarding who has access to and use of their buildings. Being physically present within a community yet providing only limited access can generate mixed messages. Unfortunately more and more congregations are being forced to lock their doors at times other than regularly scheduled main events due to the fear and likelihood of vandalism.

But beyond that, the whole challenge of availability is being exacerbated in several countries in the global north by recent legislation that has redefined institutions, such as marriage and family, that previously enjoyed much wider acceptance and understanding. Many churches have opted to limit the use of their church buildings, even for significant events such as weddings and funerals, to members only. In so doing they hope to avoid having to deal with requests from those outside the community whose lifestyles contradict certain standards. One can only surmise that it is but a matter of time before municipal and federal jurisdictions that grant charitable/non-profit status to any religious organization will call into question those that impose such restrictions on the use of their facilities. One way to avoid such a dilemma, of course, is to choose not to own a building and rely instead on rented facilities.

But sacred spaces that are built on a fear-induced fortress mentality that seeks to maintain standards by excluding others are inconsistent with the rhythm of God's redemptive mission. Am I suggesting that all biblical standards be ignored and that we capitulate to a compromised commitment to being relevant as the linchpin of our ministries? Far from it. Rather, our sacred spaces must never be allowed to become an excuse or justification for a choice to disengage from culture. It behooves all congregations to weigh these issues carefully long before concepts begin to unfold on any architect's design table.

THE ALLURE OF NEW SACRED SPACES

Despite a number of recessions that have cycled through global economies in recent decades, the most recent of which came perilously close to an eclipse of the Great Depression, consumerism continues to demonstrate a robust ability to survive. Monumental shrines to the gods of instant gratification and entitlement continue to appear and expand, exercising their alluring influence over millions and millions into faithful attendance on a far more regular basis than the majority of churches in North America enjoy. Shopping malls, however, are not designed exclusively for the exchange of currency for merchandise. Advertising for one of the largest malls in Canada clearly invites customers to an *experience*. Mall designers want their spaces to be what the founders of Starbucks intended their coffee shops to be, only on a much grander scale—that is, "the third space" next to home and work, the most important space to be.

A significant recent trend presents a notable similarity between the design of church buildings and large enclosed shopping malls. Ira G. Zepp Jr. has produced a work dedicated to this phenomenon based upon his conviction that the best way to appreciate the meaning and magnetism of the mall is through the hermeneutical lens of the phenomenology and history of religion.[70] He demonstrates how the mall is fulfilling fundamental human needs—including those of order, symmetry, and community—historically addressed and met by other institutions such as the church.

Zepp posits the notion that the shopping mall can and does become a sacred place based on Mircea Eliade's belief that anything can become sacred or can be attributed with sacrality: "The extent that the mall is space discontinuous from the trivial, ordinary world, it is understood to be potentially sacred. The sacred is always more real than the profane and therefore more powerful than the ordinary world."[71]

While malls exist primarily for the exchange of goods for money, it is clear that other purposes are incorporated intentionally into their design and construction. Advertising materials court consumers with the suggestion that the mall is "more than a shopping center, a marketplace, a collection of shops."[72] The function of the mall goes beyond the pragmatic and commercial.

Zepp contends that the mall is designed to be a place of festival, that its "construction and ritual betray its ceremonial nature."[73] He argues that there is an underlying yet unmistakably religious quality to the mall. He clarifies his use of the word "religion" by distinguishing it from an association with "denominational affiliation, adherence to belief, the practice of certain religious institutions (church or synagogue), or faith in a supreme being."[74]

He does not insinuate that the more widely accepted practice of religion is of little or no value but instead posits a broader view that considers religion as a dimension of human experience. For Zepp, any process of restoring life, wholeness, integration, or unity is a religious activity. Delicately blended in most malls is the inherent human ten-

---

70. Zepp, *New Religious Image*, 11.

71. Ibid., 51–52.

72. Ibid., 12.

73. Ibid., 13.

74. Ibid., 14.

dency to symbolize and ritualize life (*homo religiosus*) and the human propensity to play or engage in festival (*homo ludens*). To Zepp, the purchasing of goods is but a "catalyst for a community celebration."[75]

The Importance of Center

The term "center" is used in a wide variety of ways—counseling centers, shopping centers, agricultural centers, recreational centers, civic centers. Even some church congregations have chosen to refer to their main gathering place as the church center or worship center. "We find the concept of 'center' an appropriate description for a place of human empowerment, a group of people who deliver social services, and an organization whose purpose is to help, heal, or otherwise improve the world."[76]

The concept of "center," referred to in Eliadean terms as the *axis mundi*, has historically represented the place where God and humanity (or heaven and earth) connect, where power is generated. The designers of malls strive to make them places of vitality and energy, with many designs reflecting a labyrinth-like flow directing shoppers toward the center. The center, to which all walkways lead, is where people find "a replication of the primordial world in all its harmony and pristine order."[77]

As the administrator of the Findhorn Community in northern Scotland observed, even ordinary activities express spiritual values. "Our motto for business here is, 'Business is sacred.'"[78] Zepp goes further: "This gravitation toward the center implies an expectation that, as a result of being there, thought will be collected and perhaps lives will be a bit more anchored. This form of activity verges on meditation."[79]

Zepp believes that one of the reasons for the phenomenal popularity of shopping malls is that they respond to the human need for order. Humanity has a strong propensity and need to gravitate toward a center, evidenced by the prominence of circularity in many aspects of life—the shape of primitive villages, the importance of town squares or village greens, the nature of many children's games. As Zepp states,

75. Ibid., 19.

76. Ibid., 37.

77. Ibid., 51.

78. Conversation held April 27, 2001, while visiting the Findhorn Community with a class from King's College, University of Aberdeen, taught by Dr. John Drane.

79. Zepp, *New Religious Image*, 66.

> From a history of religions perspective there are good reasons for
> both the presence of the center and all those symbols found there.
> They are a response to our fundamental need to remember our
> affinity with nature and to return periodically to a stable world.
> The contemporary mall documents the pervasive and practical
> expression of this response.[80]

The church should give serious consideration to a similar response to
these needs for reflection.

One of the downfalls of enclosed, air-conditioned, orderly malls
is that they fail to allow space for brokenness in human experience.
"The orderliness of the mall is sometimes uncanny and oppressive."[81]
Zepp omits any description of what types of spaces would be more appropriate for broken people. Perhaps more suitable is a lesser degree of
predictability, or a higher degree of random arrangement. It could be
argued that the orderliness of these spaces could provide a place of re-
orientation, assisting people to move through the disorderliness of their
brokenness to a restored wholeness.

A Need for Connectedness

Mall designers have begun to consider more seriously humanity's need
to relate appropriately to our environment. For instance, many malls
include space set apart with comfortable seating accompanied by foun-
tains and natural vegetation. Aside from quenching thirst, water has
served primarily as a source of refreshing, restoration, and healing.[82]
"But the belief water has life-giving and curative function is not limited to organized religion."[83] For many people the sound of running
water provides a reprieve from the relentless cacophony of the urban
world and the ever-present infusion of canned music. Being connected
with nature while conducting more mundane activities is a feature that
continues to attract people, a subtle shift from the Western tendency to
dissect life into the distinct realms (physical-spiritual, visible-invisible,
sacred-profane) to a more unified approach in which such distinctions
are minimized or removed.

80. Ibid., 63.

81. Ibid., 146.

82. Ibid., 57. Margaret Silf describes the restorative and healing virtues of water in
Silf, *Sacred Spaces*, 84–107.

83. Zepp, *New Religious Image*, 59.

The time spent in malls is indicative of a felt need for community and social relations that are not being met in other contexts. "In a society where there are so many meetings where people do not meet and personal relationships in which nothing personal takes place, the mall, for good or ill, has filled a vacuum."[84] It is difficult to dispute the fact that people appear to be finding in malls some degree of reprieve from tedium and loneliness.

Generally, malls manage to transcend differences, fostering a welcoming, egalitarian ethos. James Rouse states, "Shopping is the most democratic of all experiences. It includes everyone, and a central city marketplace is the most democratic institution in the city."[85] Despite the North American distain for elitism, the mall is generally a middle-class reality. Rouses's suggestion regarding their all-inclusive nature requires tempering: the poor and disadvantaged are typically excluded.

Zepp makes an interesting comparison with the church:

> From an ecclesiastical point of view, the average mall, with its democratic appeal, resembles a Catholic church at worship more than a Protestant one. Since Catholics are expected to attend their parish church, you can often find a millionaire kneeling beside a laborer. The hierarchy of economic classes in the parish are leveled once a person is in the church.[86]

Yet it is within Protestantism that striking similarities between the design and construction of church buildings and malls is becoming more evident.

The vernacular of mall architecture intends to convey openness, an all-inclusive welcome, a place or orientation, and community for many. Zepp's read on the ecclesiological landscape is that many churches appeal mainly to ideological, sectarian, and class interests and have become and remain largely exclusive in nature. "The combination of festivity, ritual, and commerce make the mall as equally a significant, if not a more inclusive and egalitarian, center as most churches."[87] Seven out of ten Americans visit a mall on a weekly basis,[88] a significantly larger number than those attending church.

84. Ibid., 66.
85. Ibid., 31.
86. Ibid.
87. Ibid., 80.
88. Ibid., 155.

Humane Convictions

Zepp's convictions were clearly influenced by the work of James Wilson Rouse,[89] whose company constructed approximately forty malls across the United States from the 1950s through the 1980s. Some key convictions of the code of conduct embraced by Rouse's company include:

1. The lives of people and communities for generations to come will be affected by what we do.

2. The surest road to success is to discover the authentic needs and yearnings of people and do our best to service them.

3. People seek warm and human places with diversity and charm, full of festival and delight. They are degraded by tacky, tasteless places and are oppressed by coldness and indifference.

4. People are uplifted by beauty and order and made significant by the creative caring which that demands. We believe everything matters, that every detail is important.[90]

Rouse's conviction was that the true test of spirituality is the degree to which a person attempts to make the world a more humane place.[91] He was firm in applying this principle to the malls that he built. "The only real purpose and justification of any one of these centers," he stated, "is to serve the people in the area—not the merchants, not the architects, not the developers. The success or failure of a regional shopping center will be measured by what it does for the people it seeks to serve."[92] Statements such as these present a robust challenge for the church to consider and to assess. To what degree do our buildings reflect our mission to the people we seek to serve?

Although there is always a concern to attract new customers among mall administrators, there is increasingly an equal commitment to being a place that enriches the community in which they are located.[93] I wonder how many churches share the same desire that their presence will enrich the community in which they are situated. The church would be

89. Zepp dedicates an entire chapter to Rouse entitled "Transition: James Rouse— Mahatma of Malls" (81–93).

90. Cited in ibid., 82.

91. Cited in ibid., 90.

92. Cited in ibid., 93.

93. Ibid., 74.

well advised to consider what can be learned from the design of the mall as a ceremonial center that provides a sense of order and connectedness and measures its success by its service and community enrichment.

Thought provoking insights such as these lead us naturally into the last challenge to be considered here: How we can justify the enormous investment of funds into structures that often end up being primarily self-serving?

The challenges faced by congregations often comes down to the manner in which the building is regarded: as a tool for effective involvement in the *missio dei*, a gift of worship to God himself, a fortress to harbor us from unwanted influences, or a memorial to the leadership and congregants themselves. Involvement in the *missio dei* inevitably turns messy at times, even to the point of property damage. Maintenance and status quo are seldom if ever items for discussion in the missional church. Rather, more germane to the missional conversation are things like obedience, risk, love, and grace. However, that should never be allowed to provide an excuse to disregard the built environment we call sacred space.

Chapter 7

Where We Need to Be

THE PRAXIS OF SACRED PLACE FOR
THE TWENTY-FIRST CENTURY

I BEGAN THIS BOOK by proposing that a significant and vital connection exists between
sacred places and the fulfillment of the mission of the church. I suggested that the significance of this connection and the associated praxis
of sacred place should not only be a concern to those within the discipline of practical theology but to other disciplines within the academy. It
should be equally important to pastoral and lay leadership groups at the
local church level. The lack of previous academic study and published
research dedicated to this connection underscored the necessity of an
investigation of this nature.

We have examined a variety of sources and related disciplines and
concluded that authentic sacred places can and should convey deep
meaning as well as provide ritualistic venues. As Margaret Visser states,
"A church is no place to practice aesthetic distance, to erase content and
simply appreciate form. The building is trying to speak; not listening
to what is has to say is a form of barbarous inattention, like admir-
ing a musical instrument while caring nothing for music."[1] We have
considered sacred space through the lens of historical and theological

1. Visser, *Geometry of Love*, 14.

reflection and have dialogued with other disciplines beyond theological and biblical studies.

Lastly we thought through some of the challenges and opportunities that loom on the church's horizon. But a book dedicated to the theology of sacred space and its application to the mission of the church would be incomplete without at least in some way acknowledging that perhaps one of the greatest issues people have with respect to the construction of dedicated church buildings is the cost.

LEGITIMIZING THE COST

I am not convinced that we have done a very good job at answering the concerns and searching questions regarding the expense of buildings, particularly in the face of so many legitimate needs such as hunger and homelessness in our own communities and mission opportunities that are woefully underfunded in third world and developing countries. The statement that we are building a stronger base that would enable us to be much more effective in addressing and meeting those kinds of needs has left many unconvinced.

Though often related to a question of affordability (what limits should a congregation put on the size of project?), discussion often revolves around the more foundational issue of whether a congregation should even consider building in the first instance. Does Scripture provide anything by way of precedent or principle from which one could argue in favor of the investment of serious amounts of money, time, and energy?

One passage that has often been cited in support of such investments is found in 2 Samuel 24:24, in which David refuses to offer sacrifices to God that cost him nothing. Unfortunately history provides too many examples of situations in which that text has been misapplied to justify extravagance that exceeds a congregation's resources, let alone reasonable pragmatic needs or missional necessities. The tabernacle and temple are also identified as precedents for large financial and material expenditures on church buildings in our day. But we must be mindful of the fact that the tabernacle and Temple served vastly different functions than a church building in the twenty-first century. The Temple was never intended to accommodate masses of people or to provide educational and recreational spaces as many church buildings do today. The fact that there was one and only one Temple at a time in ancient Israel, and that both its establishment and location were justified with divine and miraculous sanction, further renders any parallel with contemporary church structures less tenable. The static, centralized location of the Temple in the specific, strategically located city of Jerusalem had religious, social, and political rationale and implications to which no twenty-first-century church may lay claim.

The legitimacy of the cost of church buildings in many sectors will be assessed on the basis of occupancy. If a new ministry space is consistently well filled then people's concerns about cost factors may be allayed to some degree. This approach may be based upon an attractional paradigm of ministry, or a "Field of Dreams" mindset toward church buildings that believes "if you build it, they will come." In some parts of North America, congregations can be quite confident that the construction of a new facility almost certainly will generate an immediate increase in attendance of up to 20 percent or higher. Demographic analysis, however, is likely to demonstrate that a significant majority of new arrivals are already believers who have been active members of varying degrees in other congregations, possibly in the same general location.

Edward Anders Sovik would have a problem with this as evidenced in his statement,

> Jesus was the "man for others"; Christians are called to be the "men for others." Their structures should not be built unless they are directed to the service of the community of people around them and become a means for the Christian community to provide as effectively as possible not only for their own needs, but for the needs of the community.[2]

Statements such as this resonate with the deeply held convictions of James Wilson Rouse regarding shopping malls. It is not difficult to demonstrate that in too many instances local congregations have committed themselves to building projects that not only mortgage their buildings but mortgage their ministries—present and future—as well, leaving them with woefully inadequate resources to be engaged in meeting community needs to any measurable degree. In so doing a church paints itself into a corner of a self-serving, inwardly-focused mindset. I would argue that it is this kind of unwise overcommitment, and not

---

2. Cited in Torgerson, *Architecture of Immanence*, 147.

the existence of church buildings per se, that has sullied the concept of sacred space and represents a *modus operandi* that is far removed from a missional paradigm of ministry. However, having said that, I would emphasize that being a congregation committed to serving others does not automatically preclude the place or need for sacred places, including church buildings.

Unfortunately, most conversations centering on the cost of any building endeavor are typically limited to financial considerations. But there are always other costs associated with the development and construction of new ministry environments that cannot be quantified in dollars and cents. Men and women who serve on committees and task forces associated with any building project know full well the onerous demand on personal and family time. The ever-present awareness of increased financial responsibilities and challenges and the subsequent stewardship or fundraising campaigns and pleas for sacrificial giving can become serious points of contention and resentment if drawn out over a long period of time. What starts out with a flurry of excitement and enthusiasm has a way of devolving into a debilitating albatross around a congregation's neck. It is often because of these costs—perceived, potential, or real—that some congregations opt out of moving into the rigorous journey of expansion.

But choosing not to build does not guarantee the avoidance of costs. There are costs to be considered seriously that will result from choosing *not* to build as well, and those costs exceed mere numerical decline. For example, obvious practical considerations such as safety can be compromised through overcrowded conditions. North American personal space is substantially larger than the comfort zones inherent in many other global cultures. People can tolerate crowded conditions in short doses on public transit even with complete strangers but are far less willing to endure the same during the spiritual experience of corporate worship. The benefit of additional or renovated square footage in any church structure must not be seen solely from the perspective of increased numbers in attendance. Though that *may* be important, making room for more people or activities falls short of providing compelling rationale for long-term indebtedness. There are other reasons that are born out of a missional mindset that do justify the presence of built environments and the costs associated. To some extent, some of these reasons will be culturally informed; that is, what might be deemed important if not essential sacred space in one context may well be superfluous in another.

There is another downside to the choice not to build that has the potential for deeper, more disconcerting implications: debt-free congregations that are not strongly motivated by a missional orientation may find themselves easily lulled into an apathetic contentment that requires little or no risk or radical dependence on God for their existence and ministry. Having said that, I offer this strong caution: unwisely calculated financial risk is no indicator of authentic faith and obedience. Rather, such rash impulsiveness may be generated by a presumptive misapplication of the faithful promises of God to provide. Pastoral and lay leadership must ruthlessly check their own hearts and motives to ensure that leading their congregation into any expansion or development program is not rooted in their own personal desire to leave their mark or establish a legacy.

The missional mindset prayerfully discerns what God is already doing, determines what involvement in that mission needs to look like in a particular setting, and creatively considers what kinds of sacred spaces will be necessary to the fulfillment of that mission. In this way, congregations can avoid what has occurred too often when function follows form and when the built environment is granted dictatorial powers over mission rather than enhancing and facilitating it. The built environment must respond to and reflect a congregation's understanding of their identity (who God has called them to be) and their purpose (what God has called them to do), not determine it.

I have to wonder if a major contributing factor to the dissatisfaction of many congregations with their facilities is not due to the fact that their built environment has been designed and constructed with little or no consideration to their unique identity and purpose. Ambivalence or lack of clarity in either our sense of identity or purpose will inevitably foster sacred spaces that at some point prove inadequate, if not altogether counterproductive. In the absence of clarity of vision, identity, and purpose, any space will do. But when congregations and their leadership are infused with a clear sense and confidence in what God has called and equipped them to do in a specific context, then the built environment becomes of paramount importance. When design is arrived at primarily if not solely on the basis of the need for increased seating capacity or what is financially feasible, one can virtually guarantee that at some point that building will prove inadequate or dysfunctional. And those who inherit it down the road, mortgage and all, will be frustrated, possibly to the point of resenting those responsible for its design and construction.

The missional church can live with the fact that no single congregation is going to reach all people and address all pressing needs. Being a missional church does not require commitment to the most current, cutting-edge strategies, ministry paradigms, and technologies, but it does require an awareness of current needs and opportunities within the local congregation and the immediate context. Therefore, because no two expressions of the missional church will necessarily look exactly alike, the built environments or sacred spaces conducive to the missional church will be as varied and numerous as contexts require. There is no such thing, then, as a one-size-fits-all missional sacred space.

Craig Hoopes, principal architect and owner of Craig Hoopes and Associates, reflected on the design he offered to his home church, United Church of Sante Fe, when they revisited their master plan for expansion and renovation:

> We generally think of only the sanctuary as sacred space, but in fact the whole church—the children's rooms, the offices, even the hallways—tell the story of the congregation. You can read architecture. It's a different "read" than a book, but if you take time to really look at and experience a place, you can read a building—learn the story of the congregation, what they believe about God, themselves, other people.[3]

Hoopes, among several others from numerous disciplines cited in throughout this book, recognize and acknowledge the impact that spaces can have on people. The places in which we live and worship are not peripheral or inconsequential to our embodied experience. Sacred places *embrace* those present and *denote something beyond* both the participant and the context, like a word or a symbol. Visser concludes, "A church is bigger than I am, but it also represents me."[4] Sacred space, like those who are embraced by it, is a key player and fundamental element. Whether desired or not, it will affect the participant and the event.

Zepp's work, in which he posits shopping malls as the emerging ceremonial centers in American life, does not lead one automatically to the conclusion that churches should convert their facilities into theme

---

3. *Sacred Space: Looking at the World Differently*, http://www.ucc.org/cgi-in/Master PFP.cgi?doc.

4. Ibid., 15.

parks or physical environments in which the core values of convenience and entertainment dominate. Rather, we must gain insight, recognizing that some malls successfully provide space that fosters a sense of connectedness with one's environment and with other people—a *quality of place* that any church would be wise to incorporate intentionally into its design.

Perhaps the most appropriate areas where qualities and insights may be translated from shopping mall designs to ecclesiastical centers is in such peripheral yet essential areas as the foyer, or narthex, and other transitional spaces intended to foster community and the development of interpersonal relationships. Until the last couple of decades, transitional spaces were given little consideration, almost to the point of being nonexistent in many settings. Spatial dimensions designed to move participants promptly into the nave or auditorium did not allow for lingering or mingling. When entering into the main worship space, worshipers were encouraged to take their place quickly and quietly, which deterred conversation. More and more, however, attention is being given to the transitional spaces outside the sanctuaries.

FIGURE 7.1. *Community Building Space, First Alliance Church, Calgary, Alberta. Photo by William R. McAlpine.*

FIGURE 7.2. *Spaces That Invite Unhurried Reflection, First Alliance Church, Calgary, Alberta. Photos by William R. McAlpine.*

Zepp's representation of the mall center as a place in which people can reorient themselves has significant potential for application to the church. Perhaps it is expecting too much for people to depart from a harried and challenging mundane world to swiftly enter a liturgical venue ready to engage in worship. Worshipers would be assisted in transitioning to a rich worship experience through the provision of spaces allowing them to collect themselves and foster connections with fellow worshipers in an informal, personal sense.

In this respect, Victor and Edith Turner's concepts of *liminality* and *communitas*[5] are particularly appropriate considerations in the design of church buildings. The inclusion of design features incorporated into some mall centers, such as generous amounts of natural light, natural vegetation, and flowing water, would greatly enhance these reorienting spaces from both an attention-restorative and aesthetic perspective. Worshipers could be reminded of the need to see themselves in proper

---

5. Particularly helpful in understanding these concepts is the material provided in Turner and Turner, *Image and Pilgrimage*, 249–51, and Turner, *Temple to Meeting House*, 94–130.

relation to their environment, a relation often blurred or eclipsed by the frenetic pace of urban and suburban realities.

The ritualistic dimension of the church's mission necessitates careful consideration of and attention to the appropriateness of the venue in which these rituals occur. As I have tried to demonstrate, sacred places do not merely provide the container or context in which rituals occur; they contribute to the content and significance of the associated rituals, to the meaning extracted from them, and to the spirituality experienced by those participating in them. The theological intentionality of sacred architectural designs will enhance the ritual experience. Conversely, failure to appropriately consider and incorporate our Christian theology into the sacred place is likely to hinder the optimal effectiveness of ritualistic expressions occurring in twenty-first century spirituality.

Ritual possesses the capacity to transform both time and space into something beyond the ordinary or profane. A given place or specified time may be considered sacred by virtue of a particular event occurring then and there. Can the same influence be attributed to the space itself, such that a particular ritual is deemed sacred based upon the location where it is administered? The fact that many spaces are dedicated to a limited number of significant activities would indicate that this is the case in some instances.

My contention is that sacrality of place is not contingent solely upon ritual or event or on those participating in it, nor is it based primarily or exclusively on context itself. However, one cannot engage in ritual in a vacuum; nor can ritual be effectively conducted in spaces that distract from a meaningful ritualistic experience, even though other legitimate purposes may be served. It is likely inconceivable for many to imagine participating in the Eucharist or conducting a Bar Mitzvah at a rock concert or in a station in the London Underground. Sacred places constitute an essential component of ritual; they impart meaning, and they do matter.

Something that those who advocate a return to an early church praxis need to keep in mind is that during the first few centuries, Christian worship was considered strange if not offensive to unbelievers. Today, however, there is a tendency to make it as familiar and comfortable as possible. Horton suggests that this trend is evident not only in the blurring of distinction between Christian and secular music and communication but also in architecture.[6] Just as congregational singing is part of the ministry of the Word as proclaimed in Ephesians 5:19, so too are the architecture and the furnishings of a church building. "In both cases something significant is proclaimed, the former orally, the latter visually. And in neither case is style neutral."[7]

I am not advocating the elevation of sacred space to a position of inordinate importance. The Reformers' concern that architecture and symbolism not be apotheosized, thus undermining the importance of the Word of God, is a truly valid one. The context for ritual must not demand our attention to the point of distraction, whether through ornate extravagance or shameful lack of beauty.

Although it is difficult to identify exactly when or how, a shift has occurred, particularly within the North American evangelical church. An emphasis on the mystery and majesty of God[8] now shares the stage with an emphasis on intimacy and fellowship within the body of Christ. In some instances interpersonal intimacy and an emphasis on divine immanence have trumped transcendence altogether. The apparent shift is from a theocentric approach to worship to a more anthropocentric approach. The vertical dimension of relationship between humanity and the divine has been balanced with, and sometimes eclipsed by, the horizontal dimension of relationships between people.

This shift has recently influenced the design of church buildings, some of which now intentionally incorporate features that will foster and enhance a sense of community. In some churches constructed during the past few years, sanctuaries have been designed to significantly and intentionally increase the visual connection with other worshipers. Focus and attention is no longer directed primarily toward the front of the sanctuary where rituals and events are conducted.

6. Horton, "Why Sacred Space Matters."

7. Ibid.

8. These were qualities consistently invested in the design of medieval cathedrals.

FIGURE 7.3. *View of the Seating Arrangements in First Alliance Church, Calgary, Alberta, Canada. Photo by William R. McAlpine.*

Of significant concern however, is the diminished attention to Christian symbolism that has accompanied this shift, particularly within some sectors of Protestantism. Specifically, the removal of a permanently ensconced cross, pulpit, baptismal, and communion table or altar arguably conveys a theological perspective which, some would argue, hinders the effective enculturation of the deep meaning and centrality of Christian sacrament and ritual. If the built environment is to augment the accomplishment of the church's mission, it must speak unambiguously.

In the twenty-first century, there must be at least one place, *a sacred place*, where the church can gather and make bold statements about its mission and faith without compromising its fundamentals or being ashamed.[9] Casting the built church environment in the role of an impartial, muted container runs the risk of neutering a significant voice in the communication of both the church's mission and message. This is the result of neglecting or denying sound principles of the function and

9. These comments were inspired by a conversation with Father Kevin Tumback, parish priest of St. Gregory the Great Roman Catholic Church, Calgary, Alberta, Canada, March 18, 2005.

meaning of place established by social science research and by minimizing the practical implications of key theological foundations.

It is my strong contention that churches should thoughtfully and intentionally consider and create sacred places that are not limited to liturgical or functionally efficient spaces. As articulated in chapter 4, social science has demonstrated the capacity of certain types of space to rejuvenate, to assist in attention recovery, and to encourage reflection in the lives of people attempting to cope in an increasingly fragmented world.

Gathering places and ministry or liturgical spaces are consistently resistant to imposed or implied neutrality. Just as Jones believes that no building is ever fully finished,[10] I would contend that church buildings should never be considered devoid of meaning or influence. Attention to detail, ambience, and theological expression should not be considered peripheral or optional in any spaces in the design of sacred places. Even hallways and foyers, designed primarily to facilitate access and egress, will have inherent capabilities to elicit a spiritual response from those lingering there or to spiritually prepare those moving through them. When designed as such, they may become those liminal or transitional places where God is encountered or may make himself known.

The evidence is overwhelming that there is a wide range of possible concepts and designs capable of contributing significantly to the fulfillment of the church's mission. The most appropriate place for churches to commence is not with the structure or design of a church building nor with a deepened understanding and appreciation of the culture in which it is to be located, despite the essential nature of those considerations. Neither architecture nor culture should exercise a hegemonic influence on determining the mission of the church or its expression in architectural form.

Returning to the diagram of the transformative-reflective approach, I make the following concluding observations:

10. Jones, *Hermeneutics of Sacred Architecture*, 263.

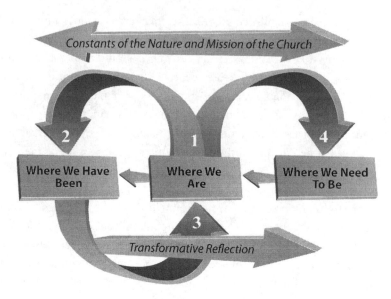

FIGURE 7.4. *Transformative Reflection Model Revisited*

It is in the *"Where We Are," "Where We Have Been"* and *"Where We Are—Revisited"* phases of transformative reflection that we identify, crystallize, and embrace those essential aspects of identity and purpose, the fundamentals of mission. Failure to reflect theologically on each of these critical phases and those essential aspects by moving directly from "Where We Are" to "Where We Need to Be" in our thinking and planning results in potentially suffering from the following liabilities:

1. Too much influence and attention is dedicated to the function, form, and economics of the space, ironically reducing it to a tool for mission at best and a receptacle at worst—a mere facility.

2. The fundamentals of mission, identity and purpose, receive too little attention, resulting in their blurring, minimization, and limitation in a new built environment that is other than *a sacred place.*

Frustration for the church and for mission invariably results when what we are able to do falls short of a previously held *raison d'etre* for a church's existence. Subsequently, the sacred space is the perceived or branded culprit for limited success and blurred identity, but I contend that the built environment is the victim, not the perpetrator. Unfortunate and unnecessary challenges have resulted when churches fail to reflect intentionally on their theology, identity, and purpose, and to consider carefully how those elements of their mission can best be communicated through the buildings they inherit or construct.

It is in these phases of transformative reflection that the perspective of a theologian is particularly necessary and effective. That is why my colleague referred to in the preface was correct. Theologians are vital contributors to any building committee. They can bolster and invigorate essential expressions of identity and purpose within the designed sacred place. Only then does the necessary symbiotic, synergistic, revelatory dynamic between sacred place and mission become a reality.

The pivotal starting point for establishing the role and nature of sacred places in the accomplishment of the church's mission is fundamentally a matter of practical theology. Only when the theological foundations of the church's mission are unambiguously embraced within architectural expressions can philosophical and effectual brilliance blossom in the design and structure of authentic, fruitful sacred places to communicate and impart redemptive truth to the next generation, thereby enhancing the fulfillment of the church's mission in the twenty-first century.

Appendix

Sacred Space Walk: A Guideline for Personal Reflection

THE FOLLOWING IS AN exercise designed to guide individual reflection and stimulate group discussion, particularly within leadership groups of local congregations considering renovation of construction of new ministry spaces. Groups may find this helpful in assessing their own present facilities or when visiting other locations. It is important that this not be a rushed activity, but that adequate time is allowed both for individual reflection and for group discussion afterward. A general suggestion would be about an hour for the whole exercise.

Entering the building:

 A. What kinds of sensations/emotions (if any) did you experience as you left the exterior and moved into the designated space?

Once inside the space:

 A. Upon first entering the gathering space what grabbed or demanded your attention or focus first?

 B. Once you were more or less settled in the auditorium, what (if anything) did this space make you want to do? Why would you say that is?

C. If possible and not disruptive, move to a few different locations within the space and gauge what kinds of reactions or responses you experienced. What became your focus of attention in each location?

D. What (if anything) does this space say to you about: God? The nature of the Church? A person's relation to God? A person's relation to others?

In Summary:

A. If there was one thing you could change about this space that would assist you in worship and reflection, what might that be?

B. List at least one feature of this space that you appreciated or enjoyed?

Bibliography

Addleshaw, G. W. O., and Frederick Etchells. *The Architectural Setting of Anglican Worship*. London: Faber and Faber, 1947.

Agnew, Una. "The World Is Charged with the Grandeur of God." *Feminist Theology* 23 (2000) 37–44.

Alexander, Christopher. *The Timeless Way of Building*. New York: Oxford University Press, 1979.

Anderson, Herbert. "Seeing the Other Whole: A Habitus for Globalization." In *Globalization and Difference: Practical Theology in a World Context*, edited by Paul H. Ballard, 3–17. Cardiff: Cardiff Academic Press, 1999.

Anderson, Kenton C. "The Place for the Pulpit." Unpublished paper.

Anderson, Robert Mapes. "Pentecostal and Charismatic Christianity." In *Encyclopedia of Religion*, edited by Lindsay Jones, 11:229–35. New York: Macmillan, 2004.

Arbuckle, Gerald. *Refounding the Church: Dissent for Leadership*. London: Geoffrey Chapman, 1993.

———. *Earthing the Gospel*. Maryknoll, NY: Orbis 1990.

Arefi, Mahyr. "Non-Place and Placelessness as Narrative of Loss: Rethinking the Notion of Place." *Journal of Urban Design* 4 (1999) 179–93.

Arnold, Talitha and Craig Hoopes. "Sacred Space: Looking at the World Differently." *United Church News*, November 2001. Available at http://www.ucc.org/ucnews/novo1/sacred-space-looking-at-the.html.

Congretation for the Clergy, "Opera Artis: Circular Letter on the Care of the Church's Historical and Artistic Heritage," April 1971. Available at http://www.adoremus.org/Opera_Artis.html.

Auge, Marc. *Non-Places: Introduction to an Anthropology of Supermodernity*. London: Verso, 1995.

Aziz, Barbara Nimri. "Personal Dimensions of the Sacred Journey." *Religious Studies* 23 (1987) 247–61.

Bachelard, Gaston. *The Poetics of Space*. Translated by Maria Jolas. Boston: Beacon 1994.

Bailey, Edward. *Implicit Religion: An Introduction*. London: Middlesex University Press, 1998.

———. *Implicit Religion in Contemporary Society*. Leuven: Peeters, 2001.

Ballard, Paul, and Pam Couture. *Globalization and Difference: Practical Theology in a World Context*. Cardiff: Cardiff Academic Press, 1999.

Banks, Robert and Julia Banks. *The Church Comes Home*. Peabody, MA: Hendrickson 1998.

Barna, George. *Grow Your Church from the Outside: Understanding the Unchurched and How to Reach Them*. Ventura, CA: Regal, 2002.

Barron, Robert. *Heaven in Stone and Glass: Experiencing the Spirituality of the Great Cathedrals*. New York: Crossroad, 2000.

Barth, Karl. "Protestantism and Architecture." *Theology Today* 19 (1962) 272, available at http://theologytoday.ptsem.edu/jul1962/v19-2-criticscorner2.htm.

Baum, Andrew and Stuart Valins. *Architecture and Social Behavior: Pschological Studies of Social Density*. Hillsdale, NJ: Lawrence Erlbaum, 1977.

Beasley-Murray, Stephen. "Development of the Concept of the Holy Since Rudolph Otto." PhD diss., Southern Baptist Theological Seminary, 1980.

Bedell, Ken. "The Christian Church's Struggle to be Faithful." March 3, 1998, available at http://www.religion-online.org/showarticle.asp?title=192.

Beidelman, T. O. *Colonial Evangelism: A Socio-Historical Study of an East African Mission at the Grassroots*. Bloomington, IN: Indiana University Press, 1982.

Benedict, Daniel T. and Craig Kenneth Miller. *Contemporary Worship for the 21st Century: Worship or Evangelism?* Nashville: Discipleship Resources, 1998.

Bennett, Vicki. *Sacred Space and Structural Style: The Embodiment of Socio-Religious Ideology*. Ottawa: University of Ottawa Press, 1997.

Berger, Peter. *The Desecularization of the World*. Grand Rapids: Eerdmans, 1999.

———. *The Heretical Imperative: Contemporary Possibilities of Religious Affirmation*. Garden City, NY: Anchor, 1979.

Berry, Harold J. "The Age-Old New Age Movement, Part II." *Confident Living*, July/August 1989, 10–13.

Bevans, Stephen B. *Models of Contextual Theology*. Maryknoll, NY: Orbis, 1992.

Bibby, Reginald W. *Restless Gods: The Renaissance of Religion in Canada*. Toronto: Novalis, 2002.

———. *Restless Churches: How Canada's Churches Can Contribute to the Emerging Religious Renaissance*. Toronto. Novalis, 2004.

Bieler, Andre. *Architecture in Worship: The Christian Place of Worship*. Edinburgh and London: Oliver & Boyd, 1965.

Bosch, Paul F. "Signs in Worship: The Altar-Table." Available at http://www.worship.ca.

———. "R. C. Church Architecture: More Lutheran Than the Lutherans?" Available at http://www.worship.ca.

Bouyer, Louis. *Liturgy and Architecture*. Notre Dame, IN: University of Notre Dame Press, 1967.

Bower, Peter. "Editorial Introduction." *Reformed Liturgy & Music* 22 (1988) 58.

Bowman, Ray and Eddy Hall. *When Not to Build: An Architect's Unconventional Wisdom for the Growing Church*. Grand Rapids: Baker, 2000.

Boyer, Mark G. *The Liturgical Environment: What the Documents Say*. Collegeville, MN: Liturgical, 1990.

Bradley, Ian. *The Celtic Way*. London: Darton, Longman and Todd, 1993.

Brereton, Joel P. "Sacred Space." In *The Encyclopedia of Religion*, edited by Lindsay Jones, 12:526–35: New York, Macmillan, 2004.

Brown, David. *Cybertrends: Chaos, Power, and Accountability in the Information Age*. London: Penguin, 1998.

Brown, Graham, and Robert Gifford. "Architects Predict Lay Evaluations of Large Contemporary Buildings: Whose Conceptual Properties?" *Journal of Environmental Psychology* 21 (2001) 93–99.

Browning, Don S. *A Fundamental Practical Theology: Descriptive and Strategic Proposals.* Minneapolis: Fortress, 1996.

———. "Integrating the Approaches: A Practical Theology." In *Building Effective Ministry: Theory and Practice in the Local Church,* edited by Carl S. Dudley, 220–37. San Francisco: Harper & Row, 1983.

———. *Practical Theology: The Emerging Field in Theology, Church, and World.* San Francisco: Harper & Row, 1983.

Brueggemann, Walter. *The Land: Place as Gift, Promise, and Challenge in Biblical Faith.* Philadelphia: Fortress, 1977.

Bruggink, Donald J., and Carl H. Droppers. *Christ and Architecture: Building Presbyterian/ Reformed Churches.* Grand Rapids: Eerdmans, 1865.

Buckley, Vincent. *Poetry and the Sacred.* London: Chatto and Windus, 1968.

Burkhart, John E. "Schleiermacher's Vision of Theology." In *Practical Theology: The Emerging Field in Theology, Church, and World,* edited by Don S. Browning, 42–57. San Francisco: Harper & Row, 1983.

Burton-Christie, Douglas. "The Wild and the Sacred." *Anglican Theological Review* 85 (2003) 493–510.

Byrd, Davis. "Designing for Corporate Worship." *Church Administration,* Winter 2002–2003, 54–55.

Calkins, Robert J. "The Cathedral as Text." *Humanities* 16 (1995) 35–39.

Canter, David. *The Psychology of Place.* London: Architectural Press, 1977.

Carey, Ann. "Ever Ancient, Ever New." *Sursum Corda* (1998). Available at http://www .catholicliturgy.com/index.cfm/FuseAction/ArticleText/Index/15/SubIndex/0/ ArticleIndex/29.

Carmichael, David et al. *Sacred Sites, Sacred Places.* London: Routledge, 1994.

Carrigan, Henry Jr. "Seeking God in Cyberspace: Religion and the Internet." *Journal of Religious & Theological Information* 4 (2001) 55–82.

Carroll, Jackson W. and Wade Clark Roof. *Bridging Divided Worlds: Generational Cultures in Congregations.* San Francisco: Jossey-Bass, 2002.

Casey, Edward S. "How to Get from Space to Place in a Fairly Short Stretch of Time." In *Senses of Place,* edited by Steven Feld and Keith H. Basso, 13–52. Sante Fe: School of American Research Press, 1996.

———. *Remembering: A Phenomenological Study.* Bloomington, IN: Indiana University Press, 1987.

Champlin, Joseph M. *Inside a Catholic Church: A Guide to Signs, Symbols and Saints.* Maryknoll, NY: Orbis, 2003.

Chan, Simon. *Spiritual Theology: A Systematic Study of the Christian Life.* Downers Grove, IL: InterVarsity, 1998.

Chang, Amos Ih Tiao. *The Tao of Architecture.* Princeton: Princeton University Press, 1956.

Chapell, Bryan. *Christ-Centered Preaching.* Grand Rapids: Baker, 1994.

Chiat, Marilyn J. *America's Religious Architecture: Sacred Places for Every Community.* New York: Wiley, 1997.

Chidester, David, and Edward T. Linenthal. *American Sacred Space.* Bloomington, IN: Indiana University Press, 1995.

Chinn, Nancy. *Spaces for the Spirit: Adorning the Church*. Chicago: Liturgy Training Publications, 1998.

Cimino, Richard, and Don Lattin. *Shopping for Faith: American Religion in the New Millennium*. San Francisco: Jossey-Bass, 2002.

Clark, William W. "The Recollection of the Past Is the Promise of the Future: Continuity and Contextuality—Saint-Denis, Merogingians, Capetians, and Paris." In *Artistic Integration in Gothic Buildings*, edited by Kathryn L. Brush, Peter Draper, and Virginia Chieffo Raguin, 92–113. Toronto: University of Toronto Press, 2000.

Clines, David J. A. "Space, Holy Places and Suchlike." In *On the Way to the Postmodern: Old Testament Essays, 1967–1998*, 2:542–54. Sheffield: Sheffield Academic Press, 1998.

Clowney, Edmund P. *The Church*. Downers Grove, IL: InterVarsity, 1995.

Cobb, Jennifer J. "A Spiritual Experience of Cyberspace." *Technology in Society* 21 (1999) 393–407.

Cole, Emily. *The Grammar of Architecture*. New York: Bulfinch, 2002.

Collins, Kenneth J. *Exlporing Christian Spirituality: An Ecumenical Reader*. Grand Rapids: Baker, 2000.

Colpe, Carsten. "The Sacred and the Profane." In *Encyclopedia of Religion*, edited by Lindsay Jones, 12:511–526. New York: Macmillan, 2004.

Conn, Harvie M. *Eternal Word and Changing Worlds: Theology, Anthropology, and Mission in Trialogue*. Grand Rapids: Zondervan, 1984.

Connor, Steven. *Postmodernist Culture: An Introduction to Theories of the Contemporary*. Oxford: Blackwell, 1999.

Cory, Catherine A., and David T. Landry. *The Christian Theological Tradition*. 2nd ed. Upper Saddle River, NJ: Prentice Hall, 2003.

Crowfoot, J. W. *Early Churches in Palestine*. London: Oxford University Press, 1941.

Cullmann, Oscar. *Early Christian Worship*. London: SCM, 1973.

Cunningham, Lawrence S., and Keith J. Egan. *Christian Spirituality: Themes from the Tradition*. New York: Paulist, 1996.

Currie, Robert et al. *Churches and Churchgoers: Patterns of Church Growth in the British Isles Since 1700*. Oxford: Clarendon, 1977.

Hay, David, and Kate Hunt. "Understanding the Spirituality of People Who Don't Go to Church." Center for the Study of Human Relations, University of Nottingham, August 2000.

Davies, Horton. *The Worship of the English Puritans*. Morgan, PA: Soli Deo Gloria, 1997.

———. *Worship and Theology in England: From Watts and Wesley to Maurice, 1690–1850*. London: Oxford University Press, 1961.

Davies, J. G. "The Limitations of Liturgical Revision." In *Looking to the Future: Papers Read at an International Symposium on Prospects for Worship, Religious Arachitecture and Socio-Religious Studies*, 7–12. Birmingham: University of Birmingham, 1976.

———. "Architecture and Theology." *The Expository Times* 73 (1962) 231–33.

———. *The Early Christian Church*. London: Weidenfield and Nicolson, 1965.

———. *Early Christian Arcitecture*. London: SCM, 1952.

———. *The Secular Use of Church Buildings*. London: SCM, 1968.

———. *Everyday God*. London: SCM, 1973.

———. *The Origin and Development of Early Christian Church Architecture*. London: SCM, 1952.

———. "Participation in Worship: Its Meaning and Its Relation to Literacy." Research Bulletin of the Institute for the Study of Worship and Religious Architecture. Birmingham: University of Birmingham, 1977.

Davies, W. D. *The Gospel and the Land*. Berkeley: University of California Press, 1974.

Dawe, Donald G. "A Pluralistic Church: Collapsing Tower or Growing Vine." http://www.religion-online.org/showarticle.asp?title=1316.

DeSanctis, Michael, E. *Building from Faith: Advance, Retreat, and Compromise in the Remaking of Catholic Church Architecture*. Collegeville, MN: Liturgical, 2002.

Dean, William. *The American Spiritual Culture and the Invention of Jazz, Football, and the Movies*. New York: Continuum, 2002.

Delarue, Anthony. "Liturgical Architecture: Its Abuse and Restoration." *The Catholic Liturgical Library*. Available at http://www.catholicliturgy.com/index.c.n/Article Text/Index/65/ArticleIndex/42.

Demerath, N. J. III. "The Varieties of Sacred Experience: Finding the Sacred in a Secular Grove." *Journal for the Scientific Study of Religion* 39, no. 1 (March 2000) 1–11.

Dillenberger, John, ed. "Dwelling, Space, and Time." In *Paul Tillich on Art and Architecture*, 81–85. New York: Crossroad, 1987.

Dillistone, F. W. *Traditional Symbols in the Contemporary World*. London: Epworth, 1973.

Dingemans, Gijsbert D. J. "Practical Theology in the Academy: A Contemporary Overview." *Journal of Religion* 76, no. 1 (January 1996) 82–96.

Dix, Dom Gregory. *The Shape of the Liturgy*. London: Dacre Adam and Charles Black, 1970.

Dobson, Ed. *Starting a Seeker Sensitive Service*. Grand Rapids: Zondervan, 1993.

"Doctrine and Covenants Containing Revelations Given to Joseph Smith Jr., the Prophet." Salt Lake City: Deseret, 1978.

Douglas, Mary. *Natual Symbols: Explorations in Cosmology*. New York: Pantheon, 1982.

Downing, Gerald F. "Aesthetic Behaviour in the Jewish Scriptures: A Preliminary Sketch." *Journal for the Study of the Old Testament* 28, no. 2 (2003) 131–47.

Drane, John. *Faith in a Changing Culture: Creating Churches for the Next Century*. London: Marshall Pickering, 1994.

———. *Cultural Change and Biblical Faith*. Carlisle: Paternoster, 2000.

———. *What the New Age Is Still Saying to the Church*. London: Marshall Pickering, 1999.

———. *The McDonaldization of the Church: Spirituality, Creativity, and the Future of the Church*. London: Darton, Longman and Todd, 2000.

Driver, Tom F. *The Magic of Ritual: Our Need for Liberating Rites That Transform Our Lives and Our Communities*. New York: HarperCollins, 1991.

Drummond, Andrew Landale. *The Church Architecture of Protestantism: An Historical and Constructive Study*. Edinburgh: T. & T. Clark, 1934.

Dulles, Avery. "The Gospel and Culture: Narrowing the Gap." *Woodstock Report* 37 (March 1994) 3–10, available at http://woodstock.georgetown.edu/resources/articles/The-Gospel-and-Culture-Narrowing-the-Gap.html.

Dupre, Louis. *Symbols of the Sacred*. Grand Rapids: Eerdmans, 2000.

Durkheim, Emile. *The Elementary Forms of the Religious Life*. London: George Allen & Unwin, 1964.

Eade, John, and Michael J. Sallnow. *Contesting the Sacred: The Anthropology of Christian Pilgrimage*. Urbana, IL: University of Illinois Press, 2000.

Edwall, Pehr et al. *The Ways of Worship: The Report of a Theological Commission of Faith and Order*. London: SCM, 1951.

Eisenhauer, Krannich et al. "Attachments to Special Places on Public Lands: An Analysis of Activities, Reason for Attachments and Community Connections." *Society and Natural Resources* 13, no. 5 (July-August 2000) 421–41.

Eliade, Mircea. *Images and Symbols: Studies in Religious Symbolism*. London: Harvill, 1952.

———. *Patterns in Comparative Religion*. London: Sheed and Ward, 1958.

———. *The Myth of the Eternal Return: Or, Cosmos and History*. Princeton: Princeton University Press, 1954.

———. *Myths, Dreams, and Mysteries: The Encounter Between Contemporary Faiths and Archaic Realities*. New York: Harper & Row, 1960.

———. *The Sacred and the Profane: The Nature of Religion*. New York: Harcourt, Brace & World, 1959.

Erickson, Millard J. *Postmodernizing the Faith: Evangelical Responses to the Challenge of Postmodernism*. Grand Rapids: Baker, 1998.

Estabrook, Carl B. "Ritual, Space, and Authority in Seventeenth-Century English Cathedral Cities." *Journal of Interdisciplinary History* 32, no. 4 (2002) 593–620.

Farley, Edward. "Theology and Practice Outside the Clerical Paradigm." In *Practical Theology: The Emerging Field in Theology, Church, and World*, edited by Don S. Browning, 22–41. San Francisco: Harper & Row, 1983.

Feld, Steven, and Keith H. Basso. *Senses of Place*. Sante Fe, NM: School of American Research Press, 1996.

Ferguson, Marilyn. *The Aquarian Conspiracy*. Los Angeles: J. P. Tarcher, 1980.

Fernandes-Armesto, Felipe, and Derek Wilson. *Reformations: A Radical Interpretation of Christianity and the World, 1500–2000*. New York: Scribner, 1996.

Fernie, Eric C. "Suger's 'Completion' of Saint-Denis." In *Artistic Integration in Gothic Buildings*, edited by Kathryn L. Brush, Peter Draper, and Virginia Chieffo Raguin, 84–91. Toronto: University of Toronto Press, 2000.

Fiddes, Victor. *The Architectural Requirements of Protestant Worship*. Toronto: Ryerson, 1961.

Finney, John. *Finding Faith: How Does it Happen?* London: British and Foreign Bible Society, 1992.

———. *Recovering the Past: Celtic and Roman Mission*. London: Darton, Longman and Todd, 1996.

Finney, Paul Corby. *Seeing beyond the Word: Visual Arts and Calvinist Tradition*. Grand Rapids: Eerdmans, 1999.

Firet, Jacob. *Dynamics in Pastoring*. Grand Rapids: Eerdmans 1986.

Fitzpatrick, Kevin, and Mark LaGory. *Unhealthy Places: The Ecology of Risk in the Urban Landscape*. New York: Routledge, 2000.

Flanagan, Kieran. *The Enchantment of Sociology: A Study of Theology and Culture*. London: Macmillan, 1996.

Flory, Richard W., and Donald E. Miller. "Expressive Communalism: The Embodied Spirituality of the Post-Boomer Generations." *Congregation* 30, no. 4 (2004) 31–35.

Forrester, Duncan et al. *Encounter with God*. Edinburgh: T. & T. Clark, 1998.

Fowler, James W. *Faith Development and Pastoral Care*. Philadelphia: Fortress, 1987.

———. "Practical Theology and Theological Education: Some Models and Questions." *Theology Today* 42, no. 1 (2004) 43–58.

———. "Practical Theology and the Shaping of Christian Lives." In *Practical Theology: The Emerging Field in Theology, Church, and World*, edited by Don S. Browning, 148–66. San Francisco: Harper & Row, 1983.

Freedberg, David. *The Power of Images: Studies in the History and Theory of Response*. Chicago: University of Chicago Press, 1989.

Fried, Marc. "Continuities and Discontinuities of Place." *Journal of Environmental Psychology* 20 (2000) 193–205.

Fulgham, Robert. *From Beginning to End: The Rituals of Our Lives.* New York: Ivy, 1995.

Fuller, Robert C. *Spiritual but Not Religious: Understanding Unchurched America.* New York: Oxford University Press, 2001.

Gadamer, Hans-Georg. *Truth and Method.* Translated by Joel Weinsheimer and Donald G. Marshall. 2nd rev. ed. New York: Continuum, 2003.

Gallagher, Michael Paul. *Clashing Symbols: An Introduction to Faith and Culture.* London: Darton, Longman and Todd, 1997.

Gallen, John. "Environment as Ritual." *Reformed Liturgy & Music* 23, no. 3 (Summer 1989) 121–27.

Gallup, George Jr., and Timothy Jones. *The Next American Spirituality: Finding God in the Twenty-First Century.* Colorado Springs: Victor, 2000.

Gallup, George Jr., and David Poling. *The Search for America's Faith.* Nashville: Abingdon, 1980.

Garling, Tommy. "Conceptualizations of Human Environments." *Journal of Environmental Psychology* 18 (1998) 69–73.

Geertz, Clifford. *The Interpretation of Cultures.* London: Fontana, 1993.

Gehring, Roger W. *House Church and Mission: The Importance of Household Structures in Early Christianity.* Peabody, MA: Hendrickson, 2004.

Giles, Kevin. *What on Earth Is the Church? An Exploration in New Testament Theology.* Downers Grove, IL: InterVarsity, 1995.

Giles, Richard. *Re-Pitching the Tent: Re-Ordering the Church Building for Worship and Mission.* Norwich: Canterbury, 1990.

Gill, Robin. *The Myth of the Empty Church.* London: SPCK, 1993.

Goetz, Ronald. "Protestant Houses of God: A Contradiction of Terms?" *Christian Century*, March 20–27, 1985, 294–99.

Gollink, James. "Is Implicit Religion Spirituality in Disguise?" *Implicit Religion* 6 (2003) 146–60.

Gorringe, T. J. *A Theology of the Built Environment: Justice, Empowerment.* Cambridge: Cambridge University Press, 2002.

Gottdiener, Mark. "Themed Environments of Everyday Life: Restaurants and Malls." In *The Postmodern Presence: Reading on Postmodernism in American Culture and Society,* edited by Arthur Asa Berger, 74–87. London: Alta Mira, 1998.

Gottdiener, Mark. *Postmodern Semiotics: Material Culture and the Forms of Postmodern Life.* Oxford: Basil Blackwell, 1995.

Graham, Elaine. "From Space to Woman Space." *Feminist Theology* 9 (1995) 11–34.

Greschat, Martin. *Martin Bucer: A Reformer and His Times.* London: Westminster/John Knox, 2004.

Grimes, Ronald L. "Jonathan Z. Smith's Theory of Ritual Space." *Religionswissenschaft* 29 (1999) 261–73.

Groothuis, Doug. "Christian Scholarship and the Philosophical Analysis of Cyberspace Technologies." *Journal of the Evangelical Society* 41 (1998) 631–40.

Guiness, Os. *Dining with the Devil: The Megachurch Movement Flirts with Modernity.* Grand Rapids: Baker, 1993.

Gustafson, Per. "Meanings of Place: Everyday Experience and Theoretical Conceptualizations." *Journal of Environmental Psychology* 21 (2001) 5–16.

Hageman, Howard G. *Pulpit and Table: Some Chapters in the History of Worship in the Reformed Churches.* London: SCM, 1962.

Hahn, Ferdinand. *The Worship of the Early Church*. Philadelphia: Fortress, 1973.

Hahnenberg, Edward P. "Forum: Who Is at Work? Ecclesiology and Domus Dei." *Worship* 74, no. 4 (July 2000) 365–70.

Hakken, David. *Cyborgs @ Cyberspace*. New York: Routledge, 1999.

Hall, Edward T. *The Hidden Dimension*. Garden City, NY: Doubleday, 1969.

Hall, Douglas John. "The Church: Beyond the Christian Religion." Address given to Covenant Conference, Network of Presbyterians, Atlanta, November 6, 1999, available at http://www.religion-online.org/showarticle.asp?title=529.

Hall, Coffey et al. "Self, Space and Place." *British Journal of Sociology of Education* 20 (1999) 501–13.

Hamma, Robert M. *Landscapes of the Soul: A Spirituality of Place*. Notre Dame: Ave Maria, 1999.

Hammond, Peter. *Liturgy and Architecture*. London: Barrie and Rockliff, 1960.

Harries, Karsten. *The Ethical Function of Architecture*. Cambridge, MA: MIT Press, 2000.

Hartzfeld, David F., and Charles Nienkirchen. *The Birth of a Vision: Essays on the Ministry and Thought of Albert B. Simpson, Founder of the Christian and Missionary Alliance*. Beaverlodge, AB: Buena, 1986.

Hauerwas, Stanley. *In Good Company: The Church as Polis*. Notre Dame: University of Notre Dame Press, 1995.

Hay, Robert. "Sense of Place in Developmental Context." *Journal of Environmental Psychology* 18 (1998) 5–29.

Hayes, Dawn Marie. "Mundane Uses of Sacred Places in the Central and Later Middle Ages." *Comitatus Journal of Medieval and Renaissance Studies* 30 (1999) 11–36.

Hebert, A. G. *Liturgy and Society: The Function of the Church in the Modern World*. London: Faber and Faber, 1936.

Helminiak, Daniel A. *The Human Core of Spirituality: Mind as Psyche and Spirit*. Albany, NY: State University of New York Press, 1996.

Herrick, James A. *The Making of the New Spirituality: The Eclipse of the Western Religious Tradition*. Downers Grove, IL: InterVarsity, 2003.

Herzog, Thomas R. et al. "Reflection and Attentional Recovery as Distinctive Benefits of Restorative Environments." *Journal of Environmental Psychology* 17 (1997) 165–70.

Hine, Virginia H. "Self-Generated Ritual: Trend or Fad?" *Worship* 55 (1981) 404–19.

Hitchcock, Helen Hull. "Cry Sanctuary! Will Renovated Churches Have Room for Jesus?" *Adoremus Bulletin* 2, no. 3 (May–June 1996), available at http://www.adoremus.org/5-6_96CrySanc.html.

Hoffman, Lawrence A. *Sacred Places and the Pilgrimage of Life: Meetinghouse Essays*. Chicago: Liturgy Training, 1991.

Hollenweger, Walter J. "Intercultural Theology." *Theology Today* 43, no. 1 (1986) 28–35, available at http://theologytoday.ptsem.edu/apr1986/v43-1-article3.htm.

Holmes, David. *Virtual Politics: Identity and Community in Cyberspace*. London: Sage, 1997.

Hooke, S. H. *The Kingdom of God in the Experience of Jesus*. London: Gerald Duckworth, 1949.

Horton, Michael S. "Why Space Matters." *Modern Reformation* 7, no. 3 (May–June 1998), available at http://www.modernreformation.org/default.php?page=articledisplay&var1=ArtRead&var2=578&var3=authorbio&var4=AutRes&var5=1

Hull, Lam et al. "Place Identity: Symbols of Self in the Urban Fabric." *Landscape and Urban Planning* 28, nos. 2–3 (April 1994) 109–20.

Hunsberger, George R. "Evangelical Conversion: Toward a Missional Ecclesiology." In *Evangelical Ecclesiology: Reality or Illusion?*, edited by John G. Stackhouse Jr., 105–32. Grand Rapids: Baker, 2003.

Hunt, Stephen J. *Alternative Religions: A Sociological Introduction*. Aldershot: Ashgate, 2003.

Hunter, George G. III. *How to Reach Secular People*. Nashville: Abingdon, 1992.

Hunter, Kent R. *The Jesus Enterprise: Engaging Culture to Reach the Unchurched*. Nashville: Abingdon, 2004.

Hurley, Richard. "The Eucharist Room at Carlow Liturgy Center: The Search for Meaning." *Worship* 70, no. 3 (2001) 238–51.

Hurtado, Larry W. *At the Origins of Christian Worship*. Grand Rapids: Eerdmans, 1999.

Hybels, Lynne, and Bill Hybels. *Rediscovering Church: The Story and Vision of Willow Creek Community Church*. Grand Rapids: Zondervan, 1995.

Inge, John. *A Christian Theology of Place*. Aldershot: Ashgate, 2003.

Inoue, Nobutaka. "From Religious Conformity to Innovation: New Ideas of Religious Journey and Holy Places." *Social Compass* 47, no. 1 (2000) 21–32.

Iogna-Prat, Dominique. *Order and Exclusion: Cluny and Christendom Face Heresy, Judaism, and Islam (1000–1150)*. Translated by Graham Robert Edwards. Ithaca, NY: Cornell University Press, 2002.

Jamieson, Alan. *A Churchless Faith: Faith Journey beyond the Churches*. London: SPCK, 2002.

Jantzen, Hans. *High Gothic: The Classic Cathedrals of Chartres, Reims, Amiens*. Hamburg: Constable, 1962.

Jenks, Brother Christopher Stephen. "The Akron Plan Sunday School." *American Religious Buildings*. December 1995, available at http://www.sacredplaces.org/PSP-Info-ClearingHouse/articles/American%20Religious%20Buildings.htm.

Jones, Lindsay. *The Hermeneutics of Sacred Architecture: Experience, Interpretation, Comparison*. 2 vols. Cambridge, MA: Harvard University Press, 2000.

Jones, Noragh. "A Spirituality of Place Based on the Seven Pillars of Wisdom: A Response to Una Agnew's 'The Word Is Charged by the Grandeur of God.'" *Feminist Theology* 23 (2000) 45–50.

Jones, Steven. *Virtual Culture*. London: Sage, 1997.

Kahera, Akel Ismail. "Gardens of the Righteous: Sacres Space in Judaism, Christianity, and Islam." *Cross Currents* 52, no. 3 (2002) 328–41.

Kant, Immanuel. *Critique of Judgment*. Oxford: Oxford University Press, 1952.

Kerr, Hugh T. "Discerning the Presence." *Theology Today* 44, no. 3 (1987) 305–8.

Kerr, John H., and Paul Tacon. "Psychological Responses to Different Types of Locations and Activities." *Journal of Environmental Psychology* 19 (1999) 287–94.

Kilde, Jeanne Halgren. *When Church Became Theatre: The Transformation of Evangelical Architecture and Worship in Nineteenth-Century America*. Oxford: Oxford University Press, 2002.

Kimball, Dan. *The Emerging Church: Vintage Christianity for New Generations*. Grand Rapids: Zondervan, 2003.

Klein, Patricia S. *Worship Without Words: The Signs and Symbols of Our Faith*. Brewster, MA: Paraclete, 2000.

Knez, I. "Effects of Indoor Lighting on Mood and Cognition." *Journal of Environmental Psychology* 15 (1995) 39–51.

Koch, Guntram. *Early Christian Art and Architecture: An Introduction*. London: SCM, 1996.

Korpela, Kalevi, and Terry Hartig. "Restorative Qualities of Favorite Places." *Journal of Environmental Psychology* 16 (1996) 221–33.

Kraft, Charles. "The Church in Culture: A Dynamic Equivalence Model." In *Down to Earth: Studies in Christianity and Culture,* edited by John Stott and Robert Coote, 211–30. Grand Rapids: Eerdmans, 1980.

———. *Christianity in Culture: A Study in Dynamic Biblical Theologizing in Cross-Cultural Perspective.* Maryknoll, NY: Orbis, 1979.

Krautheimer, Richard. *Early Christian and Byzantine Architecture.* Harmondsworth: Penguin, 1979.

Krell, David Farrell. *Martin Heidegger: Basic Writings.* London: Harper & Row, 1977.

Kunin, Seth. *God's Place in the World: Sacred Space and Sacred Place in Judaism.* London: Cassell, 1998.

———. "Judaism." In *Sacred Place,* edited by Jean Holm and John Bowker, 115–48. London: Pinter, 1994.

Lane, Belden C. "Fantasy and Geography of Faith." *Theology Today* 50, no. 3 (1993) 397–408.

———. *Landscapes of the Sacred: Geography and Narrative in American Spirituality.* Baltimore: John Hopkins University Press, 2001.

———. "The Spirituality of the Evangelical Revival." *Theology Today* 43, no. 2 (1986) 169–77.

Lawton, Jim. "A Walk-Through." *Call to Worship* 36, no. 3 (2002–2003) 29–34.

Lefebvre, Henri. *The Production of Space.* Translated by Donald Nicholoson-Smith. Oxford: Blackwell, 2003.

Leithart, Peter J. "Synagogue or Temple? Models for Christian Worship." *Westminster Theological Journal* 63 (2002) 119–33.

———. "Making and Mis-Making: Poesis in Exodus 25–40." *International Journal of Systematic Theology* 2, no. 3 (November 2000) 307–18.

Long, Thomas G. *Beyond the Worship Wars: Building Vital and Faithful Worship.* Bethesda, MD: Alban Institute, 2001.

Loveland, Anne C., and Otis B. Wheeler. *From Meetinghouse to Megachurch: A Material and Cultural History.* Columbia, MO: University of Missouri Press, 2003.

Lundquist, John M. *The Temple: Meeting Place of Heaven and Earth.* London: Thames and Hudson, 1993.

Luscombe, Belinda. "Building Momentum." *Time,* September 8, 2003, 66–68.

Luther, Martin, "The Misuse of the Mass." *Luther's Works.* Vol. 36, *Word and Sacrament II.* Philadelphia: Fortress, 1975.

———. "Sermon at the Dedication of the Castle Church in Torgau, 1544." *Luther's Works.* Vol. 51, *Sermons I.* Philadelphia: Fortress 1973.

Luzbetak, Louis J. *The Church and Cultures: New Perspectives in Missiological Anthropology.* Maryknoll, NY: Orbis, 1990.

Lyndon, Donlyn, and Charles W. Moore. *Chambers for a Memory Palace.* Cambridge, MA: MIT Press, 1994.

MacDonald, Fraser. "Towards a Spatial Theory of Worship: Some Observations from Presbyterian Scotland." *Social & Cultural Geography* 3, no. 1 (2002) 61–80.

———. "Producing Space in Presbyterian Scotland: Highland Worship in Theory and Practice." Research paper, Arkleton Centre for Rural Development Research, Aberdeen, 2000.

MacDonald, Gordon. *Forging a Real World Faith.* Guildford: Highland, 1993.

Maguire, Robert. "Continuity and Modernity in the Holy Place." *Architectural History: Journal for the Society of Architectural History of Great Britain* 39 (1996) 1–18.

Malina, Bruce. *Christian Origins and Cultural Anthropology*. Atlanta: John Knox, 1986.

Mann, A. T. *Sacred Architecture*. Dorset: Element, 1993.

Marcantonio, Dino. "Architecture and the Scandal of Particularity." Paper presented at the Theology and Built Environment Colloquium, Calvin College, Grand Rapids, Michigan, May 2004.

Marshall, I. Howard. "Culture and the New Testament." In *Down to Earth: Studies in Christianity and Culture*, edited by John Stott and Robert Coote, 21–46. Grand Rapids: Eerdmans, 1980.

Martin, Ralph. *Worship in the Early Church*. London: Marshall, Morgan and Scott, 1974.

Martinez, German. "Catholic Liturgical Reform." *Theology Today* 43, no. 1 (1986) 52–62.

Massey, Doreen, and Pat Jess. *A Place in the World? Places, Culture, and Globalization*. Oxford: Open University, 1995.

Mauck, Marchita B. *Places for Worship: A Guide to Building and Renovating*. Collegeville, MN: Liturgical, 1995.

———. *Shaping a House for the Church*. Chicago: Liturgy Training, 1990.

McAffe Brown, Robert. "True and False Witness: Architecture and the Church." *Theology Today* 23, no. 4 (1967) 521–37.

McGrath, Alister. "Faces, Places, and Spaces: Visualization and Spatialization in Christian Spirituality." In *Christian Spirituality: An Introduction*, 110–34. Oxford: Blackwell, 1999.

McKiver, Kenneth. *40-Year History of First Alliance Church: The Christian and Missionary Alliance Calgary, Alberta, 1938–1978*. Calgary: 1978.

McLaren, Brian D. *The Church on the Other Side: Doing Ministry in the Postmodern Matrix*. Grand Rapids: Zondervan, 2000.

McLuhan, T. C. *Cathedrals of the Spirit: The Message of Sacred Places*. London: Thorsons, 1996.

McMann, Jean. *Altars and Icons: Sacred Spaces in Everyday Life*. San Francisco: Chronicle, 1998.

McManus, Erwin Raphael. *An Unstoppable Force: Daring to Become the Church God Had in Mind*. Loveland, CO: Group, 2001.

McNeal, Reggie. *Missional Renaissance: Changing the Scorecard of the Church*. San Francisco: Jossey-Bass, 2009.

McRoberts, Duncan. "Tectonics and the Chapel of St. Ignatius at Seattle University." *The Catholic Liturgical Library* (1998), available at http://www.catholicliturgy.com/index.cfm/FuseAction/ArticleText/Index/15/SubIndex/0/ArticleIndex/26.

Mead, Loren B. *The Once and Future Church: Reinventing the Congregation for a New Mission*. Washington, DC: Alban Institute, 1994.

Meeks, Wayne. *The First Urban Christians: The Social World of the Apostle Paul*. New Haven: Yale University Press, 1983.

Menzies, Henry. "Church Renovation: An Architect's Perspective." *The Catholic Liturgical Library* (1997), available at http://www.catholicliturgy.com/index.cfm/FuseAction/ArticleText/ArticleIndex/44.

Meyrowitz, Joshua. *No Sense of Place*. New York: Oxford University Press: 1985.

Miles, Margaret R. *Image as Insight: Visual Understanding in Western Christianity and Secular Culture*. Boston: Beacon, 1985.

Miller, Samuel H. "Sacred Space in a Secular Age." *Theology Today* 19, no. 2 (1962) 212–23.

Minear, Paul S. "The Holy and the Sacred." *Theology Today* 47, no. 1 (1990) 5–12.

Mitchell, William J. *E-Topia*. Cambridge, MA: MIT Press, 1999.

Mol, Hans. *Identity and the Sacred: A Sketch for a New Social-Scientific Theory of Religion*. Oxford: Basil-Blackwell, 1976.

Moore, Robert L. "Ministry, Sacred Space, and Theological Education: The Legacy of Victor Turner." *Theological Education* 21, no. 1 (1984) 87–100.

Morgan, David. "Visual Religion." *Religion* 30 (2000) 41–53.

Morgenthaler, Sally. *Worship Evangelism: Inviting Unbelievers into the Presence of God*. Grand Rapids: Zondervan, 1995.

Morinis, Alan. *Sacred Journeys: The Anthropology of Pilgrimage*. Westport, CT: Greenwood, 1992.

Moynagh, Michael. "How Is Emerging Church Different?" November 2004, available at http://www.emergingchurch.info/reflection/michaelmoynagh/index.htm.

Newbigin, Lesslie. *The Gospel in a Pluralist Society*. Grand Rapids: Eerdmans, 1989.

———. *Foolishness to the Greeks*. Grand Rapids: Eerdmans, 1986.

———. *Signs amid the Rubble: The Purposes of God in Human History*. Grand Rapids: Eerdmans, 2003.

Nichols, J. Randall. "Worship as Anti-Structure: The Contribution of Victor Turner." *Theology Today* 41, no. 4 (1985) 401–9.

Nichols, James H., and Leonard J. Trinterud. "The Architectural Setting for Reformed Worship." Chicago: Presbytery of Chicago, 1960.

Nida, Eugene A., and C. R. Taber. *The Theory and Practice of Translation*. Leiden: Brill, 1969.

Niebuhr, H. Richard. *Christ and Culture*. New York: Harper & Row, 1951.

Nunes, Mark. "Baudrillard in Cyberspace: Internet, Virtuality, and Postmodernity." *Style* 29 (1995) 314–27.

Oosterhoff, F. G. *Postmodernism: A Christian Appraisal*. Winnipeg: Premier, 1999.

Ostwalt, Conrad. *Secular Steeples: Popular Culture and the Religious Imagination*. Harrisburg, PA: Trinity, 2003.

Otto, Rudolph. *The Idea of the Holy*. Translated by John W. Harvey. Oxford: Oxford University Press, 1958.

Paden, William Edward. "The Category of the Sacred in the History of Religious Theory." PhD diss., Claremount Graduate School, 1967.

Packer, J. I. "The Gospel: Its Content and Communication—A Theological Perspective." In *Down to Earth: Studies in Christianity and Culture*, edited by John Stott and Robert Coote, 97–114. Grand Rapids: Eerdmans, 1980.

Pahl, Jon. *Shopping Malls and Other Sacred Spaces: Putting God in His Place*. Grand Rapids: Brazos, 2003.

Pamenter, Bev. *A Centennial Celebration 1895–1995: St. Mary's Cochrane Church*. Cochrane, AB: St. Mary's Parish, 1995.

Panofsky, Erwin. *Gothic Architecture and Scholasticism: An Inquiry into the Analogy of the Arts, Philosophy, and Religion in the Middle Ages*. New York: New American Library, 1976.

———. *Abbot Suger on the Abbey Church of St.-Denis and Its Art Treasures*. Princeton: Princeton University Press, 1979.

Parker Pearson, Michael, and Colin Richards. *Architecture and Order: Approaches to Social Space*. London: Routledge, 1997.

Pattison, Stephen, and James Woodward. "A Vision of Pastoral Theology: In Search of Words That Resurrect the Dead." In *Spiritual Dimensions of Pastoral Care: Practical Theology in a Multidisciplinary Context*, edited by David Willows and John Swinton, 36–52. London and Philadelphia: Jessica Kingsley, 2000.

Peck, Scott. *In Search of Stones: A Pilgrimage of Faith, Reason and Discovery*. London: Simon & Schuster, 1995.

Peterson, David. *Engaging with God: A Biblical Theology of Worship*. Grand Rapids: Eerdmans, 1992.

Peterson, Eugene H. *Leap over a Wall: Earthy Spirituality for Everyday Christians*. New York: Harper Collins, 1998.

Potter, Taylor M. "The Building as Witness." *Theology Today* 23, no. 4 (1967) 554–59.

Pratt, Douglas. "The Dance of Dialogue: Ecumenical Inter-Religious Engagement." *Ecumenical Review* 51 (1999) 274–87.

Pred, A. "Structuration and Place: On the Becoming of Sense of Place and Structure of Feeling." *Journal for the Theory of Social Behaviour* 13, no. 1 (1983) 45–68.

Preziosi, Donald. *Architecture, Language, and Meaning: The Origins of the Built World and Its Semiotic Organizations*. The Hague: Mouton, 1979.

Price, Joseph L. "The Super Bowl as Religious Festival." *Christian Century*, February 22, 1984, available at http://www.religion-online.org/showarticle.asp?title=1375.

Quasten, Johannes, and Joseph C. Plumpe, eds. *The Didache*. Ancient Christian Writers 6. 1–26. Mahwah, NJ: Newman, 1948.

Quinn, Patrick J. "Ritual and the Definition of Space." In *The Roots of Ritual*, edited by James D. Shaughnessy, 103–19. Grand Rapids: Eerdmans, 1973.

Rae, Murray. "A Place to Dwell." Paper presented at the Theology and Built Environment Colloquium, Calvin College, Grand Rapids, Michigan, May 2004.

Raglan, Lord. *The Temple and the House*. London: Routledge, 1964.

Rahner, Karl, "The Development of Dogma." In *Theological Investigations*, vol. 1, 39–77. London: Darton, Longman & Todd, 1974.

Rapoport, Amos. "Sacred Places, Sacred Occasions, and Sacred Environments." *Architectural Design* 52 (1982) 75–82.

———. *The Meaning of the Built Environment: A Non-Verbal Communication Approach*. Tucson: University of Arizona Press, 1990.

Raskin, Eugene. *Architecture and People*. Englewood Cliffs, NJ: Prentice Hall, 1974.

Redman, Robb. *The Great Worship Awakening: Singing a New Song in the Postmodern Church*. San Francisco: Jossey-Bass, 2002.

Regev, Eyal. "Priestly Dynamic Holiness and Deuteronomic Static Holiness." *Vetus Testamentum* 51, no. 2 (2001) 243–61.

Relph, Edward. *Place and Placelessness*. London: Routledge, 1976.

Rheingold, Howard. *The Virtual Community: Homesteading on the Electronic Frontier*. New York: Addison-Wesley, 1993.

Riddell, Michael. *Threshold of the Future: Reforming the Church in the Post-Christian West*. London: SPCK, 1999.

Ritterfeld, Ute, and Gerald C. Cupchik. "Perceptions of Interior Spaces." *Journal of Environmental Psychology* 16 (1996) 349–60.

Ritzer, George. *The McDonaldization of Society*. London: Pine Forge, 2000.

Roberts, David E. "The Christian Gospel and the American Way of Life." *Christianity and Crisis*, March 1952, available at http//: http://www.religion-online.org/showarticle. asp?title=493.

Rolheiser, Ronald. *The Holy Longing: The Search for a Christian Spirituality*. New York: Doubleday, 1999.

Romain, Jonathan. *Your God Shall Be My God: Religious Conversion in Britain Today*. London: SCM, 2000.

Rose, Michael S. "Did *Sacrosantum Concilium* Promote the Reform of Church Architecture?" March 2000, available at http://www.catholic.net/rcc/Periodicals/Dossier/2000-10/article4.html.

———. "Shape and Style of the Church Tomorrow." *Theology Today* 25, no. 1 (1968) 64–80.

Rose, Michael S. *Ugly as Sin: Why They Changed Our Churches from Sacred Places to Meeting Spaces—and How We Can Change Them Back Again*. Manchester, NH: Sophia Institute, 2001.

Ross, Kristin. "Henri Lefebvre's *The Production of Space*." Available at http://www.notbored.org/space.html.

Rush, Robert T. "From Pearl Merchant to Treasure Hunter: The Missionary Yesterday and Today." *Catholic Mind* (1978) 6–10.

Rutler, Fr. George William. "Ten Myths of Contemporary Church Architecture." *The Catholic Liturgical Liturgy* (1998). Available at http://www.catholicliturgy.com/index.cfm/FuseAction/ArticleText/Index/15/SubIndex/0/ArticleIndex/24.

Rykwert, Joseph. *Church Building*. London: Burns and Oates, 1966.

Sack, Robert David. *Conceptions of Space in Social Thought: A Geographic Perspective*. London: Macmillan, 1980.

Sagovsky, Nicholas. *Liturgy and Symbolism*. London: Grove, 1978.

Saliba, John. *Christian Responses to the New Age Movement*. London: Geoffrey Chapman, 1999.

Sample, Tex. *The Spectacle of Worship in a Wired World: Electronic Culture and the Gathered People of God*. Nashville: Abingdon, 1998.

Sargeant, Kimon Howland. *Seeker Churches: Promoting Traditional Religion in a Nontraditional Way*. New Brunswick: Rutgers University Press, 2000.

Schaper, Donna. "Sacred Spaces." *Cross Currents* 50 (2000) 221–24.

Schloeder, Steven J. *Architecture in Communion: Implementing the Second Vatican Council through Liturgy and Architecture*. San Francisco: Ignatius, 1998.

Schmidt, Francis. *How the Temple Thinks: Identity and Social Cohesion in Ancient Judaism*. Sheffield: Sheffield Academic Press, 2001.

Schreiter, Robert J. *Constructing Local Theologies*. Maryknoll, NY: Orbis, 1985.

Schultze, Quentin J. *High-Tech Worship? Using Presentational Technologies Wisely*. Grand Rapids: Baker, 2004.

Seasoltz, R. Kevin. "Transcendence and Immanence in Sacred Art and Architecture Transcendence and Immanence in Sacred Architecture." *Worship* 75, no. 5 (2001) 403–31.

Segal, Robert A. "Weber and Geertz on the Meaning of Religion." *Religion* 29 (1999) 61–71.

Segler, Frankin M. *Christian Worship: Its Theology and Practice*. Nashville: Broadman, 1967.

Sheldrake, Philip. *Spaces for the Sacred: Place, Memory and Identity*. London: SCM, 2001.

———. *Life Between Two Worlds: Place and Journey in Celtic Spirituality*. London: Darton, Longman and Todd, 1995.

Sherrard, Philip. *The Sacred in Life and Art*. Louisville: Golgonooza, 1995.

Sherry Jr., John F. "Place, Technology, and Representation." *Journal of Consumer Research* 27 (September 2000) 273–78.

Shorter, Aylward. *Toward a Theology of Inculturation.* London: Geoffrey Chapman, 1988.

Silf, Margaret. *Sacred Spaces: Stations on a Celtic Way.* Oxford: Lion, 2001.

Simcoe, Mary Ann. *The Liturgy Documents: A Parish Resource.* Chicago: Liturgy Training, 1985.

Simpson, A. B. *Year Book of the Christian Alliance and the International Missionary Alliance 1893.* New York: Christian Alliance, 1894.

Simson, Wolfgang. *Houses That Change the World: The Return of the House Churches.* Carlisle: Paternoster, 2001.

Siry, Joseph M. *Unity Temple: Frank Lloyd Wright and Architecture of Liberal Religion.* Cambridge: Cambridge University Press, 1996.

Sitter, Joseph. "Faith and Form." *Theology Today* 19, no. 2 (1962) 207–11.

Siwek, Peter C. "An Architect Looks at Prayer Spaces." *Christianity and the Arts* 7, no. 2 (2000) 12–16.

Smith, Jonathan Z. *To Take Place: Toward a Theory of Ritual.* Chicago: University of Chicago Press, 1992.

———. *Map Is Not Territory.* Chicago: University of Chicago Press, 1993.

Smith, Thomas Gordon. "An Architecture to Honor the Church's Vision." *Adoremus Bulletin* 3, no. 8 (1997), available at http://www.Adoremus.org/1197-Smith.html.

Smithe, Peter F. *Third Millennium Churches.* London: Galliard, 1972.

Soja, Edward W. *Thirdspace: Journeys to Los Angeles and Other Real and Imagined Places.* Oxford: Blackwell, 1996.

Sommer, Robert. *Personal Space: The Behavioral Basis of Design.* Englewood Cliffs, NJ: Prentice Hall, 1969.

———. "Shopping at the Co-op." *Journal of Environmental Psychology* 18 (1998) 45–53.

Sopher, David E. *Geography of Religions.* Englewood Cliffs, NJ: Prentice Hall, 1967.

Sprunger, Keith L. "Puritan Architecture and Worship in a Dutch Context." *Church History* 66, no. 1 (1997) 36–53.

St. Augustine. "Tractate 80: On John 15:1–2." In *The Fathers of the Church*, vol. 90, *St. Augustine: Tractates on the Gospel of John 55–111*, trans. John W. Rettig, 115–23. Washington, DC: Catholic University of America Press, 1994.

Stackhouse, John G. Jr. *Evangelical Ecclesiology: Reality or Illusion?* Grand Rapids: Baker Academic, 2003.

Stackhouse, Max L. *Apologia: Contextualization, Globalization, and Mission in Theological Education.* Grand Rapids: Eerdmans, 1988.

Stafford, Tim. "God Is in the Blueprints." *Christianity Today*, September 7, 1998, 77–82.

Stark, Rodney. *The Rise of Christianity: A Sociologist Reconsiders History.* Princeton: Princeton University Press, 1996.

Stefanovic, Ingrid Leman. "Phenomenological Encounters with Place: Cavtat to Square One." *Journal of Environmental Psychology* 18 (1998) 31–44.

Stephens, Mitchell. *The Rise of the Image, the Fall of the Word.* Oxford: Oxford University Press, 1998.

Stewart, Cecil. *Simpson's History of Architectural Development: Early Christian, Byzantine and Romanesque Architecture.* 2 vols. London: Longmans, Green and Company, 1954.

Stipe, Claude E. "Anthropologists Versus Missionaries: The Influence of Presuppositions." *Current Anthropology* 21, no. 2 (1980) 165–79.

Stoesz, Samuel J. *Understanding My Church*. Camp Hill, PA: Christian Publications, 1983.

Stokowski, Patricia A. "Languages of Place and Discourse of Power: Constructing New Senses of Place." *Journal of Leisure Research* 34, no. 4 (2002) 368–83.

Storey, John. *Cultural Theory and Popular Culture: An Introduction*. Essex: Pearson Education, 2001.

Strinati, Dominic. *An Introduction to Theories of Popular Culture*. London: Routledge, 1995.

Stroik, Duncan. "The Roots of Modernist Church Architecture." *Adoremus Bulletin* 3, no. 7 (1997), available at http://www.adoremus.org/1097-Stroik.html.

———. "Is There a Christian Architecture: An Interview with Daniel Lee." *Re:Generation Quarterly* 4 (1998) 20.

Studsill, Randall. "Eliade, Phenomenology, and the Sacred." *Religious Studies* 36 (2000) 177–94.

Swanson, Tod D. "To Prepare a Place: Johannine Christianity and the Collapse of Ethnic Territory." *Journal of the American Academy of Religion* 62, no. 2 (1994) 241–63.

Swatos, William H. Jr. "Revisiting the Sacred." *Implicit Religion* 2, no. 1 (1999) 33–38.

Sweet, Leonard I. "From Catacomb to Basilica: The Dilemma of Oldline Protestantism." *Christian Century*, November 2, 1988, available at http://www.religion-online.org/showarticle.asp?title=961.

Swinton, John. *Spirituality and Mental Health Care: Rediscovering a "Forgotten" Dimension*. London: Jessica Kingsley, 2001.

———. *From Bedlam to Shalom: Towards a Practical Theology of Human Nature, Interpersonal Relationships, and Mental Health*. New York: Peter Lang, 2000.

Taber, Charles R. *To Understand the Word, to Save the World: The Interface Between Missiology and the Social Sciences*. Harrisburg, PA: Trinity, 2000.

Tanner, Kathryn. *Theories of Culture: A New Agenda for Theology*. Minneapolis: Fortress, 1997.

Tatusko, Andrew M. "Rootlessness and Simulacra: The Loss and Recovery of Foundations." *Quodlibet Journal* 2, no. 4 (2000), available at http://www.quodlibet.net/articles/tatusko-culture.shtml.

Thiemann, Ronald F. *Constructing a Public Theology*. Louisville: Westminster John Knox, 1991.

Tillich, Paul. *Theology of Culture*. New York: Oxford University Press, 1959.

Thumma, Scott. "Exploring the Megachurch Phenomena: Their Characteristics and Cultural Context," 1993, available at http://hirr.hartsem.edu/bookshelf/thumma_article2.html.

Tomlinson, Dave. *The Post-Evangelical*. London: Triangle, 1996.

"Topical Guide to the Scriptures of the Church of Jesus Christ of Latter-Day Saints." Salt Lake City: Deseret, 1979.

Torrance, Thomas F. *Space, Time and Incarnation*. Edinburgh: T. & T. Clark, 1997.

Tozer, A. W. *Wingspread: Albert B. Simpson—A Study in Spiritual Altitude*. Harrisburg, PA: Christian Publications, 1943.

———. *Worship: The Missing Jewel*. Harrisburg: Christian Publications, 1992.

Tracy, David. "The Foundations of Practical Theology." In *Practical Theology: The Emerging Field in Theology, Church, and World*, edited by Don S. Browning, 62–82. San Francisco: Harper & Row, 1983.

———. *Blessed Rage for Order: The New Pluralism in Theology*. New York: Seabury, 1975.

Tuan, Yi-Fu. *Space and Place: The Perspective of Experience*. London: Edward Arnold, 1977.

———. *Passing Strange and Wonderful: Aesthetics, Nature, and Culture.* New York: Kodansha, 1993.

———. "Sacred Space: Explorations of an Idea." In *Dimensions of Human Geography: Essays on Some Familiar and Neglected Themes.* Chicago: University of Chicago Press, 1978.

Turner, Harold W. *From Temple to Meeting House: The Phenomenology and Theology of Places of Worship.* The Hague: Moulton, 1979.

Turner, Victor, and Edith L. B. Turner. *Image and Pilgrimage in Christian Culture.* New York: Columbia University Press, 1978.

Twigger-Ross, Clare L., and David L. Uzzell. "Place and Identity Processes." *Journal of Environmental Psychology* 16 (1996) 205–20.

USCCB Committee on Liturgy. "Built of Living Stones: Art, Architecture, and Worship. Guidelines of the National Conference of Catholic Bishops." November 16, 2000, available at http://www.usccb.org/liturgy/livingstones.shtml.

Van der Leeuw, G. *Sacred and Profane Beauty: The Holy in Art.* Translated by Diane Apostolos-Cappadona. Nashville: Abingdon, 1963.

———. *Religion in Essence and Manifestation.* Translated by J. E. Turner. London: George Allen & Unwin, 1964.

Van Gelder, Craig. *The Essence of the Church: A Community Created by the Spirit.* Grand Rapids: Baker, 2000.

Van Reken, Calvin P. "The Mission of the Local Church." *Calvin Theological Journal* 32, no. 2 (2004) 344–67.

Vaughan, John N. *Megachurches and America's Cities: How Churches Grow.* Grand Rapids: Baker, 1993.

Venturi, Robert et al. *Learning from Las Vegas: The Forgotten Symbolism of Architectural Form.* Cambridge, MA: MIT Press, 1993.

Visser, Margaret. *The Geometry of Love: Space, Time, Mystery, and Meaning in an Ordinary Church.* New York: North Point, 2000.

Von Simpson, Otto. *The Gothic Cathedral.* Princeton: Princeton University Press, 1974.

Vosko, Richard S. "A House for the Church: Structures for Public Worship in a New Millennium." *Worship* 74, no. 3 (2000) 194–212.

———. "Designing Future Worship Spaces: The Mystery of a Common Vision." *Meeting House Essays.* Chicago: Liturgy Training, 1996.

Wainwright, Geoffrey. "Renewing Worship: The Recovery of Classical Patterns." *Theology Today* 48, no. 1 (1991) 45–55.

Wakefield, Dan. "New Age, New Opportunities." *Theology Today* 51, no. 1 (1994) 142–47.

Ward, Sally. "On Shifting Ground: Changing Formulations of Place in Anthropology." *Australian Journal of Anthropology* 14, no. 1 (2003) 80–96.

Wardlaw, Theodore J. "Protagonist's Corner: "Still Crazy after All These Years." *Journal for Preachers* 20, no. 4 (1997) 48–50.

Warren, Rick. *The Purpose-Driven Church: Growth Without Compromising Your Message and Mission.* Grand Rapids: Zondervan, 1995.

Warshall, Peter. "Liturgy of Place?" *Whole Earth,* 1997, 52.

Watson, Sophie, and Katherine Gibson. *Postmodern Cities and Spaces.* Oxford: Blackwell, 1995.

Webber, Robert. *Worship Old and New.* Rev. ed. Grand Rapids: Zondervan, 1994.

———. *The Complete Library of Christian Worship.* Nashville: Starsong, 1994.

Weightman, Barbara W. "Sacred Landscapes and the Phenomenon of Light." *Geographical Review* 86, no. 1 (1996) 59–71.

Weil, Simone. *The Need for Roots*. Boston: Beacon, 1955.

Westerfelhaus, Robert. Review of *Ugly as Sin* by Michael S. Rose. *Homiletic* 27, no. 2 (2002) 41–44.

White, James F. "A Liturgical Strategy: Four Lines of Attack." *Christian Century*, March 7, 1979, available at http://www.religion-online.org/showarticle.asp?title=1224.

———. *Christian Worship in North America: A Retrospective: 1955–1995*. Collegeville: Liturgical, 1997.

———. "From Protestant to Catholic Plain Style." In *Seeing beyond the Word: Visual Arts and the Calvinist Tradition*, edited by Paul Corby Finney, 457–77. Grand Rapids: Eerdmans, 1999.

———. *Introduction to Christian Worship*. Nashville: Abingdon, 2000.

———. *Protestant Worship and Church Architecture: Theological and Historical Considerations*. New York: Oxford University Press, 1964.

———. *Protestant Worship: Traditions in Transition*. Louisville: Westminster John Knox, 1989.

White, James F., and Susan J. White. *Church Architecture: Building and Renovating for Christian Worship*. Nashville: Abingdon, 1988.

Wilkins, Michael J., and Terrence Page. *Worship, Theology and Ministry in the Early Church*. Sheffield: JSOT, 1992.

Will, Philip Jr. "Building for Time and Eternity." *Theology Today* 19, vol. 2 (1962) 198–206.

Williams, Peter W. "Metamorphoses of the Meetinghouse: Three Case Studies." In *Seeing beyond the Word: Visual Arts and the Calvinist Tradition*, edited by Paul Corby Finney, 479–505. Grand Rapids: Eerdmans, 1999.

Wilson-Kastner, Patricia. *Sacred Drama: A Spirituality of Christian Liturgy*. Minneapolis: Fortress, 1999.

Witvliet, John D. *Worship Seeking Understanding: Windows into Christian Practice*. Grand Rapids: Baker Academic, 2003.

Wuthnow, Robert. "Church Realities and Christian Identity in the 21st Century." *Christian Century*, May 12, 1993, available at http://www.religion-online.org/showarticle.asp?title=231.

———. *After Heaven: Spirituality in America Since the 1950s*. Berkeley: University of California Press, 1998.

Yannoulatos, Archbishop Anastasios. "Rediscovering Our Apostolic Identity in the Twenty-first Century." *St. Vladimir's Theological Quarterly* 48, no. 1 (2004) 3–20.

Yates, Nigel. *Buildings, Faith, and Worship: The Liturgical Arrangement of Anglican Church 1600–1900*. Oxford: Oxford University Press, 2000.

Yoder, John H. "Sacrament as Social Process: Christ the Transformer of Culture." *Theology Today* 48, no. 1 (1991) 33–44.

Zepp, Ira Jr.. *The New Religious Image of Urban America: The Shopping Mall as Ceremonial Center*. Boulder, CO: Univeristy Press of Colorado, 1997.

Ziauddin, Sardar. *Postmodernism and the Other: The New Imperialism of Western Culture*. London: Pluto, 1998.

Zuesse, Evan M. "Ritual." In *The Encyclopedia of Religion*, edited by Lindsay Jones, 12:405–22. 15 vols. New York: Macmillan, 2004.

Subject and Author Index

aesthetics, 75, 123
Akron Plan, 62–63
altar, 36, 43, 49, 51–55, 58, 61, 89, 93,
    96, 113, 143; access to, 51–52, 54,
    93; permanent, 54–55
ambo, 56
Anderson, Herbert, 124
anthropologists, 17, 80
Aquinas, 47, 48
Arbuckle, Gerald, 16, 135n2
archaeological data, 37
architecture, 43, 44–49, 64, 68, 71;
    church, 34; Puritan, 61
Arefi, Mahyr, 107
Aristotle, 95, 96, 143
ascension of Christ, 19, 102
Atriums, 36
Attention Restoration Theory, 116
attractional paradigm of ministry, 2,
    166
auditory design, 53
Auge, Marc, 109
axis mundi, 79, 80, 96, 159

Baby boomers, 65
Banks, Robert and Julia, 154
Baptism, 36, 37, 59; sacrament of, 30
baptismal, 174; font, 57
Bar Mitzvah, 172
Barna Research Group, 10, 149
Barna, George, 10
Barth, Karl, 29, 99

basilica, 34, 40–42, 67, 69
beauty, 75, 84, 131, 162, 173
Beliefnet.com, 151
Bennett, John C., 18
Berger, Peter, ix, 9, 135
Bethel, 88, 89, 96
Bevans, Stephen, 19, 24
Bibby, Reginald, 9
Book of Common Prayer, 49–51, 59
Bosch David, 29
Bouyer, Louis, 36, 41n27
Bowman, Ray, 155
Brandenburg Missionary Conference, 29
British Airways, 31
Brown, David, 146, 152
Browning, Don S., x, 82
Brueggemann Walter, 95, 114,129
Bruggink, Donald, 90
Bucer, Martin, 49
built environment, x, xii, 1, 8, 11, 49,
    67–68, 105–6, 108, 112, 113, 119,
    122, 125–26, 136, 163, 167–69,
    174, 176; and culture, 13–15; and
    liturgy, 39; and identity, 168; appre-
    ciation for, 112, 136; consecrated,
    99; ecclesial, 71; hermeneutics of,
    11; meaning of, 56, 113; role of, 3;
    sacredness of, 68; theology of, 72

Calvin, John, 55
Canaan, 90, 96
Canter, David, 108

Carrigan, Henry L., Jr., 145
cathedrals, 20, 37, 43–45, 68, 93
Center, 79–80, 82, 96, 110, 147;
    ceremonial, 163; importance of,
    159–60; meaning of, 128; sacred,
    158; worship, 92; *see* shopping malls
Central United Church, Calgary, 62–63
chancel, 43, 49–51
Charismatic renewal, 140
Christ, 51, 99; body of, 59, 99, 173;
    incarnation of, 100, 102; real pres-
    ence of, work of, 51, 54
Christianity, x, 14, 17, 19, 34, 36n7,
    139; and culture, 24; incarnational
    nature of, 19; sixteenth century, 56
Church, 14, 19–20; acceptance of, 20;
    Apostolic nature of, 29; architec-
    ture, 44, 107; buildings, 36n6, 41,
    46, 67, 69, 119, 131, 156, 166, 174;
    Christian, 67; cruciform design,
    45; dynamic equivalent, 22; early,
    38–39, 66; evangelical, 72, 112, 131,
    173; gathered, 132; institutional,
    137; local, 20, 29, 150; medieval, 43,
    68; Methodist, 63; mission of, 15,
    16, 18, 27, 29, 31, 69, 71, 103; mis-
    sional, 27, 71, 169; multi-purpose,
    62; New Testament, 21, 91, 99,
    155; North American, 17, 155;
    Reformation, 68; Reformed, 53n73;
    role of, 26; Roman Catholic, 61,
    135; spiritual nature of, 44; struc-
    tures, 34; Western, 38, 66, 128, 135;
    universal, 20; virtual, 152
Church Growth Movement, 64
Church of England, 49, 54, 61, 68
Church of Fools, 152, 153n60
Churchill, Winston, 106
Communion rails, 53
Communion table, 51, 54, 55, 174
communitas, 171
community, 18, 19, 36n8, 39, 48, 59,
    94, 99, 110, 134; Christian, 5, 135,
    144, 153, 166; need for, 146, 161;
    virtual, 145

Constantine, 40–42, 67n118
contextualization, 19
conversion, 16, 17, 26, 124
Coote, Robert, 12
covenant, 87, 104; Abrahamic, 95
creation, 30, 76, 80, 97, 115–16, 142;
    of the world, 80, 147; original act
    of, 97
cross of Christ, 18
cruciform layout, 45
cultural romanticism, 18
culture, xi, xii, 12, 35, 56, 64, 77, 81, 104,
    113, 132, 139, 157; appreciation of,
    12, 175; definition of, 12–14; con-
    temporary, 69, 141; internet, 145;
    postmodern, 131; preincarnational,
    101; Western, 133, 136
cyberspace, 134, 144–50, 153; experi-
    ence of, 147; impact of, 143

Damascus, road to, 100
David, King of Israel, 89, 92
Davies, Char, 147
Davies, J. G., 35n6, 7, 102
Didache, 37
digital revolution, 149
Dix, Gregory, 36, 40n25, 41n27
domus Dei, 5, 42, 67, 132
domus ecclesia, 5, 40, 42, 67, 132
Douglas, Mary, 138
Drane, John, 4, 29n72
Droppers, Carl, 90
Drucker, Peter, 146
dualism, 26
Dura-Europos, 37
Durkheim, Emile, 74, 76, 77–78, 92, 140

ecclesia materialis, 44
ecclesia spiritualis, 44
ecclesiology, 51
Ecumenical dialogue, xii, 134–35, 150
Edict of Milan, 40, 41n27
edification, 39
Eliade, Mircea, 74, 76, 78–81, 83, 84,
    88, 92, 96–98, 100, 127, 147, 158

Emergent church, 3
Emmaus, road to, 100
Enlightenment, 140, 143
Eucharist, 36, 37, 40, 50, 52–54, 56, 59, 68, 172
Evangelicalism, 11, 135
evangelism, 30
experience, 46, 74, 76, 82, 110, 147; of the built environment, collective, 146; of cyberspace, 147; embodied, 146–47, 169; human, 111, 113, 116, 137, 158; of God, 143; of the holy/sacred, 73, 76, 87; of liminality, 87; of the numinous, 74–75; of the physical environment, 148; of place, 120–29; religious, 130, 142, 143; ritual-architectural, 48; ritualistic, 172; of sacred place/space, 80, 86, 106; spiritual, 134, 167; of worship, 54, 136, 148, 155, 171

Fellowship, 2, 27, 31, 35, 42, 154, 173; meals, 35
Findhorn Community, 159
First Alliance Church, Calgary, 170–71, 174
Foucault, Michel, 152
Fulghum, Robert, 138–39

Gadamer, Hans-Georg, 120–21, 123
Gallagher, Michael, 13–15, 19, 23–25
Gallup, George, 136
Geertz, Clifford, 12, 113
geometry, 83; sacred, 83
Gibson, William, 144
Giles, Richard, 86, 107, 119
Global north, xi, 4, 119, 137, 155, 156
globalization, 108n17; influence of, 107
Gorringe, Timothy, 80, 107, 108
gospel, xi, xii, 9, 11, 13, 15, 100, 128, 135; of John, 35; and culture, 22–26, 102; understanding, 16–20
Gothic structure, 43, 45, 47n49, 48n58, 49, 61, 113
grace, 16, 30, 57, 163
Groothuis, Doug, 144

Hall, Eddy, 155
Hammond, Peter, 4, 5
Harries, Karsten, 4n4, 146
Hartford Institute for Religion Research, 150
Hay, Robert, 130
healing, xii, 18, 26, 28, 30, 83, 143, 160; and place, 116
heaven, 42, 45, 52, 78n32, 83, 84, 88, 102, 159; gate of, 89. *See* heavens
heavens, 98
Hendricks, William, 133
Herzog, Thomas R., 117
heterogeneity, 77; Durkheim's complete, 76
hierophany, 74, 78, 88, 96, 147
Hine, Virginia, 140–42
Holy of holies, 50, 91, 92
Holy Place, 50, 79n43, 83, 86, 89, 97, 103
Holy Spirit, 37, 99, 143
homo ludens, 159
homo religious, 159
Hooker, Richard, 50
Hooper, John, 49, 50, 51
Hoopes, Craig, 169
house church, 39, 67n118, 154–56; movement, xii, 134, 154
human geography, 105
Huntington, Samuel, 15
Hybels, Bill, 65n112
hypostatic union, 103

immanence of God, 19, 71, 82, 90, 93, 98, 173
Incarnation, digital, 144; of Christ, 18–20, 100–103, 118, 131
incarnational perspective, 110, 125
individualism, 17
Industrial Revolution, 60, 149
Inge, John, 94, 130
injustice, 31
Internet, 127, 143–46, 149–52
Israel, 87, 89–96, 114, 166; assembly of, 98

Jacob, 88–89, 96, 100–101
Jacob's well, 101
Jamieson, Alan, 10
Jantzen, Hans, 44, 45
Jesus, 16, 18, 31, 36,54, 98, 99,101–3,
    116, 137; images of, 151; incarna-
    tion of, *see* incarnation of Christ;
    teaching of, 36
Jones, Lindsay, 112
Jones, Noragh, 125
Jones, Steven, 144
justice, 30, 94

Kilde, Jeanne Halgren, 33, 38, 42,
    43n34, 65
Klotz, Heinrich, 108
Kraft, Charles, 14, 15, 22
Kunin, Seth, 87, 88, 90–95

land, 94–96; of Canaan, 96; Promised,
    95
landedness, 94
Lane, Beldon, 98
Larson, Elena, 150
Laud, Archbishop of Canterbury,
    52–53
Lawson, Lorne, 151
Lefebvre, Henri, 130
Libeskind, Daniel, 108
lighting, 19, 125
liminality, 82, 87, 100, 171
liturgical environments, 39
liturgical focal points, 50–58
liturgical Reform, 140
liturgical spaces, 36, 49, 68, 175
liturgical theology, 131
Liturgies, rationale behind, 39
Liturgy, 5, 37, 42, 43, 53, 59, 67, 69,
    82; impact on architecture, 68;
    Reformed, 57
Lord's Supper, 8, 30, 51, 52, 57
Lundquist, John M., 141
Luther, Martin, 48n60, 56, 58, 68, 93
Lutheran church, 50, 51, 55
Luzbetak, Louis J., 135

Malina, Bruce, 107
Mann, A. T., 81, 83, 85
Marshall, I. Howard, 21, 23
McDonald's, 31
McNeal, Reggie, 29
Mead, Margaret, 139
megachurch, 34, 62, 63–67, 70, 150,
    155–56; definition, 63
Meyrowitz, Joshua, 126, 127
Milne, Courtney, 82–83
missio Dei., 29, 163. *See* Mission of
    God
Mission of God, 29, 31
Mission of the church, xi, xii, 2, 3, 6,
    11, 15, 16, 18, 20, 27, 28–31, 71,
    103, 106, 111, 118, 134, 149, 151,
    156, 164, 165, 175
Mission statements, x, 31
Mission, and missions, 2, 26–27
missional church, xii, 1, 2–4, 5, 8, 27,
    71, 156, 163, 169
modernization, 9
Moses, 87, 89, 100
Mother earth, 83
Mount Sinai, 87
mysterium fascinans, 75
mysterium tremendum, 75
mystery, 43, 47n55, 74, 75, 131, 143,
    173

narrative, 45, 87, 113, 114; and place,
    118–20
nave, 35n8, 41, 43, 50, 52, 53, 55, 58,
    61, 80, 96, 113, 170
Neuromancer, 144
New Age movement, 151
Newbigin, Lesslie, ixn1, 14, 20, 21, 24
Nicene Creed, 28
Niebuhr, H. Richard, 13
non-place, 109–10
numinous, 74, 75, 141
Nunes, Mark, 146, 148

Ornan, threshing floor of, 89
Osmose, 147–48
Otto, Rudolph, 74–76

Packer, J. I., 24
para-place, 127
Peck, Scott, 84–85
Pentecost, 17, 36
philosophy, New Age, 151
pilgrimage, 96; Jewish, 87
place, ix, 1, 4, 8, 38, 78, 106, 110; and
    action, 118, 127; attachment, 107,
    127; centralized sacred, 91–94; de-
    centralized sacred, 88–91; domestic,
    38; experience of, 123, 125, 128;
    function of, 113, 120, 131; gather-
    ing, 175; and healing, 116–18; and
    identity, 114–16; meaning of, 108;
    and memory, 114; and narrative,
    118; public, 126; sacred, x, xi, 11,
    13, 32, 34, 36, 40, 69, 72, 76, 79,
    80, 83, 85, 97, 101, 104, 130, 147,
    164, 172, 177; sense of, *see* sense of
    place, significance of, 105, 107, 112,
    130; and space, 129; spirituality of,
    transitional, 100, 175
Pope Paul II, 22
post-Christian society, 12
post-enlightenment, 140
Practical Theology, 6, 7, 11, 164, 177;
    Anthropological model of, 24
preaching, 2, 6, 30, 37, 53n73, 55, 65;
    of the apostle Peter, 17; centrality
    of, 61; Reformed emphasis on, 61;
    Luther's commitment to, 68; theol-
    ogy of, 56, 66
pre-understandings, 123
priesthood of believers, 48, 58
Principe, Walter, 136
printing press, 56, 153
private home, 3, 34, 35–40, 61, 69
pulpit, 50, 53, 54–58, 62, 65–66, 174
Puritans, 50, 53, 60; architecture of, 61

Rahner Karl, 26
Rapoport, Amos, 56, 105, 106, 109,
    119, 122
reconciliation, 29, 30
redemption, 29, 30

reflective exiles, 10
Reformation, 44, 49, 50, 51, 55, 68–69;
    Protestant, 48; theology, 59, 68
Reformed experiments, 34, 48, 70
Relph, Edward, 110, 111, 113, 124, 127
Rheingold, Howard, 145, 148, 152, 153
Riddell, Michael, 118
Ridley, Nicholas, 51
ritual, 13, 20, 42, 70, 75, 82, 84, 94, 103,
    111, 120, 127, 130, 131, 158, 164,
    172; and ceremony, 139; medieval
    dedication, 45; process, 55; and
    spirituality, 138–42. *See* experience,
    ritual-architectural
Ritzer, George, 86
Roman Empire, 35n8, 41, 69
Romanesque architecture, 48
Rouses, James Wilson, 161
Rush, Robert T., 24

sacrality, xii, 72, 73, 77, 78, 79, 82, 84,
    89, 101, 158, 172. *See* sacred
sacraments, 2, 6, 30, 47n55, 56
sacred place. *See* place
sacred space, 1, 4, 8, 11, 13, 44, 50, 61,
    70, 71, 73, 74, 74n7, 78, 78n30, 80,
    86, 87, 91, 94, 107, 114, 118, 131,
    132, 136, 157, 164, 165, 167, 173,
    176; centralized, 90, 91; and cul-
    ture, 15; and cyberspace, 143–53;
    decentralized, 88; in the New
    Testament, 99–104; interpretation
    of, 111; meaning of, need for, 134;
    Old Testament characteristics of,
    95–98; praxis of, 134; and ritual,
    138; shopping malls as, 158–63;
    within the Temple, 93
sacred, the, 76, 78, 81, 81n54, 103;
    definition of, 78; derivative, 78, 91,
    103–4n155; designation of, 83, 84,
    87, 98; function of, 85–86; impact
    of, 86–87
Saddleback Community Church, 27
Schleiermacher, Fredrick, 75
Schmidt, Francis, 93, 94

Schreiter, Robert, 18, 19, 20, 25
seeker sensitive, 2, 3
semiotics, 13, 113
sense of place, 106, 107, 109, 112, 126, 128–30
Sheldrake, Philip, 82, 100, 107, 109, 113, 114, 123, 136, 137
shopping malls, xii, 157–59, 169
Shorter, Aylward, 13
Simmel, Georg, 120
Simpson, Otto von, 43, 46, 48, 48n58
Simson, Wolfgang, 154
social action, 31
Social Sciences, x, 72, 107; dialogue with, 72, 105
Sovik, Edward Anders, 166
spiritual gifts, 21n41, 39
spirituality, xi, 74, 82, 85, 125, 136, 141, 144, 162, 172; Celtic, 82; Christian, 47, 82, 147; definition of, 136; eclectic, 142–43; embodied, 147; experiential, 11, 74; human, 129; post-modern, and ritual, 138; twenty-first century, 136–38, 172
St. Paul's cathedral, 53
St. Peter's basilica, 42
St.-Denis, 46–47
Stackhouse, Max, 135
Stott, John, 12
Strasbourg, 56
Suger, Abbot, 46–48
supermodernity, 110
Swatos Jr., William H., 80–81
Swinton, John, 6n7
symbolism, 69, 173; Christian, 5, 45, 174
synagogues, 40, 84
syncretism, 25–26

tabernacle, 36n11; 90–91, 92, 94, 96, 165
technology, 73, 110, 122n73, 144, 148, 151; benefits of, 143; communication, 152; computer, 148; cyber, 145–46

temple, 36, 39, 42, 50, 79, 84, 90, 91, 96; of God, 36; in Jerusalem, 36, 92, 97; in the New Testament, 99; place of encounter, 91–92
Tent of meeting, 90
Third space, 157
Thumma, Scott, 150
Torrance, T. F., 95, 131
Tozer, A. W., 72
transcendence, 19, 43, 71, 82, 90, 93, 98, 138, 173
Transformative reflection model, 5, 176
Tuan, Yi Fu, 73–74, 106, 109
Turner, Harold, 35, 85, 99, 132
Turner, Victor, 55, 87

Udnall, Ephraim, 54

Van Gelder, Craig, 28
Van Reken, Calvin P., 6, 29–30
Vatican II, 24, 135
virtual reality, 147, 148, 151–53
vision casting, 31
Visser, Margaret, 164, 169

Walker, E. V., 130
Warren, Rick, 27
Williams, John, 53
Willow Creek Community Church, 65
Wilson-Kastner, Patricia, 73, 80, 85
World Council of Churches, 23, 135
worship arts, 30
worship, 4, 27, 30, 31, 35n7, 38, 40n25, 42, 49, 53, 56, 73; alternative expressions of, 70; and the Book of Common Prayer, 49; Calvinistic, 55; center, 159; Christian, 36, 38, 41, 42, 67, 172; corporate, 5, 37, 57, 155, 167; of the early church, 38–39; emperor, 42; neglect of, 72; participative, 48, 54; places dedicated to, 40–41, 67, 90; priest-led, 48; purpose of, 56, 61; and ritual, 139; Sabbath, 60; Temple, 91–92; theology of, 44, 67; visual nature of, 56

worship environment, 44, 45, 85, 136

worshipers, 4, 19, 43, 49, 52, 78, 99, 103, 112, 171; Reformed, 59

Wren, Matthew, 54

Wren, Sir Christopher, 53

Zepp, Ira G., Jr., 158–62, 169, 171

Zion, 97

Zurich, 56

Zwingli, Ulrich, 56–57, 68